Instructor's Manual

to accompany

Art across Time
Volumes I, II, and Combined

Second Edition

Laurie Schneider Adams
John Jay College and Graduate Center
City University of New York

Revised by
Eric Berman

Boston Burr Ridge, IL Dubuque, IA Madison, WI New York San Francisco St. Louis
Bangkok Bogotá Caracas Kuala Lumpur Lisbon London Madrid Mexico City
Milan Montreal New Delhi Santiago Seoul Singapore Sydney Taipei Toronto

McGraw-Hill Higher Education

A Division of The McGraw-Hill Companies

Instructor's Manual to accompany
ART ACROSS TIME, VOLUMES I, II, AND COMBINED

2 3 4 5 6 7 8 9 0 QSR/QSR 0 9 8 7 6 5 4 3 2

ISBN 0-07-249849-8

www.mhhe.com

Contents

This manual is intended to help art history instructors get the maximum benefit from Laurie Schneider Adams' *Art across Time*, Volumes I, II, or combined.

Student Study Guides

The first part of the *Instructor's Manual* is coordinated to the *Student Study Guides (Volumes I and II)*, which are workbooks to accompany both Volumes of *Art across Time*. For each chapter of the textbook, the *Study Guide* has several sets of questions: fill in the blanks, matching artists with works, works with style, time, place, and identifications of quotations relevant to the history of art. Most questions involve works of art directly, but some also deal with their context while other exercises ask students to label maps, plans, and diagrams.

Answers are not provided to students in the *Study Guide*, but are provided in this *Instructor's Manual*. This means that instructors can use the *Guides* for take-home and/or open-book assignments. The pages of the *Guides* are perforated, making it easy for students to tear them out neatly and hand them in. Questions are designed to engage students in a detailed reading of the text and in reviewing lecture notes. After completing the *Study Guide* workbook, students will be well equipped to take the multiple choice questions that comprise the *Instructor's Manual*.

How the material is organized

Each chapter of the manual has the following parts:
- A list of **Key Works** covered in each chapter of *Art across Time*
- A list of **Key Terms** introduced in the chapter and bolded in the text
- A list of **Maps, Diagrams, and Projections** appear in every chapter to help orient the student
- **Audiovisual Resources** suggested to complement each chapter including videos, CD-ROMs, and Web sites
- **Multiple-Choice Questions** designed to text students on the key concepts

About Brownstone

The sample test questions at the end of each chapter are available on Brownstone's Diploma for Windows or Exam IV for Macintosh, a powerful but easy-to-use test-generating program. With Brownstone, you can easily view and select the test item file questions, then print a test and answer key. You can customize questions, headings, and instruction, you can add or import questions of your own, and you can print you test in a choice of fonts allowed by your printer.

Art across Time website (www.mhhe.com/artacrosstime)

Please be sure to visit the *Art across Time* Web site. Highlights include:

For Students:
- an online image bank (correlated to each chapter)
- audio pronunciation guides for works of art, artists, and glossary terms
- self-testing multiple choice questions (students can email answers to their professors)
- essay questions (students can email answers to their professors)
- links for research topics in art
- links on how to get involved in the arts

For Instructors:
- an online version of this Instructor's Manual
- PageOut Lite: designed for the professor just beginning to explore Web site options. In just a few minutes, even a novice computer user can have a course Web site.
- a McGraw-Hill sales representative locator

Art across Time Core Concepts CD-ROM

The *Art across Time* Core Concepts CD-ROM provides interactive exercises, video clips, research guidelines, and self-quizzing for art history students. The CD was developed to help demonstrate art concepts that benefit from exploration beyond the printed page.

The following page of this Instructor's Manual provides an overview of the CD-ROM and suggests ways of incorporating it into the classroom.

Please consult your McGraw-Hill representative for policies, prices, and availability of all ancillaries, You can find your local McGraw-Hill representative by visiting us on the Web at: <http://www.mhhe.com>

ART ACROSS TIME'S
CORE CONCEPTS IN ART CD-ROM

The *Art across Time* Core Concepts CD-ROM provides interactive exercises, video clips, research guidelines, and self-quizzing for students. The CD was developed to help demonstrate art concepts and applications that benefit from exploration beyond the printed page.

This part of the Instructor's Manual provides an overview of the CD-ROM and suggests ways of incorporating it into the classroom. As with the chapters of the text, we expect that there will be as many ways to use this CD in your class as there are ways of using the text. What follows are just a few examples. If you or your students would like to contribute to this section of the manual, please send your suggestions to us at art@mcgraw-hill. We will be posting these listings to the text's Online Learning Center, www.mhhe.com/artacrosstime.

CD-ROM TABLE OF CONTENTS

Chapter Summaries
Key Terms
Self-Assessments
CRITICISM EXERCISES

Internet Resources
Internet Primer
Guide to Electronic Research
Link to the *Art across Time* Online Learning Center (www.mhhe.com/artacrosstime)

Study Skills Primer
Doing Well in College
Study Strategies
References

INTEGRATING THE TEXT & CD-ROM

The CD-ROM works particularly well in conjunction with the Introduction: Why Do We Study the History of Art?, in which students are presented with the most basic concepts of art. Additionally, throughout the history of art, you are encouraged to direct students back to the CD for examples of lost wax casting, painting techniques, and others in the Art Techniques section of *Core Concepts*. In the following section, we list the areas of the text where the CD-ROM can be especially useful. The column on the left provides chapter title, heading, and page references for specific topics in the text, while the column on the right lists the corresponding material in the CD-ROM.

__TEXT__	__CD-ROM__
Introduction: Why Do We Study the History of Art?	**Elements of Art**
LINE, pgs. 18–19	LINE: Exercise 1, Line Quality; Exercise 3, Linear Perspective (one-, two-, and three-point)
SHAPE, pgs. 19–20	SHAPE: Exercise 1: Defining Shape
LIGHT AND COLOR, pgs. 20–22	COLOR: Exercise 2: Properties of Color; Exercise 3: Expressive Qualities
TEXTURE, p. 22	TEXTURE (entire)
Introduction: Why Do We Study the History of Art?	**Chapter Resources / CRITICAL EXERCISES**
FORMALISM, p. 14	Formalism Exercise
ICONOGRAPHY AND ICONOLOGY, p. 15	Iconography and Iconology Exercise
MARXISM, p. 15	Marxism Exercise
FEMINISM, p. 15	Feminism Exercise
BIOGRAPHY AND AUTOBIOGRAPHY, pgs. 15–16	Biography and Autobiography Exercise
SEMIOLOGY, p. 16	Semiology Exercise
DECONSTRUCTION, pgs. 16–17	Deconstruction Exercise
PSYCHOANALYSIS, p. 17	Psychoanalysis Exercise
Chapters 1–29	**Chapter Resources:** chapter summaries, key terms, and quizzes for each chapter of *Art across Time*.
	Internet Resources

A quick starter for students not yet up-to-speed on using the internet.	INTERNET PRIMER
Guides students from idea stage to writing a paper using the internet as a research tool. Provides guidance on citation usage and style, searching tools, and organizing research materials.	GUIDE TO ELECTRONIC RESEARCH
More quizzing options, links for research topics, the complete instructor's manual, and more.	LINK TO THE *ART ACROSS TIME* ONLINE LEARNING CENTER
	Study Skills Primer
An overview of both time and course management.	DOING WELL IN COLLEGE
Systematic strategies to help students master the wide range of material they will encounter every semester.	STUDY STRATEGIES

Study Guide Answer Key

VOLUME 1

Introduction

p. 1

1. pictures, sculpture, and architecture; 2. before Christ; 3. anno Domini; 4. "circa" or around; 5. ka; 6. patron; 7. trompe-l'oeil; 8. garbha griha, womb chamber; 9. ground plan; 10. archaios, old, logos, word; 11. portrait.

p.2

12. graphe, writing, eikon, image; 13. Taj Mahal, Shah Jahan
1.B, 2.C, 3.E, 4.A, 5.D
1.D, 2.E, 3.A, 4.B, 5.H, 6.G, 7.F, 8.C

p. 3

1.C, 2.E, 3.F, 4.D, 5.B, 6.A, 7.H, 8.J, 9.N, 10.K, 11.M, 12.I, 13.G, 14.L, 15.P, 16.O, 17.R, 18.Q

p. 6

1.J, 2.H, 3.G, 4.A, 5.I, 6.K, 7.L, 8.F, 9.C, 10.D, 11.E, 12.B

Chapter 1

p. 16

1.C, 2.B, 3.L, 4.K, 5.C, 6.J, 7.A, 8.I, 9.H, 10.F, 11.D, 12.E, 13.G

p. 19

1.a, 2.d, 3.a, 4.c, 5.b

Chapter 2

p. 23

1. Inanna, goddess of fertility, love and war; Mesopotamian hymn
2. Giglamesh; *The Epic of Giglamesh*
3. Ur-Nammu; cuneiform tablet

p. 24

1.E, 2.I, 3.K, 4.J, 5.A, 6.B, 7.H, 8.F, 9.G, 10.C, 11.D

p. 29

1. Neolithic; Jericho; Joshua
2. primal sea; clay; gods; and afterlife below the earth
3. Mesopotamians; clay tablets
4. rivers; Tigris; Euphrates
5. Base; capital; shaft; a bull

p. 30

1.E, 2.E, 3.F, 4.B, 5.D, 6.C, 7.C, 8.D, 9.A, 10.A, 11.A

p. 31

1.H, 2.G, 3.A, 4.A, 5.A, 6.E, 7.D, 8.I, 9.D, 10.K, 11.F, 12.J, 13.L, 14.B, 15.K, 16.C, 17.C, 18.M

Chapter 3

p. 34

1. a. Hapy; b. *Hymn to Hapy*; c. because of the drought
2. a. King of Egypt (6th Dynasty); b. Boat which will take Teti to Re; c. Opening of the Mouth ritual; d. Pyramid Text, Utterance 407.

p. 35

1. Africa; 3000 B.C.; King Menes; pharaoh
2. 4th; Manetho; dynasties; Predynastic, Early Dynastic, Old, Middle, New, and Late Dynastic.
3. Alexander the Great; Macedonians; 30 B.C.
4. Upper Egypt; red; Lower Egypt
5. step; 2600 B.C.; Imhotep; Saqqara; mastabas (red-brick and limestone)
6. Carnarvon; Tutankhamon; Valley of the Kings

p. 43

1. Papyrus; 2. Foliated; 3. Palm leaf; 4. Papyrus blossom 5. Reed bundle; 6. Lotus

p. 44

1.D, 2.J, 3.G, 4.C, 5.K, 6.L, 7.H, 8.M, 9.B, 10.A, 11.I, 12.E, 13.F

p .45

1.D, 2.I, 3.A, 4.B, 5.J, 6.K, 7.G, 8.H, 9.E, 10.C, 11.F

Chapter 4

p. 49

1. circle; islands; Aegean; 3000; 1200 B.C.; Bronze; females; males; graves; marble
2. Evans; twentieth; Knossos; house of the double axe
3. Marinatos; volcanic eruption; 1500
4. Schliemann; The Trojan War; mainland; 1600; 1200; fortified; temples

p. 50

Agamemnon; Klytemnestra; Iphigenia; Orestes; Elektra;
Agamemnon; Helen; Menelaus; Sparta; Paris; Priam; Troy
Troy; Agamemnon; Artemis; stag; Iphigenia
Agamemnon; Klytemnestra; Aesgisthos; Orestes; Elektra
Aeschylos; Euripides

p. 51

1.E, 2.F, 3.A, 4.A, 5.C, 6.B, 7.B, 8.F, 9.B, 10.A, 11.D

Chapter 5

p. 58

1200; 800; writing; Phoenician; Eastern; Semitic; Hellenes; Dorians; Ionians; Doric; Ionic; Corinthian; barbarian; they spoke foreign languages with words which sounded like "bar-bar," therefore the Greeks considered them less civilized.; Olympiads; Olympic Games.

p. 59

omphalos; oracle; Gaia; eighth century; Apollo; darkness/light; Pythian; Python; dragon; Olympic; Panhellenic.
"know thyself"; Socrates; exile; *Dialogues*.
Republic; artists; Aristotle; Alexander the Great.

p. 66

1.H, 2.J, 3.Q, 4.G, 5.K, 6.A, 7.F, 8.P, 9.I, 10.E, 11.L, 12.C, 13.M, 14.N, 15.O, 16.D

p. 67

1. steps; 1a. stereobate; 1b. stylobate; 2. shaft; 2a. Doric drum; 2b. flute; 2c. base; 3. capital; 3a. necking; 3b. echinos; 3c. abacus; 3d. volute; 4. column; 5. architrave; 6. frieze; 6a. metope; 6b. triglyph; 7. cornice; 8. entablature

p. 69

1.A,E; 2.I,F; 3.C,H;4.G; 5.A; 6.A; 7.I; 8.D; 9.B or D; 10.A; 11.B or D; 12.J; 13.C; 14.C; 15.C; 16.B or D; 17.C

p. 70

1.D, 2.E, 3.C, 4.G, 5.F, 6.A, 7.B
1.C, 2.A, 3.F, 4.B, 5.E, 6. D

p. 71

1.C, 2.F, 3.A, 4.G, 5.E, 6.B, 7.D
1.E, 2.D, 3.A, 4.C, 5.B

Chapter 6

p. 77

1000; 100; Villanovans; Bologna; North; Tuscany; Tiber; Arno.

Herodotos; Lydia; Turkey; Italy; no other; Greeks;
Phoenician; right; left.
Rome.
p. 78
1.D, 2.E, 3.A, 4.B, 5.G, 6.C, 7.F, 8.G
1.C, 2.D, 3.A, 4.B
P.82
Xia; Five Rulers; second; Yellow River; bronzes; Shang;
1700; 1050; Zhou; 1050; 221.
Qin; 211; 206 B.C.; Warring States.

Chapter 7
p. 87
caput mundi; forth; Alexander the Great; 323; Latin; 510;
Republic; senate; an assembly; of March; Julius Caesar;
Octavian; Augustus; emperor; 180; 180 to 192; 235; 235 to
284.
Tertrarchs; Constantine I; Milan; 313; Christianity.
p. 88
domus; "house"; atrium; insulae; "islands"
Pompeii; Herculaneum; volcanic ash/lava; Mount
Vesuvius; 79; Issos; Darius III; 333 B.C.; Bucephalos;
Darius; tesserae; opus vermiculatum; worm-work; Faun;
Pompeii; Greek; 300 B.C.
p. 89
1.D, 2.E, 3.G, 4.A, 5.C, 6.B, 7.F
1.E, 2.G, 3.B, 4.C, 5.D, 6.A
p. 90
1.G, 2.F, 3.H, 4.I, 5.A, 6.N, 7.C, 8.M, 9.O, 10.J, 11.K, 12.D;
13.L, 14.B, 15.E
p. 91
1a. The Greeks; b. Greek leaders, subjects of Greek art; c.
The Romans
2a. Suetonius; b. Nero's; c. Golden House; d. A.D. 64-68
3a. Josephus; b. History of the Jewish Wars; c. the honor
Jews felt for the number seven
4a. Marcus Aurelius; b. A Stoic philosopher and Emperor
of Rome; c. artists
p. 97
1.D, 2.G, 3.H, 4.C, 5.A, 6.I, 7.J, 8.B, 9.F, 10.E
Jupiter; Alkmene; Juno; Jupiter; snakes; Hercules;
Amphitryon; Vettii; Laocoön.
p. 100
2700; 1750; Pakistan; India; Mohenjo-daro; Harappa; mud-
brick; baked brick; sewage; bronze; copper; potter's wheel;
terracotta, bronze, and stone; grid; religious; royal
square; stamp; knob; raised
eighteenth; Aryans; Sanskirt; *Vedas.*
p. 101
Siddhartha Gautama; mid-sixth; Nepal; Maya; side; sal;
Lumbini; elephant; Siddhartha; Shakya; Siddhartha;
meditation, extreme austerities and poverty; knowledge;
Middle Way; pipal; Mara; enlightenment; bodhi; bodhagaya;
Deer Park; Sarnath; Wheel; Law; Mahaparinirvana; eighty;
pearls.
p. 107
1.C, 2.G, 3.D, 4.F, 5.A, 6.E, 7.H, 8.B
1.B, 2.D, 3. A, 4.C
Chapter 8
p. 109
Christianity: 33, Jerusalem; Roman; Christianity; fourth
Near East; Passover; bread; wine; Mass; Eucharist; Bible;
Old; New; Apocrypha; Evangelists; Matthew, Mark, Luke,
and John; apostles; Saint Paul; Apocalypse; Second; Christ
Mary; Joseph; Christ; saint; martyr.

p. 111
1.   narthex, 2. ambulatory, 3. nave, 4. sanctuary, 5. apse,
      6. nave
1.   atrium, 2. narthex, 3. nave, 4. apse, 5. baptistry, 6.
      minaret, 7. pendentive, 8. dome
p. 113
1. Annunciation; 2. Visitation; 3. Nativity; 4. Adoration of
the Magi; 5. Presentation in the Temple; 6. Massacre of the
Innocents; 7. Flight into Egypt; 8. Christ among the
Doctors; 9. Baptism; 10. Resurrection of Lazarus; 11.
Marriage at Cana; 12. Transfiguration; 13. Entry into
Jerusalem.
p. 114
14. Last Supper; 15. Kiss of Judas; 16. Flagellation; 17.
Road to Calvary; 18. Crucifixion; 19. Deposition; 20.
Lamentation; 21. Harrowing of Hell; 22. Resurrection; 23.
Noli me Tangere; 24. Ascension; 25. Pentacost; 26.
Judgement.
p. 118
1.D, 2.G, 3.G, 4.A, 5.A, 6.E, 7.F, 8.G, 9.C, 10.H, 11.B,
Chapter 9
P. 127
Goths; Visigoths; Moors; Spain; Moors; Islam; Granada;
1492; Columbus
"Surrender to God"; the Prophet Muhammad; Mecca;
Arabia; 570; Sunni; Shiite; worship; figurative; Allah;
Muhammad; Koran; Allah; 622; hijra; five; Mecca; hadj.
p. 128
800; Roman Emperor; Peter's; thirteenth; Holy Roman;
Rome; Latin; monasteries; Alcuin; York; 800; Aachen;
Alcuin; trivium; quadrivium; trivium; quadrivium
Otto I the Great; Ottonian; Saint Michael's; Hildesheim;
Germany; Benedictine; Bernard; Otto III; 1015; the Old
and New Testament.
p. 135
1. Islamic calligraphy. 2. *Beowulf,* Scyld's burial ship; icy
because it takes place in Denmark, eager because the ship
has been prepared for the burial at sea. 3. Scyld Scefing;
Akkad; Moses. 4. Saemund's Edda; Snorri Sturlson;
Scaldic; thirteenth; in the beginning of time; a Norse ice-giant
who emerged from the ice that filled the abyss.
p. 136
1.J, 2.K, 3.A or L, 4.M, 5.N, 6.O, 7.A, 8.B, 9.A or C, 10.D,
11.E, 12.F, 13.I, 14.A or G, 15.H
p. 137
1.E, 2.G, 3.A, 4.F, 5.H, 6.J, 7.I, 8.C, 9.D, 10.B
p. 139
Siberia; Bering Strait; 900 B.C.; Columbus; American;
Spanish; Columbian; conquest
Preclassic; c. 2000 B.C. to A.D. 250/300; Classic; c. 300 to
900; Postclassic; 900 to 1500
calender round; "long count"; three; sky, earth, and
underworld; crocodile; the underworld; nine; *Popal Vuh;*
ball-game; sun; planet Venus.
p. 140
1.D, 2.E, 3.E, 4.E, 5.D, 6.C, 7.F, 8.B, 9.A, 10.E, 11.G, 12.none
1.C, 2.B, 3.A
Chapter 10
p. 149
1.   nave, 2. aisle, 3. crossing, 4. choir, 5. transparent, 6.
      chancel, 7. apse, 8. ambulatory, 9. radiating chapel
1.   voussoir, 2. archivolts, 3. tympanum, 4. lintel, 5. door
      jamb, 6. trumeau
p. 150

embroidery; Norman; 1066; Bayeux; Normandy; France; Odo; Bayeux; William the Conqueror; left to right; Latin; William; Hastings; Harold; England; Scandinavians; oars; sail; carved dragon heads; bow; antiramming devices secular; Norman; red and yellow; wavy.

Chapter 11
p. 151
12th, Ile-de-France; France; Abbot Suger; Louis VI and Louis VII; Saint-Denis; north; Carolingian; eighth century; Suger; light; Saint-Denis; narthex; west façade; towers; Portals; ambulatory; apse; radiating chapels; chevet; choir; ambulatory; apse; ribbed; pointed; buttresses.
p. 152
1.   flyer, 2. clerestory, 3. buttress pier, 4. triforium, 5. arcade
p. 153
1.   tower, 2. nave, 3. side aisle, 4. crossing, 5. north transept, 6. south transept, 7. choir, 8. apse, 9. radiating chapel, 10. buttress, 11. west façade
p. 154
1.   bay, 2. nave, 3. side aisle, 4. nave arcade, 5. clerestory, 6. cluster pier, 7. triforium; 8. buttress, 9. flying buttress, 10. wooden roof, 11. colonette
p. 155
1. Abbot Suger; Saint-Denis; *The Book of Suger, Abbot of Saint-Denis.* 2. Saint Augustine; *The City of God,* non-Christians or pagans. 3. William Wordsworth; sonnet; 1822; King's College Chapel.
p. 163
1.I; 2.G and I; 3.G and I; 4.A; 5.B; 6.J; 7.C; 8.D; 9.E, G and I; 10.I; 11.M; 12.K; 13.L
P. 166
Shilpa Shastras; anthropomorphic; mandalas; houses; Garbha griha; cella; puja; sunrise; womb chamber; salutes; negative spirits; mantras; mundras; cleans and anoints; circumambulates.
1.C. Vaishya (Brahmin: elite, priests); 2.B; 3.A; 4.D
p. 168
Cambodia; Devaraja; Indravarman; Suryavarman II; Vishnu; rectangular; east-west; five; cosmos; Mount Meru; mortuary; balustrades; water serpents; fertility
Apsareses
Jayavarman VII; "Great Angkor"; Devaraja's; Bayon; cosmic; cosmic ocean; mountain; Mount Meru.

Chapter 12
p. 170
1.H, 2.G, 3.G, 4.F, 5.D, 6.D, 7.C, 8.E, 9.A, 10.B
p. 171
1.Bd, 2.Hc, 3.Ab, 4.Ea, 5.Ea, 6.Fa, 7.Gd, 8.Dd, 9.Ca, 10.Ie
p. 175
1.   Ceninno Ceninni; *The Craftsman's Handbook;* Turn of the Century (1400); painting
2.   Saint Francis of Assisi; The Stigmata; *The Canticle* of *Brother Sun*
3.   Boccaccio; *Decameron;* bubonic plague; 1348; Orcanga, *Triumph of Death*

VOLUME II
Introduction
p. 1
pictures; sculpture; architecture; inborn; pictures, sculptures and model buildings; material; Nationalistic; Intrinsic; religious; psychological
bronze; Brancusi; bird; Edward Steichen; Gertrude Vanderbilt Whitney.
p. 2
1. illusionistic or trompe-l'oeil; 3. representational or figurative; 4. nonrepresentational; 5. idealized; 6. romanticized; 7. stylized; 8. naturalistic; 9. texture; 10. shading; 11. shadow; 12. plane; 13. composition; 14. line; 15. shape; 16. red, yellow and blue.
p. 3
1.D, 2.E, 3.A, 4.B, 5.H, 6.G, 7.F, 8.C
1.H, 2.E, 3.G, 4.I, 5.A, 6.C, 7.F, 8.D, 9.B

Chapter 12
p. 12
1.H, 2.G, 3.G, 4.F, 5.D, 6.D, 7.C, 8.E, 9.A, 10.B
1.Bd, 2.Hc, 3.Ab, 4.Ea, 5.Ea, 6.Fa, 7. Gd, 8.Dd, 9.Ca, 10.Ie
p.16
1.   Ceninno Cennini; *The Crafsman's Handbook;* Turn of the Century (1400); painting
2.   Saint Francis of Assisi; The Stigmata; *The Canticle of Brother Sun*
3.   Boccaccio: *Decameron;* bubonic plague; 1348; Orcagna, *Triumph of Death*

Chapter 13
p. 21
Humanism: Man, Petrarch; Latin; Gothic; Greek; Latin; Bruni; Athens; republic; Plato; Medici; Neoplatonism
The Humanist Tomb: *City of Florence; Florentine People;* Rossellino; sarcophagus; bier; Nikes; Corinthian; round; putti; wreath; Marzocco.
p. 22
1.   nave; 2. side aisle; 3. apse; 4. dome; 5. campanile
2.   nave; 2. aisle; 3. transept; 4. choir; 5. crossing
p. 23
1. steps; 1a. stereobate; 1b. stylobate; 2. shaft; 2a. Doric drum; 2b. flute; 2c. base; 3. capital; 3a. necking; 3b. echinos; 3c. abacus; 3d. volute; 4. column; 5. architrave; 6. frieze; 6a. metope; 6b. triglyph; 7. cornice; 8. entablature
p. 25
1.E (Ghiberti), 2.J, 3.J, 4.B, 5.A, 6.F, 7.G, 10.A, 11.H, 12.L, 13.K, 14.C, 15.D, 16.O, 17.K, 18.I, 19G, 20.D, 21.M, 22.H, 23.J, 24.N
p. 26
1.C, 2.D, 3.B, 4.E, 5.A
1., 2.F, 3.A, 4.B, 5.A, 6.A, 7.E, 8.D, 9.C, 10.A, 11.A, 12.A, 13.A, 14.B
p. 27
Perspective: linear; smaller; surface; painting; relief sculpture; window; perpendicular; orthogonals; right angles; vanishing
figure on a rearing horse; grid; horizontal; perpendicular
Uccello; square; rectangular; spinning; aerial
clearer; thickly; two; three.

Chapter 14

p. 35

<u>Leonardo Da Vinci</u>: Florence: Verrocchio; angel; Verrocchio's; 1470; *The Last Supper;* Santa Maria delle Grazie; Milan; Judas; Thomas; John; Perer; Christ a pyramid; Saint Anne; Mary; Christ; a lamb; sfumato; chiaroscuro

Notebook; right; left; human anatomy.

p. 36

<u>Michelangelo</u>: Ghirlandaio; Florence; Pietà; Rome, Saint Peter's; David; Palazzo Vecchio; Florentine republicanism; Julius II; Moses; Sistine Chapel; Old; ancestors; Christ; Creation; Adam; Eve; Noah; 1508; 1512; 1534; altar; right; Left; Hades; Charon; Styx; Saint Bartholomew.

p. 38

1.E, 2.H, 3.G, 4.E, 5.B, 6.G, 7.A, 8.F, 9.B, 10.F, 11.C, 12.C, 13.C, 14.G, 15.F, 16.G, 17.D, 18.D, 19.A, 20.E, 21.I, 22.C, 23.D

p. 39

1.D, 2.E, 3.B, 4.C, 5.A, 6.B, 7.B

1.D, 2.E, 3.F, 4.A, 5.C, 6.B

1.B, 2.C/A, 3.B, 4.H, 5.D, 6.F, 7.G, 8.E, 9.C/A

p. 40

1. dome, 2. apse, 3. pier

p. 41

1.   Raphael; Baldassare Castiglione; Galatea; an ideal/perfect model
2.   Michelangelo; Raphael; "And you? Alone like the executioner?"
3.   Vasari; painting; Giorgione; painting; sculpture
4.   With Time; an old woman; Giorgione; Venice; 16th; *The Tempest* and *Sleeping Venus*

Chapter 15

p. 47

Indulgences; Martin Luther; 1517; Wittenberg (Saxony); 95 theses; 1520; Reformation; Protestant; Counter-Reformation; Inquisition; Gregory IX

Trent; Veronese; *Last Supper*, changing the title to *Christ in the House of Levi;* Galleria dell'Accademia; Venice

p. 49

1.   nave, 2. aisle, 3. transept, 4. crossing, 5. choir, 6. apse
1.   nave, 2. side chapel, 3. dome, 4. transept, 5. apse

p. 50

1.G, 2.F, 3.F, 4.H, 5.E, 6.B, 7.A, 8.C, 9.D, 10.C

1.B, 2.A (or Francis I), 3.C

P. 51

1.D, 2.C, 3.E, 4.B, 5.A

P. 52

1.   Versari; Parmigianino; *Self-Portrait in a Convex Mirror* or *Madonna and Child with Angels*
2.   Loyola; 1540; *Spiritual Exercises;* Ecclesiastics 1:2
3.   Saint Teresa; *The Way of Perfection*; Avila, Spain; Carmelites

Chapter 16

p. 60

1.E, 2.C, 3.F, 4.D, 5.C, 6.A, 7.B, 8.G

1.C, 2.F, 3.E, 4.D, 5.A, 6.B, 7.C

1.C, 2.D, 3.E, 4.A, 5.B

P. 61

Antwerp; Italy; *Icarus*; landscape; down at the ground; up at the sky; Icarus; myth; Daedauls; wings; wax; Daedalus; Icarus; sun; Icarus disobeyed; Aegean; "No plow stops for A dying man."

Tower of Babel; unrealistic ambition; hubris; *The Alchemist;* irrational ambition; *Netherlandish Proverb; Adagia*; Erasmus.

Chapter 17

p.68

1618; 1648; Catholics; Protestants; Phillip II; Phillip IV; Westphalia; Holland; Catholic; Belgium; Phillip; Charles I; Charles II; Louis XIV

Dutch; Hanseatic; Copernicus; Kepler; Galileo; same; Newton; Hobbes; Locke; citizens; Hobbes; Locke; governed.

p. 69

1.   dome, 2. sacristy, 3. Transept of Saint Peter, 4. Sistine Chapel, 5. Papal Palace, 6. piazza, 7. obelisk, 8. colonnade.

1. nave, 2. choir, 3. entrance, 4. side chapel

p. 70

1.   bell tower, 2. nave, 3. aisle, 4. Lord Mayor's vestry, 5. Minor Canon's vestry, 6. Dean's vestry, 7. transept, 8. crossing under the dome, 9. choir, 10. Jesus chapel

p. 73

1.G, 2.J, 3.G, 4.K, 5.C, 6.B, 7.F, 8.P, 9.D, 10.A, 11.B, 12.L, 13.O, 14.C, 15.E, 16.N, 17.M, 18.I, 19.H, 20.P, 21.G, 22.C, 23.G, 24.G, 25.D

p. 74

1.B, 2.C, 3.A

1.B, 2. Versailles, 3.H, 4.I, 5.J, 6.A, 7.F, 8.G, 9.E, 10.C, 11.D,

p. 75

1.F, 2.E, 3.G, 4.H, 5.B, 6.A, 7.D, 8.C

Karel Van Mander; Caravaggio; god or war; goddess of wisdom and the arts; one cannot be both a lover of art and a lover of war.

Chapter 18

p. 84

1.D, 2.F, 3.A, 4.E, 5.B, 6.C

p.85

1.J, 2.I, 3.H, 4.F, 5.K, 6.G, 7.E, 8.L, 9.C, 10.N, 11.A, 12.D, 13.O, 14.B, 15.M, 16.R, 17.P, 18.Q

p. 86

1.F, 2.E, 3.F, 4.H, 5.A, 6.G, 7.D, 8.I, 9.C, 10.B, 11.J, 12.M, 13.K, 14.L, 15.N

1. Louis VIV; monarchy

2. William Hogarth: on his etching *Time Smoking a Picture,* time increases the value of a work of art

Chapter 19

p. 94

<u>French History</u>: True Style; Rococo; Revolution; Napoleon; imperial; 1789; Bastille; Terror; old regime; Marie Antoinette; 1793; Directoire; 1804; emperor; Rome; Julius Caesar; eagle; laurel wreath; Russia; 1814; monarchy; XVII; 1815; 1821.

p. 95

1.C, 2.E, 3.A, 4.A, 5.E, 6.C, 7.D, 8.F, 9.H, 10.B, 11.A, 12.G,

1.C, 2.E, 3.F, 4.I, 5.H, 6.G, 7.D, 8.A, 9.B

p. 97

1.D, 2.B, 3.E, 4.C, 5.A

Chapter 20

p. 103

1. A (1824), 2.B, 3.C, 4.E, 5.D

p.104

1.I, 2.G, 3.F, 4.G, 5.G, 5.B, 6.C, 7.D, 8.A, 9.E, 10.I

p.105

1.E, 2.F, 3.G, 4.H, 5.D, 6.B, 7.C, 8.A, 9.D, 10.J, 11. K, 12.M, 13.N, 14.L, 15.I

p. 107
1. Shelley; English; King of Kings; desert
2. Keats; "La Belle Dame sans Merci"
3. Wordsworth; " The Solitary Reaper"; A woman reaping; oneness of humanity with nature
4. Coleridge; *Lyrical Ballads*; Royal Pavilion; John Nash Brighton, England
p. 108
1. Lord Byron; English; fighting for Greek independence from Turkey; Greek poet; Greek island—legendary birthplace of Apollo and Artemis; Apollo as the sun god.
2. Thomas Cole; American Romantic; he liked them

Chapter 21
p. 118
1.D, 2.H, 3.G, 4.J, 5.A, 6.F, 7.I, 8.E, 9.A, 10.C, 11.B
1.D, 2.F, 3.M, 4.H, 5.J, 6.L, 7.I, 8.K, 9.A, 10.C, 11.E, 12.G, 13.B
p.120
1. Karl Marx and Friedrich Engels; 1848; England; the working class; the superstructure
2. A gigantic prince; Rabelais; very large; Louis Philippe
3. William Holman Hunt, Dante Gabriel Rossetti, and John Everett Millais; London; looked to the past to find an ideal; his aim had been to achieve beauty through idealization. Esthetic is artificial and sentimental.

Chapter 22
p. 127
Paris; 1860; optical; light; color; bourgeois; bohemian; Guerbois; Montmarte
Napoleon III; Georges; Eugène Haussmann; Square of Saint Peter's; Palace de l'Etoile; Garnier; Baroque; Ionic; pediment; mirrors; social rank
p.128
1.E, 2.F, 3.G, 4.H, 5.I, 6.A, 7.D, 8.B, 9.C, 10.B, 11.J
1.C, 2.F, 3.L, 4.K, 5.I, 6.J, 7.A, 8.H, 9.D, 10.B, 11.G, 12.E
P. 130
1. *Torso of a Woman in the Sun*; Renoir
2. Edward Steichen; photographer; *Balzac* by Rodin
3. Whistler; He struggles with these as he struggles with the male and female forces within himself.
4. Ruskin; Whistler's *Nocturne in Black and Gold*

Chapter 23
p. 139
1.J, 2.E, 3.I, 4.H, 5.C, 6.A, 7.B, 8.G, 9.D, 10.F
1.D, 2.I, 3.E, 4.J, 5.A, 6.G, 7.F, 8.H, 9.B, 10.C, 11.K
P. 141
1. Cézanne; by painting apples in a new structured abstraction
2. Vincent Van Gogh; his brother Theo; *Bedroom at Arles*; none, two
3. Edgar Allen Poe; American; *The Raven;* Gauguin
4. Gauguin; to music; Tahiti
p. 142
1. Edvard Munch; Norwegian; *The Scream*; Symbolist and Post-Impressionism
2. Henri Rousseau; *The Dream*; nude women in *The Dream*; reclining on a couch in the jungle; lions, an elephant, birds
3. Van Gogh; *Wheatfield with Reaper*; the power of the sun; one

Chapter 24
p. 152
1. Gertrude Stein; Paris was the center of the Western art world in the twentieth century.
2. Donatello among the wild beasts!; 1905; Paris; exhibition at the Salon d'Automne
3. Pablo Picasso; African tribal masks and sculpture; by giving form to threatening spirits, we are no longer affected by our fears.
p. 153
1.E, 2.F, 3.D, 4.B, 5.C, 6.G, 7.F, 8.A, 9.B, 10.B, 11.C
1.H, 2.E, 3.I, 4.F, 5.B, 6.G, 7.D, 8.A, 9.C

Chapter 25
p. 162
1.E, 2.F, 3.M, 4.N, 5.B, 6.A, 7.E, 8.J, 9.G, 10.D, 11.A, 12.H, 13.K, 14.A, 15.J, 16.J, 17.I, 18.L, 19.C, 20.A, 21.F, 22.A, 23.A, 24.E
p. 163
1.B, 2.F, 3.G, 4.I, 5.P, 6.Q, 7.N, 8.O, 9.A, 10.E, 11.A, 12.J, 13.K, 14.L, 15.D, 16.H, 17.M
1.B, 2.F, 3.E, 4.D, 5.C, 6.A
P. 164
1. Gertrude Stein; Pablo Picasso; *Prose Portraits;* Cubism
2. Filippo Marinetti; *Le Figaro;* Futurism; Futurism would replace the old Academic traditions.
3. Fernard Léger; the city; Modern art, influenced by industrialism, changes the way we see our surroundings and the way it is represented
p. 165
1. "Lines to a Lady Egg"; *Mademoiselle Pogany;* Constantin Brancusi; her reductive, essential form—eggshaped head.
2. Marcel Duchamp, *Nude Descending a Staircase, No.2*; Futurism, Cubism and photography
3. Alfred Barr, Jr.; International Style; Schroeder House; Utrectht, The Netherlands; Gerrit Rietveld

Chapter 26
p. 171
1.G, 2.F, 3.C, 4.A, 5.J, 6.R, 7.H, 8.K, 9.G, 10.I, 11.B, 12.H, 13.G, 14.E, 15.M, 16.L, 17.Q, 18.D, 19.O, 20.P, 21.N
p. 172
1.F, 2.E, 3.I, 4.H, 5.L, 6.D, 7.O, 8.C, 9.S, 10.C, 11.J, 12.C, 13.G, 14.N, 15. M, 16.K, 17.B, 18.R, 19.Q, 20.P, 21.A, 22.O, 23: Steiglitz; 24: Duchamp.
p. 174
1. Hugo Ball; Dada; World War I
2. Man Ray; photography
3. Paul Klee; the creative process

Chapter 27
p. 181
1940s; New York; 1942; Art of this Century; avant-garde; Hans Hofman; Josef Albers
Alfred Barr, Jr.; Vassily Kandinsky; Surrealist; unconscious; action; Navaho; floor; Jungian; Regionalist; *Going West.*
p. 182
1. Francis Bacon; English; That technique is just as important as the work itself.
p. 183
1. Adolf Hitler; July 19, 1937; The opening of the first "Great German Art Exhibition"
2. Josef Albers; Art should not represent nature but concentrate on the shapes furthest from nature to explore color and geometry.
3. Jackson Pollock; That it is unconscious.

p. 184

1.D, 2.E, 3.G, 4.H, 5.J, 6.K, 7.C, 8.F, 9.B, 10.A, 11.I

1.E, 2.F, 3.H, 4.J, 5.K, 6.B, 7.I, 8.C, 9.G, 10.A, 11.D

Chapter 28

p. 192

1.H, 2.J, 3.I, 4.G, 5.K, 6.D, 7.F, 8.O, 9.L, 10.K, 11.C, 12.E, 13.B, 14.N, 15.M, 16.P

1.C, 2.E, 3.F, 4.A, 5.D, 6.B

p. 193

1.   Pop Art; Richard Hamilton; English
2.   Andy Warhol
3.   Dan Flavin; fluorescent lights; Minimalist

Chapter 29

p. 201

Controversy and Pollsters: New York; Brancusi; Edward Steichen; "Kitchen Utensils and Hospital Supplies"; Andres Serrano; National Endowment for the Arts; Cincinnati Contemporary Arts; Robert Mapplethorpe; acquitted; Komar and Melamid.

p. 202

1.D, 2.G, 3.I, 4.N, 5.C, 6.O, 7.A, 8.H, 9.B, 10.K, 11.L, 12.M, 13.F, 14.J, 15.E, 16.D

1.F, 2.C, 3.E, 4.A, 5.B, 6.D

p. 203

1.F, 2.D, 3.E, 4.A, 5.B, 6.C

1.G, 2.F, 3.B, 4.A, 5.K, 6.I, 7.C, 8.D, 9.E, 10.J, 11.H

p. 205

1.   Richard Rogers; The Lloyd's Building; London.
2.   Nam June Paik; Korean; That today, in an electronic age, we need art more than ever.

Sources for Art History Programs

The addresses for the media companies who publish the films, videos, and videodiscs cited in this manual, usually in an abbreviated form, are listed below. In addition to the up-to-date catalogs that may be obtained from writing or calling these companies, instructors in search of audiovisual resources should consult *The Video Source Book*, 2 volumes, 23rd edition, 1999 (Detroit: Gale Research Inc., 1999).

AIMS Multimedia
1-800-367-2467
www.aimsmultimedia.com

Agency for Instructional Technology
1-800-457-4509
www.ait.net

Applause Productions Inc
516-883-2825
apptora@aol.com

Arts America, Inc.
1-800-553-5278
artsamerica@echonyc.com

Blackwood Productions
212-247-4710
www.panix.com/~blackwoo
blackwoo@panix.com

Britannica Films & Video
1-800-554-9862

Carousel Film & Video
1-800-683-1660
carousel@pipeline.com

Cambridge Educational
1-888-744-0100
www.cambridgeol.com/cambridge

Clearvue/EAV, Inc.
1-800-253-2788
www.clearvue.com

Coronet/MTI Film & Video
1-800-777-8100

Creative Arts Television Archive (CATA)
860-868-1771
catarchive@aol.com

Crystal Productions
1-800-255-8629
www.crystalproductions.com

Direct Cinema
1-800-525-0000
dclvideo@aol.com

Electronic Field Productions Services/Saw Mill River Productions
413-548-8058
www.the-spa.com/srp

Facets Multimedia
1-800-331-6197
www.facets.org

Films for the Humanities & Sciences
1-800-257-5126
www.films.com

Green Acre Video
416-536-2711
www.greenacrevideo.com

Home Vision Cinema (HVC)
1-800-826-3456
www.homevision.com

Home Vision Select
1-800-826-3456
classics@homevision.publicmedia.com

International Film Bureau (IFB)
312-427-4545

Maysles Films, Inc.
1-800-336-0634
directcinema@worldnet.att.net

Media for the Arts (MFA)
1-800-554-6008
www.art-history.com
artmfa@art-history.com

Metropolitan Museum of Art (MMA)
212-535-7710
www.metropolitan.org

Museum of Modern Art (MOMA)
212-708-9530
www.moma.org

National Gallery of Art - Dept. of
Education Resources
202-842-6273
www.nga.gov
mail@nga.gov

New Dimension Media, Inc.
1-800-288-4456
www.btsb.com/ndm/

New York State Education Dept.
518-474-3852
www.nysed.gov/

PBS Home Video
1-800-531-4727
www.pbs.org

Phoenix Films & Video
1-800-221-1274
phoenixfilms@worldnet.att.net

RMI
1-800-745-5480
www.rmimedia.com

The Roland Group (TRC)
1-800-597-6526

Sumeria
415-904-0800
www.sumeria.com

Total Marketing Service (TMS)
1-800-469-7977

United Learning (UL)
1-800-424-0362
www.unitedlearning.com

The Video Catalog
1-800-733-6656
kyle@rivertrade.com

Video Marketplace (VM)
1-800-383-8811
www.videomarketplace.com

The Voyager Group
1-888-292-5584
http://voyager.learntech.com/cdrom/

WNET/Thirteen
212-560-2000
www.wnet.org

Zane Publishing
1-800-460-0444
www.zane.com

Key Works

Vincent van Gogh, *Self-Portrait Before his Easel*, 1888

Bodyguard of the Emperor Qin, Qin Dynasty, Lintong, Shaanxi Province, China, 221 – 206 B.C.

Taj Mahal, Agra, India, 1632 – 1648

Constantin Brancusi, *Bird in Space*, 1928

René Magritte, *The Betrayal of Images*, 1928

God as Architect (God Drawing the Universe with a Compass), from the Bible moralisée, Reims, France, mid-13th century

Pieter Bruegel the Elder, *The Tower of Babel*, 1563

Joseph Wright of Derby, *The Corinthian Maid*, 1782 – 1784

James Abbott McNeill Whistler, *Arrangement in Black and Gray* (Portrait of the Artist's Mother), 1871

Jan van Eyck, *The Virgin in a Church*, c. 1410 – 1425

Meret Oppenheim, *Fur-Covered Cup, Saucer, and Spoon, (Le Déjeuner en Fourrure)*, 1936

Alexander Calder, *Cat*, 1976

Theo van Doesburg, Study 1 for *Composition (The Cow)*, 1916

Theo van Doesburg, Study 2 for *Composition (The Cow)*, 1917

Theo van Doesburg, Study 3 for *Composition (The Cow)*, 1917

Theo van Doesburg, Study for *Composition (The Cow)*, (c. 1917; dated 1916)

Theo van Doesburg, Study for *Composition (The Cow)*, c. 1917

Maps, Diagrams, and Projections

Lines

Lines used to create facial expressions

Shapes

Drawing of solid shapes showing hatching and crosshatching

The visible spectrum of light

The color wheel

The ten-step value scale breaks the various shades from white to black into ten gradations

A color value scale

Key Terms

abstract

achromatic

archaeometry

chromatic

circumambulate

color wheel

complementary color

composition

content

contrast

dendrochronology
diptych
figurative
formalism
garbha griha
ground plan
hatching, crosshatching
hue
icon
iconography
iconology
idealized
illusionism, illusionistic
intensity
landscape
modeling
naturalism, naturalistic
non-figurative
non-representational
patron
plane

portrait
primary color
program
realistic
radiocarbon dating
representational
romanticize
saturation
secondary color
seriation
shading
still life
stratigraphy
stupa
stylization
terracotta
trompe-l'oeil
underpainting
value
ziggurat

Videos

Adventures in Perception
22 min, 1973, Phoenix/BFA Films

Art: What is it? Why is it?
30 min, 1963, Britannica Films

General Histories-multipart
Art of the Western World (4 parts)
55 min, VM

Art History: A Survey of the Western World (12 progams)
15 min, 1989, AIT

Art History: Mastery in Three Media (10 programs)
15 min, 1989, AIT

The Artist and his Environment (6 programs)
30 min, 1991, Green Acre Video

At the Met: Curator's Choice (6 programs)
25 min, (198?), HVC, Crystal Productions

Introduction
Why Do We Study the History of Art?

Civilisation (13 programs)
50 min, 1970, VM

Multiple-Choice Questions

1. The three major categories of the visual arts are

        a. painting, drawing, photography
        b. painting, drawing, sculpture
        c. painting, sculpture, architecture
        d. pictures, sculptures, architecture*
        e. drawing, architecture, sculpture

2. The material value of art refers to

        a. its materialism
        b. the value of its media*
        c. its expensive production
        d. the amount paid to the artist

3. Intrinsic value means

        a. the genetic value of a work
        b. the assessment of esthetic character*
        c. the patriotic assessment of a work
        d. the religious value of a work

4. The famous forger of Vermeer's works was

        a. Hermann Goering
        b. Steichen
        c. Brancusi
        d. van Meegeren*

5. Brancusi's Bird was admitted into the U.S. as a

        a. bronze work of art
        b. stolen work of art
        c. kitchen supply*
        d. forgery

6. The "art train" refers to

    a. Goering's cache of stolen art*
    b. a national museum housed in a railroad station
    c. a trail of stolen art
    d. a training school

7. The Betrayal of Images is

    a. a sculpture of a pipe
    b. a painting of a pipe*
    c. a nonfigurative painting
    d. an example of trompe l'oeil

8. The Apocrypha refer to

    a. the end of the world
    b. the last book of the Bible
    c. the unaccepted books of the Bible*
    d. a commentary on the Bible

9. A painting of fruit and flowers on a table is a

    a. still life*
    b. nonrepresentational work
    c. portrait
    d. drawing

10. Who said "One does like to make one's mummy just as nice as possible?"

    a. van Gogh
    b. van Eyck
    c. Oppenheim
    d. Whistler*
    e. Bruegel

11. A diptych is a

    a. two-part sculpture
    b. two-paneled painting*
    c. double building
    d. repeated image

12. Iconography refers to

    a. formal elements
    b. feminism
    c. Marxism
    d. subject matter*

13. Which is <u>not</u> a formal element of art?

    a. lines
    b. shapes
    c. deconstruction*
    d. planes

14. The philosopher Jacques Derrida is most associated with

    a. deconstruction*
    b. psychoanalysis
    c. formalism
    d. iconology

15. Ferdinand de Saussure is most associated with

    a. deconstruction
    b. psychoanalysis
    c. semiology*
    d. iconology
    e. formalism

16. Sigmund Freud is most associated with

    a. deconstruction
    b. psychoanalysis and psychobiography*
    c. semiology
    d. iconology
    e. feminism

17. In semiotics, the four letters p-i-p-e constitute

    a. a sign
    b. etymology
    c. a signifier*
    d. a signified

18. Alexander the Great's portraitist was

    a. Protogenes
    b. Rhodes
    c. Aristotle
    d. Apelles*

19. Morphe is the Greek word for

    a. shape*
    b. sleep
    c. line
    d. movement

20. Complementary colors are

    a. next to each other on the color wheel
    b. one removed from each other on the color wheel
    c. opposite each other on the color wheel*
    d. not on the color wheel

21. The Greek word chroma means

    a. chrome
    b. color*
    c. colorless
    d. value

22. The primary colors are

    a. red, yellow, blue, green
    b. red, blue, green
    c. blue, red, yellow*
    d. green, red, yellow
    e. black, gray, white

23. Additive sculpture uses

    a. clay*
    b. marble
    c. wood
    d. granite

24. All these terms refer to color purity <u>except</u>

     a. intensity
     b. saturation
     c. chroma
     d. hue*

25. Which color is used to convey that objects are at a distance?

     a. yellow
     b. blue*
     c. red
     d. orange

26. When a vertical plane slices through buildings, the cross-section that results is a

     a. floor plan
     b. pendentive
     c. structure
     d. section*

27. Two-dimensional space defines
     a. area*
     b. volume
     c. mass
     d. depth

28. An artist creates a feeling of volume by using

     a. mass
     b. visual perspective
     c. aerial perspective
     d. modeling*

29. The brightness of a color is called its _____.

     a. value*
     b. hue
     c. saturation
     d. angle

CHAPTER 1:
The Art Of Prehistory

Key Works

Venus of Willendorf, Austria, c. 25,000 – 21,000 B.C.
Venus of Laussel, France, c. 25,000 – 23,000 B.C.
Bison with turned head, La Madeleine, France, c. 11,000 – 9,000 B.C.
Bison, Tuc d'Audoubert, France, 13,000 – 8,000 B.C.
Ceiling view, Altamira cave, Spain, c. 12,000 B.C.
Standing bison, Altamira cave, Spain, c. 12,000 B.C.
Handprints from Pech-Merle, France, c. 16,000 B.C.
Shaman, Trois-Frères cave, Ariège, France, 13,000 – 11,000 B.C.
Hall of Running Bulls, Lascaux, France, c. 15,000 – 13,000 B.C.
"Chinese Horse," Lascaux, France, c. 15,000 – 13,000 B.C.
Reindeer, Lascaux, France, c. 15,000 – 13,000 B.C.
Jellyfish, Cosquer cave, France, c. 25,000 B.C.
Hyena and panther, Chauvet cave, France, c. 25,000 – 17,000 B.C.
Mammoths and horses, Chauvet cave, France, c. 25,000 – 17,000 B.C.
"Lion Panel," Chauvet cave, France, c. 25,000 – 17,000 B.C.
Saharan rock painting, Tassili, Algeria, 5th-4th millennium B.C.
Mother Goddess, Tarxien, Malta, before 2500 B.C.
Menhirs, Carnac, France, c. 4000 B.C.
Dolmen, Crucuno, France, c. 4000 B.C.
Stonehenge, Salisbury Plain, England, c. 2800 – 1500 B.C.
The inside ring of Stonehenge

Maps, Diagrams, and Projections

Map of prehistoric Europe
Map of Australia
Diagram of Lascaux cave system
Reconstruction drawing of temple at Ggantija, Malta
Plan of Stonehenge
Post-and-lintel construction
Lintel and tenon

Window on the World: Rock Paintings of Australia

Wandjina, Rowalumbin, Kimberley, Australia
Mimi hunters, Kakadu National Park, Australia
Men and women hunting kangaroos, Unbalanya Hill, Australia
Kangaroo with Lightning Man, Nourlangie Rock, Kakadu National Park, Australia

Key Terms

abstract
binder
cromlech
dolmen
façade
fire
incised
kiln
lintel
medium
megalith
menhir
modeling
monolith

necropolis
parapet
pigment
plane
polychrome
post-and-lintel construction
relief (low relief, high relief)
sculpture in the round
support
tenon
twisted perspective
trilithon
vehicle

Videos

Aboriginal Art—Past, Present, and Future
13 min, Crystal Productions

Australia's Aborigines
60 min, 1988, VM

Australia's Art of the Dreamtime: Quinkin County
60 min, 1989, Great Plains National, (GPN)

The Caves of Altamira
26 min, 1991, IFB; FFTH

The Lascaux Cave: A Look at Our Prehistoric Past
23 min., 1990, IFB

Lascaux, Cradle of Man's Art, film
17 min, 1976, IFB

Lascaux Revisited: Exploring Prehistoric Cave Art
35 min., Clearvue, Crystal

Marks of the Ancestors: Ancient Indian Rock Art of Arizona
40 min, Clearvue

Native American Rock Art of the Southwest
37 min, Clearvue

Prehistoric Man in Europe
23 min., 1991, IFB

Sacred Sites: Prehistoric Monuments of Europe
43 min, 1994, VM

CD-ROMs

MOODITJ – Australian Indigenous Cultural Expressions on CD-ROM
Mac/Windows
Development for Instructional Technology (DUIT)

Multiple-Choice Questions

1. The term "prehistory" means

       a. before people wrote history books
       b. before people had written language*
       c. before people had libraries
       d. before people could count
       e. before people could talk

2. The term "Paleolithic" refers to the

       a. Old Stone Age*
       b. Middle Stone Age
       c. New Stone Age
       d. Old Stones
       e. Old Dispensation

3. Old Stone Age people

       a. had stone houses
       b. used stone tools*
       c. worshipped in stone temples
       d. built stone tombs
       e. used stone for building

4. The term *Homo sapiens* literally means

     a. simple man
     b. stupid man
     c. stoic man
     d. wise man*
     e. genius

5. A good example of a Paleolithic sculpture-in-the-round is

     a. the Venus of Laussel
     b. the Tuc d'Audoubert Bison
     c. the Venus of Willendorf*
     d. the Wandjina
     e. the Mimi

6. The main shapes in the Venus of Willendorf are

     a. rectangular
     b. oval*
     c. cubic
     d. trapezoidal
     e. triangular

7. As used in this text, a relief refers to

     a. a rest
     b. a vacation
     c. a category of sculpture*
     d. a painted image
     e. a post-and-lintel

8. Which of the following is a logical interpretation of the Venus of Willendorf?

     a. an obese figure
     b. a wealthy figure
     c. a fertility figure*
     d. a pregnant figure
     e. a blind figure

9. Pigment is

    a. a racial characteristic
    b. color*
    c. paint
    d. painted relief
    e. watercolor

10. Paleolithic man's art has been found in the form of sculpture, friezes and paintings, but _____ is earliest.

    a. "fertility figurines" like the the Venus of Willendorf*
    b. animal frieze at Lascaux
    c. Stonehenge
    d. animal frieze at Altamira

11. The artists at Lascaux and Altamira seemed to have done their art as

    a. decoration for the cave
    b. part of a ceremony to ensure success in the hunt*
    c. the totem of the tribal chief
    d. an ex-voto for a man killed in a hunt

12. Which of the following is not Paleolithic?

    a. Venus of Laussel
    b. Handprint of Pech-Merle
    c. Mother Goddess from Tarxien*
    d. Stag from Lascaux
    e. Jellyfish from Cosquer

13. The most important Paleolithic cave paintings are located in

    a. Spain
    b. France
    c. England
    d. a and b*

14. Which of the following does not have a representation of a bison?

    a. Altamira
    b. Stonehenge*
    c. Tuc d'Audoubert
    d. La Madelaine

15. Which is not related to making sculpture?

    a. carving
    b. modeling
    c. relief
    d. post-and-lintel*
    e. incising

16. A kiln is

    a. for cooking dinner
    b. for heating pigments
    c. for baking clay*
    d. for cooking herbs
    e. for drying wet paint

17. The so-called Shaman cave painting is at

    a. Lascaux
    b. Pech-Merle
    c. Chauvet
    d. Trois-Freres*
    e. Altamira

18. Who of the following was never involved in studying cave paintings?

    a. Leroi-Gourhan
    b. Henri Breuil
    c. Pech-Merle*
    d. Reinach
    e. Chauvet

19. By definition, Paleolithic paintings are not

    a. endowed with life
    b. abstract*
    c. naturalistic
    d. designed to conjure up game for hunters

20. The caves at Altamira share certain things in common with Lascaux

    a. they are in France
    b. they are in flat, lake country
    c. they contain remarkable Paleolithic depictions of animals*
    d. a, b, and c

21. When an animal's body is shown in perspective, but its head is shown full front, the artist is using

    a. twisted perspective*
    b. atmospheric perspective
    c. linear perspective
    d. aerial perspective

22. Lascaux cave paintings of animals could be described as

    a. painted relief
    b. stylized
    c. old fashioned
    d. superimposed*
    e. stick figures

23. Which of the following is <u>not</u> found at Lascaux?

    a. a horned owl*
    b. a stag
    c. horses
    d. bulls
    e. humans

24. Paleolithic paintings of animals usually have been found

    a. in the uninhabited depths of caves*
    b. at the mouths of caves
    c. in Neolithic shelters
    d. on rock faces open to the light of day

25. In which of the following modern countries have the least number of megaliths been found?

    a. France
    b. Spain*
    c. Malta
    d. Britain

26. To what does the Aboriginal Dreaming most refer?

    a. Australian rituals
    b. Australian myth*
    c. Australian dreams
    d. Australian art
    e. Australian folk tales

27. Which is not a subject of Aboriginal rock painting?

    a. Mimi
    b. kangaroos
    c. Wandjina
    d. buffalo*

28. The oldest known Aboriginal rock painting style is

    a. Mimi*
    b. x-ray
    c. megalithic
    d. Dreaming

29. Wandjina are

    a. Mimi hunters
    b. Aboriginal kangaroos
    c. shaman
    d. cloud spirits*
    e. Aboriginal X-rays

30. Taboo means that something or someone is

    a. a saint and a sinner
    b. good and evil
    c. sacred and profane*
    d. magic and sacred
    e. untouchable

31. Civilization received its greatest push forward from the

    a. discovery of fire
    b. agricultural revolution*
    c. discovery of the potter's wheel
    d. domestication of animals

32. An important cultural change from Paleolithic to Neolithic is

    a. from nomadic to agricultural*
    b. from megalithic to caves
    c. from pottery to sculpture
    d. from warlike to peaceful
    e. from illiterate to literate

33. Which is not connected to Malta?

    a. Gozo
    b. Cosquer*
    c. Ggantija
    d. Tarxien

34. Which is not a Celtic term?

    a. Dolmen
    b. Cromlech
    c. Menhir
    d. Wessex*
    e. Druid

35. A trilithon is a

    a. single post-and-lintel*
    b. three posts-and-lintels
    c. a fossil
    d. a three-part painting
    e. a triple stone

36. Stonehenge dates from the _____ period.

    a. Paleolithic
    b. Late Jurassic
    c. Mesolithic
    d. Neolithic*

37. Stonehenge is located at

    a. Marlborough Downs
    b. Carnac
    c. Crucuno
    d. Sussex
    e. Salisbury Plain*

38. Which is not connected to Stonehenge?

    a. Aubrey Holes
    b. Camelot*
    c. Sarsen
    d. Marlborough Downs
    e. Heel Stone

39. Who built Stonehenge?

    a. Druids
    b. Merlin
    c. King Arthur
    d. Men of Wessex*
    e. Men of Camelot

40. Which is true of the Beaker People?

    a. they hunted ducks
    b. they were nomads
    c. they made pottery*
    d. they destroyed Stonehenge
    e. they were literate

41. The last Ice Age in western Europe was around

    a. 18,000 to 15,000 B.C.*
    b. 25,000 to 22,000 B.C.
    c. 100,000 to 98,000 B.C.
    d. 52,000 to 50,000 B.C.
    e. 12,000 to 11,000 B.C.

42. The sun rises over the Heel Stone at Stonehenge at

    a. the winter solstice
    b. the summer solstice*
    c. Easter
    d. Christmas
    e. dawn

CHAPTER 2:
The Ancient Near East

Key Works

Neolithic plastered skull, Jericho, c. 7000 B.C.

Anatolian goddess giving birth, Çatal Hüyük, Turkey, c. 6500 – 5700 B.C.

Two leopards, Shrine Vla, Çatal Hüyük, Turkey, c. 6000 B.C.

Cone mosaics, Uruk, c. 3500 B.C.

Carved vase (both sides), Uruk, c. 3500 – 3100 B.C.

Female head, Uruk, c. 3500 – 3000 B.C.

The White Temple on its ziggurat, Uruk, c. 3500 – 3000 B.C.

Cylinder impression and seal, Uruk, c. 3500 – 3000 B.C.

Clay tablet with the pictograph text that preceded cuneiform, Jemdet Nasr, Iraq, c. 3000 B.C.

Statues from the Abu Temple, Tell Asmar, c. 2700 – 2500 B.C.

Head of a large male figure dedicated to the god Abu.

Lyre soundbox from the tomb of Queen Puabi, Ur, c. 2685 B.C.

Inlay from front of soundbox of lyre from the tomb of Queen Puabi, Ur.

Reconstructed harp, from Ur.

Head of an Akkadian ruler (Sargon I?), Nineveh, Iraq, c. 2300 B.C.

Victory stele of Naram-Sin, Susa, c. 2254 – 2218 B.C.

Head of Gudea, Lagash, Iraq, c. 2100 B.C.

Gudea with temple plan, Lagash, Iraq, c. 2100 B.C.

Detail of temple plan on Gudea's lap, Lagash, Iraq, c. 2100 B.C.

Nanna ziggurat, Ur, c. 2100 – 2050 B.C.

Stele inscribed with the Law Code of Hammurabi, Susa, (Iran), c. 1792 – 1750 B.C.

Detail of Stele with the Law Code of Hammurabi.

Lion Gate (Royal Gate), Hattusas, Boghazköy, Turkey, c. 1400 B.C.

Hittite war god, from the King's Gate at Hattusas, Boghazköy, Turkey, c. 1400 B.C.

King Assurnasirpal II, Nimrud, Iraq, c. 883 – 859 B.C.

King Assurnasirpal II hunting lions, Nimrud, Iraq, c. 883 – 859 B.C.

City attacked with a battering ram, palace of King Assurnasirpal II, Nimrud, Iraq.

Dying Lioness (detail of *The Great Lion Hunt*), from the palace of King Assurbanipal, Nineveh, c. 668 – 627 B.C.

Lamassu, from the gateway, Sargon II's palace at Dur Sharrukin (Khorsabad), Iraq, c. 720 B.C.

Ishtar Gate (reconstructed), Babylon, c. 575 B.C.

Beaker, Susa, capital of Elam Iran, c. 5000 – 4000 B.C.

Kneeling bull, southwest Iran, Proto-Elamite, 3100 – 2999 B.C.

Stag, Kostromskaya, Russia, 7th century B.C.

Stag (Scythian?), near Caspian Sea, 4th Century B.C.

Apadana (Audience Hall) of Darius, Persepolis, c. 500 B.C.

Royal guards, relief on the stairway to the Audience Hall of Darius, Persepolis, c. 500 B.C.

Bull capital, Persepolis, c. 500 B.C.

Achaemenid drinking vessel, Persian, 5th century B.C.

Maps, Diagrams, and Projections

Map of the ancient Near East and the Middle East
Reconstruction of Çatal Hüyük, Turkey
Plan of White Temple
Plan of Sargon II's palace

Key Terms

arch
armature
attribute
bas-relief
base
capital
citadel
column
cone mosaic
convention
crenellated
cuneiform
cyclopean construction
cylinder seal
facing
glaze
glyptic art
hierarchical proportions
impost block
inlaid
lamassu
lapis lazuli
load-bearing construction
pillar
plinth
provenience or provenance
register
shaft
stele
votive

Videos

Ancient Mesopotamia
10 min, 1976, Coronet/MTI

Art in Ancient Lands, Part 1
36 min, Clearvue

Art of the Near East and Ancient Egypt
66 min, Clearvue

Elements of Sculpture: Monuments, Temples and Tombs, filmstrip
15 min, Clearvue

Iraq: Cradle of Civilization
60 min, 1992, VM

Treasures of the British Museum: Sumer, Babylon, Assyria: The Wolves
26 min, FFTH

Multiple-Choice Questions

1. Neolithic in the Near East developed about _____ years later than in Europe.

    a. 1,000
    b. 2,000
    c. 3,000
    d. 4,000*
    e. 5,000

2. The oldest fortified city, and a place of continuous habitation, is

    a. Malta
    b. Çatal Hüyük
    c. Stonehenge
    d. Jericho*

3. Plastered Neolithic skulls were found in

    a. Uruk
    b. Jericho*
    c. Ur
    d. Tell Asmar

4. The oldest planned town excavated so far is located at:

    a. Çatal Hüyük*
    b. Jerusalem
    c. Jericho
    d. Babylon

5. The largest Neolithic site so far discovered in the ancient Near East is located in modern

    a. Iraq
    b. Iran
    c. Turkey*
    d. Jordan

6. Which of the following is <u>not</u> a Mesopotamian god?

    a. Anu
    b. Isis*
    c. Ishtar
    d. Inanna

7. Shamash is the Akkadian

    a. moon god
    b. lightning god
    c. sun god*
    d. supreme god

8. Nergal and Ereshkigal are the

    a. king and queen of the underworld*
    b. king and queen of the sky
    c. king and queen of nature
    d. king and queen of the sea

9. The Mesopotamians believed in

    a. a heavenly afterlife
    b. a gloomy afterlife*
    c. a joyous afterlife
    d. a materialistic afterlife

10. The *hieros gamos* refers to

    a. a festival of the new year
    b. a fertility ceremony
    c. a sacred marriage*
    d. a holy game

11. *Machtkunst* refers to

    a. divine masochism
    b. power art*

c. megaliths

d. monumental art

12. Which of the following was found at Uruk?

    a. The White Temple*
    b. The Abu Temple
    c. The Ur Temple
    d. The Stele of Urnammu

13. A Ziggurat is a

    a. pyramid
    b. fort
    c. building made by Gudea
    d. Mesopotamian temple platform*

14. Ziggurats are

    a. symbolic temples
    b. symbolic rivers
    c. symbolic sculptures
    d. symbolic mountains*

15. Ziggurats are an example of

    a. post-and-lintel construction
    b. arcuated construction
    c. load-bearing construction*
    d. cantilever construction

16. The earliest known writing is called

    a. cuneiform*
    b. hieroglyphics
    c. the alphabet
    d. Akkadian

17. The first recorded epic is about

    a. Noah
    b. Odysseus
    c. Abraham
    d. Gilgamesh*
    e. Inanna

18. Summerian art is characterized by

 a. symmetrical when seen from the front
 b. clasped hands
 c. large eyes in upturned faces
 d. all of the above*

19. The staring, wide eyes of the Tell Asmar statues are believed to indicate that the figures

 a. are apotropaic
 b. are praying
 c. are in the presence of a god*
 d. are terrified by evil spirits

20. The beards of the Tell Asmar statues are best described as

 a. red and stylized
 b. naturalistic and black
 c. stylized and curvilinear
 d. black and stylized*
 e. black and curvilinear

21. "The one who saw the abyss...." refers to

 a. Inanna
 b. Achilles
 c. Enki
 d. Gilgamesh*
 e. Abu

22. Sir Leonard Woolley discovered the site of

 a. Ur*
 b. Tell Asmar
 c. Uruk
 d. Persepolis
 e. Lagash

23. Tigris and Euphrates are

 a. Mesopotamian gods
 b. Hittite gods
 c. Mesopotamian rivers*
 d. Mesopotamian mountains
 e. Mesopotamian rulers

24. Sargon was

    a. an Akkadian ruler*
    b. a Sumerian ruler
    c. a Hittite ruler
    d. the ruler of Lagash
    e. the ruler of Ur

25. _____ ruled Akkad and waged war on his neighbors around 3000 B.C.

    a. Ashurnasirpal
    b. Naram-Sin*
    c. Narmer
    d. Alexander the Great

26. Which is not true of the Stele of Naram-Sin?

    a. it is a relief
    b. it represents landscape as well as human figures
    c. it commemorates the death of Naram-Sin*
    d. it dates to the third millennium B.C.
    e. it is Akkadian

27. The figure of Naram-Sin is shown

    a. with frontal shoulders and profile legs*
    b. with a frontal head and shoulders
    c. with frontal legs and a profile head
    d. with frontal shoulders and legs
    e. holding a rod and scepter

28. Gudea ruled

    a. c. 2100 B.C.*
    b. c. 1800 B.C.
    c. c. 3000 B.C.
    d. c. 1500 B.C.
    e. c. 2600 B.C.

29. Gudea thought of himself mainly as a patron of

    a. cuneiform tablets
    b. sculpture
    c. temples*
    d. paintings
    e. poetry

30. Lagash was:

    a. a Persian city
    b. an important city in Babylon*
    c. the center of the Neolothic Anatolia
    d. an Assyrian city

31. The statues of Gudea are best described as

    a. of diorite, stylized and organic*
    b. of marble and naturalistic
    c. idealized and naturalistic
    d. naturalistic and organic
    e. of gold, and with long, flowing hair

32. A Stele is

    a. a knife
    b. a weapon
    c. a boundary marker*
    d. a clay tablet
    e. a city wall

33. Hammurabi is known for

    a. the Epic of Gilgamesh
    b. building the walls of Uruk
    c. worshipping the sun god
    d. making stelai
    e. a law code*

34. The Hittite civilization was located in

    a. modern Israel
    b. modern Jordan
    c. modern Iraq
    d. modern Iran
    e. modern Turkey*

35. Lions were traditional guardians because

    a. they were kings of the animals
    b. they were thought never to sleep*
    c. they were powerful enough to keep enemies away
    d. they symbolized the human king
    e. they protect their cubs

36. A Lamassu is

    a. a guardian lion
    b. a guardian bull
    c. a guardian genius*
    d. a guardian king
    e. a guardian angel

37. Which of the following does a Lamassu <u>not</u> have?

    a. five legs
    b. wings
    c. horned cap
    d. a sword*
    e. a beard

38. Most Assyrian wall decoration includes

    a. domestic scenes
    b. war*
    c. b and d
    d. royal hunting scenes

39. Assurbanipal was known for

    a. his cruelty and culture*
    b. his cruelty and virtue
    c. his culture and learning
    d. his power and his generosity
    e. his charm and his diplomacy

40. Palace reliefs are most likely to have been found in

    a. Uruk
    b. Lagash
    c. Babylon
    d. Khorsabad*
    e. Hattusas

41. The Ishtar Gate is from

    a. Paris
    b. Babylon*
    c. Akkad
    d. Persepolis

42. The Ishtar Gate used

    a. glazed brick
    b. a true arch
    c. patterns of horses
    d. a and b but not c*

43. The Ishtar Gate was dedicated to

    a. the god of war
    b. the goddess of fertility*
    c. the goddess of the moon
    d. the god of the underworld
    e. the goddess of the hearth

44. The Scythians are best known for

    a. gold*
    b. diorite
    c. pottery
    d. temples
    e. irrigation

45. A documented, excavated object is said to have a

    a. provenance
    b. value
    c. provenience*
    d. valuation
    e. meaning

46. Which of the following are most logically connected?

    a. Darius, Gudea, Sargon, Hammurabi
    b. Ishtar, Sargon, Woolley, Ur
    c. Cyrus, Darius, Persepolis, Susa*
    d. Gilgamesh, Susa, Tell Asmar, Uruk
    e. Urnammu, Abu, Inanna, Ishtar

47. An Apadana is

    a. a gateway
    b. a storage room
    c. a sanctuary
    d. an audience hall*
    e. an altar

48. Whereas early Mesopotamian figures are shown with twisted perspective, Persian human figures

       a. show shoulders in profile*
       b. have of extremely large eyes
       c. have their hands clasped
       d. appear on bas-relief

49. A bull capital is most likely found at

       a. Persepolis*
       b. Lagash
       c. Babylon
       d. Anatolia
       e. Assyria

50. Cuneiform literally means

       a. cone-shaped
       b. cylindrical
       c. wedge-shaped*
       d. rectangular
       e. triangular

Key Works

Palette of Narmer ("Upper Egypt" side), Hierakonpolis, c. 3100 B.C.

Palette of Narmer ("Lower Egypt" side), Hierakonpolis, c. 3100 B.C.

Rosetta Stone, 196 B.C.

Canopic jars of Neshkons

Vignette from Paynedjem's *Book of the Dead*, Thebes, Twenty-First Dynasty, c. 990 – 969 B.C.

Step pyramid, funerary complex of King Zoser, Saqqara, Egypt, c. 2630 – 2611 B.C.

Pyramids at Giza, Egypt, c. 2555 – 2472 B.C.

Colossal statue of Khafre, known as the Great Sphinx, Giza, c. 2520 – 2494 B.C.

Seated statue of Khafre, Giza, c. 2520 – 2494 B.C.

Menkaure and Queen Khamerernebty, Giza, 2490 – 2472 B.C.

Prince Rahotep and his wife Nofret, c. 2551 – 2528 B.C.

Seated scribe, Saqqara, c. 2551 – 2528 B.C.

Lady Senuwy, 12th Dynasty, c. 1971 – 1926 B.C.

Detail of Lady Senuwy, 12th Dynasty, c. 1971 – 1926 B.C.

Sesostris I, Lisht, 12th Dynasty, c. 1971 – 1926 B.C.

Sesostris I, Lisht, 12th Dynasty, c. 1971 – 1926 B.C.

Sesostris III, c. 1878 – 1841 B.C.

Painted coffin of Djehuty-nekht, Bersheh, 12th Dynasty, c. 1971 – 1926 B.C.

Court and pylon of Ramses II (1279 – 1213 B.C.) and colonnade and court of Amenhotep III
(1390 – 1352 B.C.), temple of Amon-Mut-Khonsu, Luxor, 19th Dynasty

Statue of Hatshepsut as pharaoh, 18th Dynasty, c. 1473 – 1458 B.C.

Funerary temple of Queen Hatshepsut, Deir el-Bahri, Egypt, c. 1460 B.C.

Statue of Senemut and Nefrura, 18th Dynasty, c. 1473 – 1458 B.C.

Nebamun hunting birds, from the tomb of Nebamun, Thebes, Egypt, c. 1390 – 1352 B.C.

Opening of the Mouth ceremony, *Book of the Dead* of Hunefer, New Kingdom, 19th Dynasty, c.
1295 – 1186 B.C.

Akhenaten, Karnak, Egypt, 1353 – 1350 B.C.

Bust of Nefertiti, Amarna Period, 1349 – 1336 B.C.

Akhenaten and Nefertiti and their children, Amarna Period, 1349 – 1336 B.C.

Mask of Tutankhamon, c. 1327 B.C.

Canopic coffinette (coffin of Tutankhamon), c. 1327 B.C.

King and Queen of Punt, from Hatshepsut's funerary temple, Deir el-Bahri, c. 1473 – 1458 B.C.

Nubian "eggshell" vessels, c. 3100 – 2890 B.C.

Western Deffufa, Kerma, 17th – 16th century B.C.

Nubians bringing offerings to Egypt, Thebes, 19th Dynasty, c. 1295 – 1186 B.C.

Presentation of Nubian tribute to Tutankhamon, tomb chapel of Huy, Thebes, 18th Dynasty, c.
1336 – 1327 B.C.

Temple of Ramses II, Abu Simbel, Nubia, 1279 – 1213 B.C.

Sphinx of Taharqo, Temple T, Kawa, Nubia, 690 – 664 B.C.

Statuette of Amenirdis I, Kush, Nubia, late 8th century B.C.

Ruins of the Meroë pyramids, Nubia, 3rd – 1st century B.C.
Tomb of Amanishakheto, Meroë, Nubia, late 1st century B.C.
Shield ring with Amon as a ram, Meroë, Nubia, c. 200 B.C.

Maps, Diagrams, and Projections

Map of Ancient Egypt and Nubia
The step pyramid with a mastaba base
Cross section of the pyramid of Khufu
Plan of the Giza funerary complex
Plan of typical pylon temple
Plan of temple of Aman-Mut-Khonsu, Luxor, Egypt, begun c. 1390 B.C.

Key Terms

apotropaion
canon
cartonnage
clerestory
corbelling
engaged column
faience
fresco
frieze
gesso
hypostyle hall
ka
mastaba
obelisk
papyrus
pharaoh
pier
pilaster
pylon
pyramidion
sarcophagus
sphinx
vellum

Videos

Ancient Egypt
11 min, 1976, Coronet/MTI

Ancient Egypt – Alarion
Crystal

Ancient Egypt: The Habit of Civilization
60 min, 1992, VM

King Tut: Tomb of Treasure
26 min, 1992, Home Vision

King Tut: The Face of Tutankhamon
200 min, 1992, VM

Mummies and The Wonders of Ancient Egypt, four-pack set
200 min, 1996, VM

Mysteries Of The Pyramids
60 min, 1989, VM

Nile, River of Gods
100 min, 1995, VM

CD-ROMs

Ancient Egypt & The Middle East, Queue Inc.

Ancient Egyptian Art—The Brooklyn Museum
Mac/Windows
Clearvue, Crystal Productions

Multiple-Choice Questions

1. The world's longest river is

    a. the River Jordan
    b. the Tigris
    c. the Nile*
    d. the Mississippi
    e. the Amazon

2. Hapy is the god of

    a. hymns
    b. happiness
    c. the Nile*
    d. Nubia
    e. Cairo

3. Which of the following is true?

    a. Upper Egypt is north and Lower Egypt is south
    b. the Blue Nile is north of the White Nile
    c. Upper Egypt is south and Lower Egypt is north*
    d. The Nile delta is in the south
    e. The Nile floods every year without fail

4. "Gift of the Nile" refers to

    a. Hapy
    b. Moses
    c. Osiris
    d. Egypt*
    e. Lake Victoria

5. The annual flooding of the Nile is symbolized by the birth and death of

    a. Artemis
    b. Horus
    c. Rameses
    d. Osiris*

6. Egyptian history is divided into

   a. chronological dates
   b. king lists
   c. dynasties*
   d. months and years

7. Narmer was associated with

   a. Menes*
   b. Manetho
   c. Alexander the Great
   d. Menkaure
   e. Nefertiti

8. The _____ shows the uniting of Upper and Lower Egypt and the establishment of the First Dynasty.

   a. Palette of Naram-Sin
   b. Palette of Narmer*
   c. Palette of Khafre
   d. Rosetta Stone

9. Which of the following is true?

   a. Isis is the mother of Horus*
   b. Bes is a death god
   c. Anubis is in the shape of a crocodile
   d. Horus opens the mouth of the dead
   e. Amon is the sun disk

10. Which of the following is true?

   a. Hatshepsut was the first queen of Egypt
   b. Akhenaten was an Old Kingdom pharaoh
   c. Narmer worshipped Aten
   d. Nefertiti was Akhenaten's mother
   e. Amenhotep III was Akhenaten's father*

11. Which of the following is not true?

   a. The Palette of Narmer is an example of *Machtkunst*
   b. The Palette of Narmer is a ceremonial object
   c. The Palette of Narmer is decorated in high relief*
   d. The Palette of Narmer is made of slate
   e. The Palette of Narmer dates to c. 3000 B.C.

12. The Rosetta Stone is important because

    a. it led to the decipherment of hieroglyphics*
    b. it is a unique stele
    c. it has Greek, cuneiform, and Egyptian writing on it
    d. it has Greek, Coptic, and Egyptian writing on it

13. The Book of Two Ways is

    a. a funeral text
    b. a pyramid text
    c. a map of the underworld*
    d. a coffin text
    e. ritual incantation

14. Imhotep was

    a. the sun god
    b. an architect*
    c. a sculptor
    d. a painter
    e. a pharaoh

15. The forerunner of the Pyramid appears to be the

    a. Ziggurat
    b. obelisk
    c. mastaba*
    d. stone-cut temple

16. The only surviving step pyramid was built for

    a. Menkaure
    b. Khufu
    c. Khafre
    d. Narmer
    e. Zoser*

17. The three great pyramids are located at

    a. Saqqara
    b. Cairo
    c. Alexandria
    d. Giza*
    e. Thebes

18. The Old Kingdom Egyptian pharaoh who built his tomb at Gizeh was

    a. Seti
    b. Akhenaton
    c. Khafre*
    d. Tutankhamun

19. In Egyptian artistic convention, all of the following were true <u>except</u>

    a. head full front*
    b. eyes full front
    c. shoulders full front
    d. feet in profile

20. For the most part, pyramids are believed to have been built by

    a. Slaves
    b. Jews
    c. Seasonal workers*
    d. Nubians

21. The conventions for representing the human figure that dominated Egyptian art first occur about 3500 B.C. in the

    a. Rosetta Stone
    b. Standard of Heliopolis
    c. Palette of Narmer*
    d. Stele of Ramses

22. The Egyptian canon of proportion was organized according to

    a. nature
    b. a grid*
    c. curves and rectangles
    d. triangles and trapezoids

23. Royal figures in Egyptian art are

    a. naturalistic and assertive
    b. hieratic and naturalistic
    c. assertive and stylized*
    d. stylized and miniature
    e. monumental and unassuming

24. The seated statue of Khafre dates to around

    a. 3000 B.C.
    b. 2500 B.C.*
    c. 2000 B.C.
    d. 3500 B.C.

25. Menkaure and Khamerernebty are

    a. sculptures in the round
    b. wall paintings
    c. architects
    d. sculptures in very high relief*
    e. Egyptians gods

26. The closest meaning of the word ka is

    a. ego
    b. double*
    c. alter-ego
    d. self-image
    e. twin

27. Rahotep and Nofret are <u>not</u>

    a. a prince and a princess
    b. two seated sculptures
    c. a king and a queen*
    d. depicted in high relief
    e. seated in rigid poses

28. An Egyptian scribe was

    a. a slave
    b. a scribbler
    c. a well-educated person*
    d. an author of scripture

29. Lady Senuwy was

    a. a courtesan
    b. a princess*
    c. a queen
    d. a slave
    e. a lady-in-waiting

30. Egyptian paintings of royal figures are generally

    a. naturalistic
    b. stylized*
    c. colossal
    d. colorful

31. The source of Egyptian column types is generally

    a. human forms
    b. animal forms
    c. plant forms*
    d. architectural forms
    e. symbolic forms

32. The Egyptians used which of the following columns?

    a. papyrus reeds with flower capitals l
    b. animal or human figure supports
    c. smooth, widening shaft with bud-shaped capita
    d. fluted pillar with acanthus leaf capital*

33. A building technique commonly used in Egyptian temples was:

    a. post-and-lintel*
    b. adobe
    c. the true arch
    d. mortise and tenon

34. Which is not true of the hypostyle hall?

    a. it has columns with a base, shaft, and capital
    b. the center columns are shorter than the side columns*
    c. the center columns are taller than the side columns
    d. it has columns with a shaft and capital, but no base
    e. the shafts of its columns are covered with hieroglyphs

35. A cartouche

    a. is a form of cartonnage
    b. is a serekh
    c. is a scarab
    d. frames the name of a king*
    e. frames a plan of the king's palace

36. The Temple of Amon-Mut-Khonsu is in

    a. Karnak
    b. Thebes
    c. Cairo
    d. Amarna
    e. Luxor*

37. Most pyramids were built by pharaohs in

    a. Nubia
    b. the Middle Kingdom
    c. the Old Kingdom*
    d. the New Kingdom

38. Tomb fresco were most popular in

    a. Nubia
    b. the Middle Kingdom
    c. the Old Kingdom
    d. the New Kingdom*

39. The obelisks were derived from

    a. the pylons
    b. the pyramids
    c. the benbens*
    d. the sphinxes
    e. the hypostyle

40. Hatshepsut declared herself the offspring of

    a. Osiris
    b. Amon*
    c. Anubis
    d. Hathor
    e. Aten

41. Hatshepsut's chief architect was

    a. Nefrure
    b. Ahmose
    c. Tuthmose
    d. Senenmut*
    e. Imhotep

42. The ankh is a symbol of

    a. god
    b. life*
    c. happiness
    d. immortality
    e. death

43. Hatshepsut's greatest architectural achievement is

    a. The Temple at Karnak
    b. The Temple at Thebes
    c. The Temple at Amarna
    d. The Temple at Deir-el-Bahri*
    e. The Temple at Luxor

44. Most Egyptian wall paintings were made of

    a. tempera
    b. encaustic
    c. buon fresco
    d. fresco secco*
    e. oil

45. Akhenaten was a

    a. polytheist
    b. prince
    c. monk
    d. sun-worshipper*
    e. mason

46. The Amarna period is associated with

    a. Akhenaten and Amenhotep III
    b. Akhenaten and Nefertiti*
    c. Akhenaten and Tiy
    d. Akhenaten and Amon
    e. Akhenaten and Isis

47. Styles under Akhenaten were more _____ than before his reign.

    a. stylized
    b. hieratic
    c. conventional
    d. naturalistic*
    e. religious

48. The Amarna style showed

    a. caricatured face and posture
    b. intimate, relaxed poses
    c. the pharaoh in the traditional twisted view
    d. a and b*

49. Tutankhamon is a well-known pharaoh because

    a. he lived a long time
    b. his tomb was discovered intact*
    c. he was a great scribe
    d. he was a revolutionary thinker
    e. his mummy was discovered and preserved

50. The temple at Abu Simbel honors?

    a. Ramses II*
    b. Hatshepsut
    c. Akhenaton
    d. Nefertiti

51. Canopic jars contain

    a. preserved foods
    b. preserved works of art
    c. preserved items of clothing
    d. preserved organs*
    e. preserved texts

52. For Egypt, Nubia was a source of

    a. pottery
    b. weapons
    c. gems and metals*
    d. artists
    e. art and architecture

53. Which is <u>not</u> a Nubian culture?

    a. Kerma
    b. Kush
    c. Meroë
    d. Punt*

54. The function of the Deffufa is

    a. funerary
    b. religious
    c. commercial
    d. artistic
    e. unknown*

55. Which of the following was <u>not</u> significant in Nubian culture?

    a. elephants
    b. tombs
    c. arrows
    d. pottery
    e. Aten*

56. The Kandake refers to

    a. an Egyptian queen
    b. a Nubian queen*
    c. an Egyptian sphinx
    d. a Nubian sphinx
    e. a Nubian priestess

CHAPTER 4:
The Aegean

Key Works

Female Cycladic idol, Amorgos, 2700 – 2300 B.C.

Female Cycladic idol (side view)

Male Cycladic flute player, Keros, c. 2700 – 2300 B.C.

Detail of the palace showing wooden columns and limestone "horns of consecration" near the south entrance, palace of Minos, Knossos, Crete

Partly restored west portico of the north entrance passage with a reconstructed relief fresco of a charging bull, palace of Minos, Knossos

Toreador Fresco, Knossos, c. 1500 B.C.

The queen's *megaron*, palace of Minos, Knossos, c. 1600 – 1400 B.C.

View of the "throne room," with heavily restored fresco depicting griffins, palace of Minos, Knossos, Crete

Snake Goddess, Knossos, Crete, c. 1600 B.C.

Harvester Vase, from Hagia Triada, Crete, c. 1650 – 1450 B.C.

A spouted jar, Kamares ware, c. 1800 B.C.

Octopus Vase, Palaikastro, Crete, c. 1500 B.C.

Ship Fresco, Akrotiri, Thera, c. 1650 – 1500 B.C.

Ship Fresco (detail of boats)

Ship Fresco (detail of two stags pursued by a mountain lion)

Boxing Children, Akrotiri, Thera, c. 1650 – 1500 B.C.

Crocus-Gatherer, Thera, before 1500 B.C.

"Goddess," from the citadel of Mycenae, c. 1200 B.C.

Lion Gate, Mycenae, thirteenth century B.C.

Façade and *dromos* of the Treasury of Atreus, Mycenae, thirteenth century B.C.

Interior of a *tholos* tomb, showing the entrance lintel and a door to the side chamber, Treasury of Atreus, Mycenae, thirteenth century B.C.

Vault, interior of the Treasury of Atreus, Mycenae, thirteenth century B.C.

Aerial view of Grave Circle A and its surroundings, Mycenae

"Mask of Agamemnon," Mycenae, c. 1500 B.C.

Minoan and Mycenaean cups from Vapheio, near Sparta, sixteenth century B.C.

Maps, Diagrams, and Projections

Map of the ancient Aegean.

Plan of the palace of Minos, Knossos, Crete, 1600 – 1400 B.C.

Diagram showing the original arrangement of the *Ship Fresco* at Akrotiri, in isut.

Plan of Mycenaean *megaron*.

Plan and section of a *tholos*.

Key Terms

capital
citadel
corbelling
engobe
frieze
megaron
repoussé
rhyton
terracotta
tholos (tholoi)

Videos

The Aegean Age
14 min, 1965, Coronet

Ancient Moderns: Greek Island Art and Culture, 3000 – 2000 B.C.
19 min, 1979, Britannica

Crete and Mycenae
54 min, VM

Odyssey of Troy
50 min, 1995, VM

CD-ROMs

Exploring Ancient Cities
Mac/Windows, Sumeria

Multiple-Choice Questions

1. The Aegean civilizations include

      a. Egypt, Santorini, and Mycenae
      b. Greece, Egypt, and Thera
      c. Cycladic, Egyptian, and Greek
      d. Mycenaean, Cycladic, and Minoan*

2. The Cyclades are

     a. mythical giants
     b. marble idols
     c. islands*
     d. bodies of water
     e. Minoan cities

3. Cycladic idols are generally found in

     a. temples
     b. graves*
     c. storage jars
     d. caves
     e. the sea

4. Cycladic idols can be described as

     a. geometric*
     b. organic
     c. naturalistic
     d. non-figurative
     e. non-representational

5. Cycladic civilization is prehistoric because

     a. it had not invented the wheel
     b. it did not have monumental architecture
     c. it did not have a writing system*
     d. it had no agriculture

6. The Aegean is named after

     a. Aegisthus
     b. Zeus
     c. the father of Theseus*
     d. the Minotaur
     e. the daughter of Minos

7. Minoan Civilization is generally dated

     a. 4000 to 1000 B.C.
     b. 3000 to 1500 B.C.*
     c. 3500 to 1000 B.C.
     d. 2500 to 1500 B.C.
     e. 4500 to 2000 B.C.

8. The Minotaur was _____.

    a. the king of Crete
    b. half bull, half man*
    c. the son of Icarus and Daedalus
    d. a hero of many happy legends

9. Minos was the son of

    a. the Minotaur and Europa
    b. Zeus and Ariadne
    c. Theseus and Ariadne
    d. Europa and Theseus
    e. Zeus and Europa*

10. The Minoan civilization was discovered by

    a. Schliemann
    b. Evans*
    c. Marinatos
    d. Plato
    e. Theseus

11. The Palace at Knossos was not fortified because

    a. the inhabitants of Crete were peace-loving
    b. the Minoans thought of themselves as invincible
    c. Crete is an island*
    d. Crete ruled the Aegean

12. Minoan frescoes were

    a. fresco secco
    b. more stylized than in Egypt
    c. more abstract than in Egypt
    d. more numerous than in Egypt
    e. true fresco*

13. As far as one can tell, the most sacred animal on Minoan Crete was:

    a. the lion
    b. the bull*
    c. the griffin
    d. the snake
    e. the duck

14. Which is true of Minoan scripts?

    a. Linear A was used for lists and Linear B was the written script
    b. Linear A and Linear B were written scripts
    c. Linear B and Linear A were Egyptian scripts
    d. Linear B was used for records and Linear A was the written language*
    e. Linear A was used on papyrus and Linear B was inscribed on tablets

15. The statue of the so-called Snake Goddess is made of

    a. terracotta
    b. fresco
    c. marble
    d. faïence*
    e. Kamares

16. The Minoan column has

    a. a lotus capital, a straight shaft, a square base
    b. a floral capital, a tapering shaft, a pillow base
    c. a pillow capital, a round base, a tapering shaft*
    d. a papyrus capital, a round base, a tapering shaft
    e. a bull capital, a round base, a tapering shaft

17. A *pithos* is a

    a. snake
    b. core
    c. Kamares jar
    d. storage jar*
    e. tholos

18. Kamares ware can be characterized as

    a. monochrome
    b. decorated with dynamic designs*
    c. organic
    d. figurative
    e. decorated with Linear B script

19. Which is not a Minoan site?

    a. Mycenae*
    b. Phaistos
    c. Palaikastro
    d. Knossos

20. The modern name for Thera is

    a. Knossos
    b. Cairo
    c. Anatolia
    d. Santorini*
    e. Atlantis

21. Which is not a Theran fresco?

    a. the Ship Fresco
    b. the Boxing Children
    c. the Griffins*
    d. the Crocus Gatherer

22. Thera seems to have been destroyed by a volcanic eruption in

    a. 1628 B.C.*
    b. 1400 B.C.
    c. 1250 B.C.
    d. 1500 B.C.

23. The most likely interpretation of the Boxing Children is as

    a. a Cycladic sport
    b. a personal dispute
    c. a theatrical performance
    d. an initiation ritual*
    e. a religious ritual

24. A pinched waist, profile pose, and "floating" forms are typical of the frescoes of _____.

    a. Assyria
    b. Crete*
    c. Egypt
    d. Rome

25. The general dates for the Mycenaean civilization are

    a. 1800 to 1600 B.C.
    b. 1600 to 1400 B.C.
    c. 1400 to 1200 B.C.
    d. 1800 to 1400 B.C.
    e. 1600 to 1200 B.C.*

26. Schliemann found

    a. Knossos*
    b. Mycenae
    c. Troy
    d. b and c

27. The term Helladic comes from

    a. Helen of Troy
    b. the Greek name for Greece*
    c. the Greek name for Helen
    d. the islands of the Hellades
    e. the Greek name for Troy

28. Mycenaean shrines were

    a. on hillsides
    b. in temples
    c. in palaces*
    d. at the edge of the sea
    e. on hilltops

29. The Mycenaean megaron had

    a. a front and a back porch, a hearth, a throne room
    b. columns, a back porch, a hearth, a throne room
    c. columns, a throne room, an antechamber, a back porch
    d. a front porch, a hearth, a throne room, columns*

30. Agamemnon and Klytemnestra were the parents of

    a. Elektra, Orestes, Cassandra
    b. Iphigenia, Cassandra, Orestes
    c. Elektra, Iphigenia, Cassandra
    d. Elektra, Orestes, Iphigenia*

31. Mycenaean civilization was discovered by

    a. Evans
    b. Schliemann*
    c. Marinatos
    d. Aeschylos
    e. Euripides

32. The heroes of Homer's *Iliad* and *Odyssey* may have come from

    a. Minoan Crete
    b. Athens
    c. Mycenaean Greece*
    d. Santorini

33. Who of the following was <u>not</u> a Trojan?

    a. Priam
    b. Paris
    c. Menelaus*
    d. Cassandra

34. A corbeled vault is

    a. concentric stone rings piled to make an arch or domed room*
    b. a means of transporting water
    c. a kind of tomb
    d. the level of windows above the central passageway to let light in from outside

35. Cyclopaean refers to

    a. a group of islands
    b. a kind of wall*
    c. a citadel
    d. a style of painting
    e. a grave circle

36. Polyphemos was

    a. a Greek artist
    b. a Greek city
    c. a Greek hero
    d. a Cyclops*
    e. a friend of Odysseus

37. Minoan features suggest that although found in Mycenae, the _____ is(are) Minoan

    a. the Vaphio Cups*
    b. the Harvester Vase
    c. the Octopus Vase
    d. the Agamemnon Mask

38. The column flanked by lions at the entrance to Mycenae symbolized

    a. a phallus
    b. a tree
    c. a goddess*
    d. a building
    e. an altar

CHAPTER 5:
The Art of Ancient Greece

Key Works

Temple of Apollo, Delphi, east view, 346 – 320 B.C.

Socrates, 1st or 2nd century A.D., Roman copy of an original by Lysippos

Geometric *amphora*, 8th century B.C.

Polyphemos Painter, *amphora*, 675 – 650 B.C. (two views)

Polyphemos Painter, *amphora* neck showing the blinding of Polyphemos, 675 – 650 B.C.

Exekias, *amphora* showing *Achilles and Ajax Playing a Board Game*, 540 – 530 B.C.

Exekias, *amphora* showing *Achilles and Penthesilea*, c. 525 B.C.

Berlin Painter, bell *krater* showing the *Abduction of Europa*, c. 490 B.C.

Penthesilea Painter, Cup interior showing *Achilles and Penthesilea*, c. 455 B.C.

Niobid Painter, *kalyx krater*, side showing unidentified scene, c. 455 – 450 B.C.

Niobid Painter, *kalyx krater*, side showing *Death of the Children of Niobe*, c. 455 – 450 B.C.

Reed Painter, *Warrior by a Grave* (detail of a white ground *lekythos*), c. 410 B.C.

The *Battle of Issos*, from the House of the Faun, Pompeii, 1st century B.C., after an original Greek fresco of c. 300 B.C.

Detail of *Battle of Issos*, showing Alexander and Bukephalos

Detail of *Battle of Issos*, showing a dying Persian

Terrace of the Lions, Delos, 7th century B.C.

New York Kouros, Attica, c. 600 B.C., three views

The Cheramyes Master, *Hera of Samos*, Samos, c. 560 B.C.

Peplos Kore, c. 530 B.C., two views

Attributed to Kritios, *Kritios Boy*, Acropolis, Athens, c. 480 B.C.

Poseidon/Zeus, found in the sea off Cape Artemision, c. 450 B.C.

Myron, *Diskobolos (Discus Thrower)*, 460 – 450 B.C.

Warrior from Riace, Reggio Calabria, c. 450 B.C.

Warrior from Riace, Reggio Calabria, c. 450 B.C. (back view)

Polykleitos*, Doryphoros (Spear Bearer)*, c. 440 B.C.

Attributed to Polykleitos, *Wounded Amazon*, c. 430 B.C.

View of the Temple of Apollo, Corinth, c. 550 B.C.

Reconstruction of the façade of the Siphnian Treasury in the sanctuary of Apollo at Delphi, 530 – 525 B.C.

Seated gods from the Ionic frieze of the Siphnian Treasury

After Phidias, *Head of Zeus* and *Enthroned Zeus*, 2nd century B.C., obverse and reserve of a coin minted by Hadrian to celebrate the 228th Olympiad in A.D. 133

Herakles and Atlas, the Golden Apples of the Hesperides, metope from the east side of the temple of Zeus at Olympia

Apollo with Lapith and Centaur, center of the west pediment of the temple of Zeus at Olympia

View of Acropolis, Athens

East end of the Parthenon, Athens, 447 – 438 B.C.

Reconstruction of the Parthenon, Athens

Maps, Diagrams, and Projections

Olympia, diagram of the east end of the *naos* from the temple of Zeus, showing the labors of Herakles

Plan of the Acropolis, Athens

Plan of the Parthenon, Athens

Sculptures from the left-hand side of the east pediment of the Parthenon, finished by 438 B.C.

Sculptures from the right-hand side of the east pediment of the Parthenon

Cutaway perspective drawing (after G. Niemann) of the Parthenon showing the Doric and Ionic friezes and a pediment

Sectional drawing showing the cult statue of Athena from the entrance of the Parthenon

Plan of the theater at Epidauros.

Key Terms

abacus

acanthus

agora

amphora

architrave

balustrade

black-figure

caryatids

cella

colonnade

cornice

contrapposto

Corinthian

Doric

drum

echinus

egg-and-dart

encaustic

entablature

entasis

finial

flutes, fluting

foreshortening

frieze

geometric

hydria

Ionic

isocephaly, isocephalic

kore

kouros

krater

kylix

leaf-and-dart

lekythos

lost-wax bronze casting (*cire-perdue*)

meander pattern

metope

naos

necking

oenochoe

Order

pediment

peripteral

peristyle

portico

protome, protoma

red-figure

scroll

shaft

slip

stoa

stylobate

triglyph

volute

white-ground

Videos

Art in Ancient Lands, Part 2
36 min, Clearvue

Art of the Western World
Volume 1: The Classical Ideal
55 min, VM

Elements of Sculpture: Aesthetics in Contrasting Cultures, filmstrip
15 min, Clearvue

Greek Temple
54 min, VM

History Through Art: Ancient Greece
49 min, Clearvue

The Greeks: Greek Pottery
20 min, 1987, TRC

Treasures of the British Museum Series—The God-Haunted: Ancient Greece
27 min, FFTH

CD-ROMs

History Through Art: Ancient Greece
Mac/Windows, Clearvue, Zane Publishing

History of Art: Ancient Greece, Zane Publishing

The Perseus Project
Mac, Clearvue

Multiple-Choice Questions

1. Greek history first becomes well documented around

     a. 1200 B.C.
     b. 1000 B.C.
     c. 900 B.C.
     d. 800 B.C.*
     e. 450 B.C.

2. The Greek alphabet came from

    a. Egypt
    b. Mycenae
    c. Crete
    d. Phoenicia*
    e. Syria

3. The Pythian Games originated at

    a. Delos
    b. Olympia
    c. Athens
    d. Delphi*
    e. Pylos

4. "Know Thyself" was inscribed in stone at

    a. Athens
    b. Olympia
    c. Delphi*
    d. Delos
    e. Eleusis

5. Apollo's sacred island was

    a. Thera
    b. Crete
    c. Delphi
    d. Delos*
    e. Atlantis

6. An oracle was a

    a. temple
    b. shrine
    c. altar
    d. priest*
    e. magician

7. Which of the following was not a famous woman in ancient Greece?

    a. Sappho of Lesbos
    b. Iaia of Kyzikos
    c. Aspasia
    d. Artemisia*

8. Greek Geometric art was in the _____.

       a. eighth century B.C.*
       b. seventh century B.C.
       d. sixth century B.C.
       d. fifth century B.C.

9. A Dipylon vase was

       a. an Egyptian treaty marker
       b. an Athenian funerary vessel*
       c. the respository of the law in Chaldea
       d. a place of safekeeping during the Olympiads

10. Black-figure pottery is from the

       a. Geometric period
       b. late Classical period
       c. Archaic or early Classical*
       d. Hellenistic period

11. A nude standing figure of a young man is known in Greek art as a(n) _____.

       a. kore
       b. entasis
       c. lapith
       d. kouros*

12. A Greek two-handled storage jar is known as a(n) _____.

       a. hydria
       b. kylix
       c. krater
       d. amphora*

13. A Greek drinking cup was called a(n) _____.

       a. krater
       b. amphora
       c. lekythos
       d. kylix*

14. The Classical Greek style can best be described as

    a. stylized and organic
    b. stylized and idealized
    c. figurative and non-representational
    d. idealized but non-figurative
    e. naturalistic but idealized*

15. Which best describes Greek government during the Classical period?

    a. democracy*
    b. autocracy
    c. tyranny
    d. monarchy
    e. aristocracy

16. The main Greek media used by sculptors were

    a. bronze and iron
    b. marble and terracotta
    c. terracotta and bronze
    d. bronze and marble*
    e. gold and marble

17. Which of the following is not a Greek god or goddess?

    a. Ares
    b. Artemis
    c. Hestia
    d. Poseidon
    e. Venus*

18. Which of the following is not a pair?

    a. Zeus and Jupiter
    b. Dionysos and Bacchus
    c. Demeter and Ceres
    d. Hades and Hebe*
    e. Athena and Minerva

19. Which of the following do <u>not</u> belong together?

    a. Zeus — thunderbolt
    b. Juno — peacock
    c. Hephaestos — hearth*
    d. Neptune — trident
    e. Hermes — caduceus

20. Which of the following did <u>not</u> take part in the Trojan War?

    a. Achilles
    b. Ajax
    c. Odysseus
    d. Sophokles*
    e. Agamemnon

21. Which of the following do <u>not</u> belong together?

    a. hydria — water jar
    b. amphora — storage jar
    c. krater — flask for pouring oil*
    d. kylix — drinking cup
    e. oenochoe — jug for pouring wine

22. Which do <u>not</u> belong together?

    a. Exekias — Geometric*
    b. Myron — Early Classical
    c. Polykleitos — Classical
    d. Lysippos — Fourth Century B.C.
    e. Phidias — Classical

23. Which was <u>not</u> a technique or process used by the Greeks?

    a. lost-wax
    b. black-figure
    c. red-figure
    d. white ground
    e. mummification*

24. "Classical" means

    a. old-fashioned and valuable
    b. traditional and of high quality*
    c. out-of-date and trite
    d. traditional and stylized
    e. idealized and valuable

25. Contrapposto is

    a. a twist at the neck
    b. a counter position
    c. a twist at the waist*
    d. stepping forward
    e. standing at attention

26. The earliest example of the use of contrapposto was in the sculpture of the _____.

    a. Kouros from Tenea
    b. Kritios Boy*
    c. Laocoön
    d. Perikles

27. The Riace bronzes were found in

    a. Riace
    b. a cave
    c. the sea*
    d. a grave
    e. a temple

28. Which do not belong together?

    a. volute, shaft, base, flutes
    b. abacus, volute, base, frieze
    c. metope, triglyph, abacus, echinus
    d. abacus, volute, echinus, metope*
    e. stylobate, drums, echinus, metope

29. Which set is correct?

    a. Nike Temple (427 – 424 B.C.)*
    b. Parthenon (439 – 419 B.C.)
    c. Erechtheum (421 – 405 B.C.)
    d. Propylaea (480 – 450 B.C.)

30. The general who commissioned the Parthenon was

    a. Alkiabiades
    b. Sophokles
    c. Herodotos
    d. Xenophon
    e. Perikles*

31. The director of the sculptural programs of the Parthenon was _____.

    a. Praxiteles
    b. Polykleitos
    c. Myron
    d. Phidias*

32. To the Greeks, barbarians were

    a. cannibals
    b. Persians
    c. Egyptians
    d. Scythians
    e. foreigners*

33. Which is not part of the Parthenon plan?

    a. naos
    b. treasury
    c. pronaos
    d. propylaea*
    e. peristyle

34. What subject was portayed on the frieze around the Parthenon?
    a. Panathenaic Procession*
    b. Dionysiac Procession
    c. Labors of Herakles
    d. Battle of Gods and Giants

35. The Parthenon metopes represented

    a. the battle between Greeks and Trojans
    b. the battle between Lapiths and Centaurs
    c. the battle between the gods and Titans
    d. the battle between Greeks and Amazons
    e. all of the above*

36. Which is not a pair?

    a. pediment — triangle
    b. metope — trapezoid*
    c. triglyph — vertical
    d. shaft — cylinder
    e. architrave — rectangle

37. Which is not an aspect of Athena?

    a. virginity
    b. victory
    c. fertility*
    d. war
    e. wisdom

38. The statue of Athena in the Parthenon naos was made of

    a. marble and bronze
    b. ivory and bronze
    c. ivory and marble
    d. gold and marble
    e. gold and ivory*

39. Which is found in the Parthenon sculptures?

    a. contrapposto
    b. isocephaly
    c. symmetry
    d. neither a, b, or c
    e. a, b, and c*

40. Which of the following is not predominantly Doric?

    a. Temple of Athena Nike, Acropolis*
    b. Parthenon
    c. Temple of Poseidon, Paestum
    d. Basilica, Paestum

41. Which is not part of the Erechtheum?

    a. the Ionic Order
    b. caryatids
    c. Doric columns*
    d. an irregular plan

42. A female figure used as column is known as a

    a. caryatid*
    b. kore
    c. kouros
    d. atlantid

43. Greek theater began

    a. inside of temples
    b. outside of temples
    c. in the hills*
    d. by the sea
    e. around trees

44. Which is not part of Greek theater architecture?

    a. orchestra
    b. pronaos*
    c. proscenium
    d. skene
    e. parodos

45. The first known Greek artist to celebrate the female nude was

    a. Praxiteles*
    b. Phidias
    c. Perikles
    d. Lysippos
    e. Exekias

46. Demosthenes was

    a. a tragedian
    b. an orator*
    c. a historian
    d. a poet
    e. a sculptor

47. Alexander the Great was

    a. an Athenian
    b. a Persian
    c. a Pergamene
    d. a Macedonian*
    e. a Mycenaean

48. The Winged Victory was found in

    a. Sparta
    b. Athens
    c. Macedon
    d. Samothrace*
    e. Rhodes

49. Greek Hellenistic art is

    a. realistic
    b. in a typical "corkscrew" arrangement
    c. more passionate
    d. all of the above*

50. The priest who warned the Trojans not to bring in the giant wooden horse was

    a. Herakles
    b. Laocoön
    c. killed by snakes
    d. b and c*

51. Which was <u>not</u> a Greek tragedian?

    a. Aristophanes*
    b. Sophokles
    c. Aeschylus
    d. Euripides

52. Herodotos is called

    a. the father of poetry
    b. the father of theater
    c. the father of rhetoric
    d. the father of history*
    e. the father of philosophy

53. Plato's spokesman in the Dialogues was

    a. Perikles
    b. Herodotos
    c. Sophokles
    d. Demosthenes
    e. Socrates*

54. Which did Alexander the Great <u>not</u> conquer?

    a. Egypt
    b. Rome*
    c. Persia
    d. Palestine
    e. Phoenicia

55. The Trojan War took place around

    a. 800 B.C.
    b. 1000 B.C.
    c. 1200 B.C.*
    d. 900 B.C.
    e. 600 B.C.

56. Troy was located in

    a. East Greece
    b. the Cyclades
    c. Persia
    d. Anatolia*
    e. Mycenae

57. Which was a Greek mathematician?

    a. Solon
    b. Praxiteles
    c. Pythagoras*
    d. Plato
    e. Socrates

58. Who wrote the *Oresteia*?

    a. Aeschylus*
    b. Sophokles
    c. Euripides
    d. Herodotos
    e. Plato

59. Who wrote the *Republic*?

    a. Homer
    b. Plato*
    c. Socrates
    d. Perikles
    e. Herodotos

60. Which of the following is true?

    a. Homer wrote the Laws
    b. Plato wrote the Iliad
    c. Socrates wrote Dialogues
    d. Demosthenes wrote speeches*
    e. Euripides wrote comedies

61. Which one was <u>not</u> a Greek mathematician?

    a. Euclid
    b. Archimedes
    c. Pythagoras
    d. Solon*

62. Which one was <u>not</u> a Greek sculptor?

    a. Praxiteles
    b. Myron
    c. Phidias
    d. Polykleitos
    e. Exekias*

Key Works

Reconstruction drawing of the temple at Veii, c. 515 – 490 B.C.
Capitoline Wolf, c. 500 B.C.
Wounded Chimera, Arezzo, 2nd quarter of the 4th century B.C.
Apollo of Veii, Veii, c. 515 B.C.
Mars of Todi, early 4th century B.C.
Scene from the back of a mirror, showing Uni (Hera) nursing Herakles in the presence of other gods, Volterra, c. 300 B.C.
Cinerary urn, Chiusi, 7th century B.C.
Mater Matuta, Chianciano, Chiusi, 460 – 440 B.C.
Urn in the shape of a hut, Tarquinia, 9th – 8th century B.C.
Cinerary urn in the form of a house, Chiusi, c. 700 – 650 B.C.
Interior of the central room in the Tomb of the Shields and the Chairs, Cerveteri, c. 600 B.C.
Sarcophagus, Cerveteri, c. 520 B.C. (front and back)
Sarcophagus of Ramtha Visnai, Vulci, c. 300 – 280 B.C.
Mourners at the Door of the Other World, Tomb of the Augurs, Tarquinia, c. 510 B.C.
Tomb of the Leopards, Tarquinia, 480 – 470 B.C.

Maps, Diagrams, and Projections

Map of Etruscan and Roman Italy
Plan of the Tomb of the Shields and the Chairs, Cerveteri, c. 550 B.C.

Key Terms

canopic urn
lost-wax (*cire perdue*)
pilasters
sarcophagus
tempera
tufa
tumulus, tumuli
wattle and daub

Key Works

The Great Wall, near Beijing, China, begun third century B.C.
Four-ram wine vessel, Ningziang Xian, Hunan Province, China, Shang Dynasty, c. 1300 – 1030 B.C.
Detail of a four-ram wine vessel, Ningziang Xian, Hunan Province, China, Shang Dynasty, c. 1300 – 1030 B.C.
Dragon finial, Qin-Zun, China, late Zhou Dynasty, third century B.C.
Kneeling archer, Tomb of Emperor Qin, Lintong, Shaanxi Province, 221 – 206 B.C.
Detail of kneeling archer from the Tomb of Emperor Qin, Lintong, Shaanxi Province, 221 – 206 B.C.
Officer, Tomb of Emperor Qin, Lintong, Shaanxi Province, 221 – 206 B.C.
Detail of Officer from the Tomb of Emperor Qin, Lintong, Shaanxi Province, 221 – 206 B.C.
Calvaryman, Tomb of Emperor Qin, Lintong, Shaanxi Province, 221 – 206 B.C.

Maps, Diagrams, and Projections

Map of archaeological sites of China
Diagram showing the Chinese system of bronze casting
Evolution of Chinese characters

Key Terms

calligraphy, calligraphic
finial
ideograph
interlace
pictograph
spacer

Videos

Art in Ancient Lands, Part 2
36 min, Clearvue

Art of the Western World
Volume 1: The Classical Ideal
55 min, VM

Elements of Sculpture: Aesthetics in Contrasting Cultures, filmstrip
15 min, Clearvue

Greek Temple
54 min, VM

History Through Art: Ancient Greece
49 min, Clearvue

The Greeks: Greek Pottery
20 min, 1987, TRC

Treasures of the British Museum Series - The God-Haunted: Ancient Greece
27 min, FFTH

CD-ROMs

History Through Art: Ancient Greece
Mac/Windows, Clearvue, Zane Publishing

History of Art: Ancient Greece , Zane Publishing

The Perseus Project
Mac, Clearvue

Multiple-Choice Questions

1. The inclusive dates of Etruscan civilization are about

   a. 1200-300 B.C.
   b. 1400- 600 B.C.
   c. 800-100 B.C.
   d. 1000-300 B.C.
   e. 1000-100 B.C.*

2. The term "Etruscan" is

   a. Lydian
   b. Roman*
   c. Greek
   d. Tyrrhenian

3. The Etruscan script was derived from

   a. Anatolian

b. Latin
c. Phoenician*
d. Egyptian
e. Linear B

4. The Apollo of Veii is made of _____.

   a. bronze
   b. wood
   c. marble
   d. terracotta*

5. The Capitoline Wolf and the Wounded Chimera were made by

   a. the lost-wax method*
   b. baking terracotta in a kiln
   c. carving stone
   d. modeling clay

6. The Wounded Chimera is closest in style to

   a. Greek Classical sculpture
   b. Greek Hellenistic sculpture
   c. Mycenaean goldwork
   d. Greek Orientalized sculpture*
   e. Greek Black-Figure

7. Which of the following make the best pair?

   a. tombs and temples
   b. mirrors and media
   c. urns and sarcophagi*
   d. frescoes and finials

8. Which of the following do not match?

   a. Hera and Herakles*
   b. Uni and Hera
   c. Aplu and Apollo
   d. Nethuns and Neptune

9. The arch was invented in

   a. Etruria
   b. Mesopotamia*
   c. Greece

d. Rome

e. Egypt

10. The Etruscans buried their dead in

a. citadels

b. pyramids

c. above-ground graves

d. tombs made like houses in "cities of the dead"*

11. Which is least likely to be found in large-scale Etruscan tombs?

a. mirrors

b. chairs

c. frescoes

d. ashes*

12. Etruscans thought of their large-scale tombs as

a. pyramids

b. houses*

c. urns

d. underground temples

13. Important Etruscan tombs were discovered at _____.

a. Cerveteri*

b. Paestum

c. Rome

d. Athens

14. Terracotta sarcophagi showing life-sized reclining figures are most typical of the _____.

a. republican Romans

b. Etruscans*

c. Greeks

d. Sumerians

15. The Etruscans used _____ for sculpture?

a. bronze

b. gold

c. terracotta*

d. a and c

16. The wall paintings in Etruscan tombs show

    a. events from everyday life
    b. banqueters and dancers*
    c. battle scenes
    d. scenes of female admiration of male heroism

17. Which is not true of the sarcophagus from Cerveteri?

    a. it is made of terracotta
    b. it dates to around 520 B.C.
    c. it is close to Greek Archaic in style
    d. it is now in Rome
    e. it shows a sleeping couple on the lid*

18. Etruria was located in what today is

    a. west-central Italy*
    b. southern Italy
    c. northern Italy
    d. southwestern Italy
    e. Sicily

19. A popular Etruscan building material was

    a. concrete
    b. tufa*
    c. travertine
    d. terracotta

20. Etruscan metalwork is seen in

    a. lost-wax sculpture
    b. jewelry
    c. everyday objects
    d. all of the above*

21. Etruscan art is _____.

    a. lively*
    b. functional
    c. rigid frontality and symmetry
    d. geometric

22. The Etruscan's used a _____-style column.

    a. Doric*
    b. Ionic
    c. Corinthian
    d. Bull-capital

23. An Etruscan temple was entered from _____.

    a. the side only
    b. the back only
    c. the front only*
    d. any side

24. The Etruscan temple differed from the Greek temple because it had _____.

    a. exterior decoration
    b. a columned porch
    c. a pitched roof
    d. a podium reached by climbing many steps *

25. Architectural sculpture decorated the _____ of the Etruscan temple?

    a. interior
    b. roof*
    c. pediment
    d. sides

26. A necropolis is a

    a. someone who likes dead people
    b. an underground city
    c. a city beneath the sea
    d. a city of the dead*

Key Works

Atrium and peristyle, House of the Silver Wedding, Pompeii, early 1st century A.D.
Insula, Ostia, reconstruction, 2nd century
View from the west of the ruins of Timgad, Algeria, early 2nd century
Piranesi, *The Great Baths, Hadrian's Villa, Tivoli*, from *Views of Rome*, 1770
Canopus, Hadrian's Villa, Tivoli, A.D.. 123 – 135
Reconstruction of the forums, Rome, c. A.D. 46 – 117
Reconstruction drawing of the interior of the Basilica Ulpia
The remains of Trajan's markets as seen from the west
Analytical drawing of the *aula* (main hall) of Trajan's markets
Aerial view of the ruins of the Baths of Caracalla, Rome, A.D. c. 211 – 217
Restoration drawing of the Baths of Caracalla
Aerial view of the Colosseum, Rome, A.D. c. 72 – 80
Reconstruction model of the Colosseum, Rome
View of the Colosseum, Rome, A.D. 72 – 80
Pont du Gard, near Nîmes, France, late 1st century B.C.
Temple of Portunus, Rome, late 2nd century B.C.
Temple of the Sibyl, Tivoli, early 1st century B.C.
Exterior view of the Pantheon, Rome, A.D. 117 – 125
Giovanni Paolo Panini, *The Interior of the Pantheon*, c. 1740
West side of the Ara Pacis (Altar of Peace), Rome, 13 – 9 B.C.
South side of the Ara Pacis, showing a detail of an imperial procession
Ara Pacis, detail of a child tugging at an adult's toga
Trajan's Column, Trajan's Forum, Rome, dedicated A.D. 113
Dacian vase in the shape of a human head, 4th century
Dacian helmet, 4th century
The three lowest bands of Trajan's Column
Arch of Titus, Rome, A.D. 81
Relief from the Arch of Titus, detail showing *The Spoils of the Temple of Jerusalem Exhibited in Rome*
Arch of Constantine, Rome, c. A.D. 313
Medallions (Hadrianic A.D. 117 – 138) and frieze (Constantinian, early 4th century) from the Arch of Constantine, Rome
Bacchus and the Four Seasons (the so-called Badminton Sarcophagus) c. A.D. 220
Bust of Julius Caesar, Tusculum, mid-1st century B.C.
Bust of Trajan, 1st half of 2nd century A.D.
Patrician with Two Ancestor Busts, A.D. c. 13
Portrait of a young Flavian lady, A.D. c. 90
Portrait of an older Flavian lady, A.D. c. 90
Augustus of Prima Porta, early 1st century A.D.
Antinous, c. A.D. 131 – 138

Maps, Diagrams, and Projections

Key Terms

aisle
amphitheater
annular or ring vault
apse
aqueduct
arcade
arena
atrium
attic
axis
barrel vault, tunnel vault
bust
buttress
castrum, castra
cella
centering
circus
coffer, coffering
concrete
dome
dressed stone
groin vault, cross-vault

highlight
keystone
nave
oculus
peripteral
pier
podium
portico
rotunda
rustication
Serapaeum
spolia
springing
stylus
tessera, tesserae
tracery
travertine
vault, vaulting
villa
voussoir

Window on the World
Developments in South Asia – The Indus Valley Civilization
(to the 3rd century A.D.)

Key Works

Square stamp seal showing a zebu, Mohenjo-daro, Indus Valley, c. 2300 –1750 B.C.
Square stamp seal showing a yogi, Indus Valley civilization, c. 2500 – 1500 B.C.
Bearded Man, Mohenjo-daro, Indus Valley, c. 2000 B.C. (three views)
Dancing Girl, Mohenjo-daro, Indus Valley Civilization, c. 2300 – 1750 B.C. (front and back)
Nude Male Torso, Harappa, Indus Valley, c. 2000 B.C. (three views)
Birth of the Buddha, Gandhara, India, 2nd – 3rd century
Dream of Queen Maya, Madhya Pradesh, India, Shunga period, 2nd century B.C.
Lion capital, Ashoka pillar, Sarnath, Uttar Pradesh, India, Maurya period, mid-3rd century B.C.
Bull capital, Ashokan pillar from Rampurva, Bihar, India, Maurya period, 3rd century B.C.
Great Stupa at Sanchi, Madhya Pradesh, India, Shunga and early Andhra periods, 3rd century B.C.
Reconstruction drawing of the Sanchi complex

North *torana* at Sanchi, Shunga and early Andhra periods, 1st century B.C.
Yakshī, from the east *torana* at Sanchi, Sunga and early Andhra periods, 1st century B.C.
Standing Buddha, Gandhara, Afghanistan or Pakistan, Kushan period, 2nd – 3rd century
Seated Buddha, Gandhara, Afghanistan or Pakistan, Kushan period, 2nd century
Model of stupa from Loriyan Tangai, Gandhara, Afghanistan or Pakistan, Kushan period, 2nd century
Seated Buddha, from the Katra Mound, Mathura, Uttar Pradesh, India, Kushan period, early 2nd century

Maps, Diagrams, and Projections

Map of South Asia
Map of the Buddhist world
Plan and elevation of the Great Stupa at Sanchi
Reconstruction drawing of the Sanchi complex

Key Terms

abhaya	*harmikā*
anda	*mudrā*
aniconic	*prana*
bodhisattva	stupas
chattra	*tribhanga*
chaurī	*ushnīsha*
dhyāna	*vedikā*

Videos

History Through Art: Ancient Rome
40 min, Clearvue

Rome: Art and Architecture - Part 1
31 min, 1995, VM

Rome: Art and Architecture - Part 2
39 min, 1995, VM

CD-ROMs

History Through Art: Ancient Rome
Mac/Windows, Clearvue

History of Art: Ancient Rome, Zane Publishing

Multiple-Choice Questions

1. Republican Roman art depicted

   a. all of these*
   b. realistic subjects
   c. portraits
   d. celebration of age and character

2. Which was not part of the Roman Empire in the first century A.D.?

   a. Gaul
   b. Britain
   c. Egypt
   d. Nubia*
   e. Judaea

3. Greek art was championed during the reign of

   a. Caesar in the Roman Republic
   b. Augustus, the emperor *
   c. Pliny the Elder
   d. Constantine

4. Virgil wrote the Aeneid for

   a. Julius Caesar
   b. Augustus*
   c. Trajan
   d. Constantine
   e. Caracalla

5. Which of the following was not associated with the founding of Rome?

   a. Venus
   b. Aeneas
   c. Romulus
   d. Remus
   e. Virgil*

6. The Goths were

   a. Gauls
   b. Dacians
   c. Germans*

d. Trojans

e. Greeks

7. Roman concrete was a mixture of

a. water, tufa, travertine, and rubble

b. water, mortar, gravel, and rubble*

c. stucco, plaster, water, mortar, and rubble

d. tufa, rubble, gravel, and mortar

8. Which was not a Roman architectural type?

a. the private house

b. the round temple

c. the peripteral temple*

d. the circus

e. the Colosseum

9. Pompeii was destroyed in

a. A.D. 79*

b. the first century B.C.

c. under Nero

d. A.D. 121

10. Pompeian wall paintings of the Second Style are characterized by

a. scenes like theater sets

b. painted inlaid stone

c. pictures showing paintings on the wall

d. illusionistic landscapes*

11. Which of the following was not built under Trajan?

a. Timgad

b. Dacia*

c. markets

d. a forum

e. basilica

12. Nero, as described by Suetonius, exemplifies

a. political know-how

b. generosity

c. grandiosity*

d. military strategy

13. Hadrian was especially influenced by

   a. Egyptian religion
   b. Greek styles*
   c. Virgil's Aeneid
   d. Homer's Iliad
   e. Marcus Aurelius

14. The Golden House belonged to

   a. Suetonius
   b. Caracalla
   c. Constantine
   d. Nero*
   e. Trajan

15. Which of the following is the best pair?

   a. Virgil and Odysseus
   b. Ovid and the Metamorphoses*
   c. Trajan and the Meditations
   d. Marcus Aurelius and the Commentarii

16. The first known Roman forum dates from

   a. the 6th century B.C.*
   b. the reign of Julius Caesar
   c. the first century A.D.
   d. the reign of Augustus

17. The Ides of March are

   a. when Roman emperors are killed
   b. the middle of the month*
   c. the birthday of the Roman emperor
   d. the end of the month
   e. the beginning of the month

18. Which was least likely to be in a forum?

   a. temples
   b. libraries
   c. markets
   d. baths*
   e. basilicas

19. Two streets intersecting at right angles in ancient Roman cities were the

   a. castra and cardo
   b. insula and decumanus
   c. castra and decumanus
   d. cardo and decumanus*

20. The Pont du Gard at Nimes was

   a. an aqueduct
   b. a temple
   c. a bridge
   d. a and c*

21. Which of the following was not a use of the Roman basilica?

   a. commerce
   b. worship*
   c. law courts
   d. administration

22. In contrast to Greek temples, Roman temples usually were _____.

   a. set on tall podiums
   b. approached from a single side
   c. pseudoperipteral
   d. a, b, and c*

23. Which best describes the architectural features of the basilica?

   a. aisles, apses, nave, clerestory windows*
   b. aisles, nave, clerestory windows, impluvium
   c. apses, nave, impluvium, aisles
   d. atrium, nave, aspe, clerestory windows

24. Which is least likely to have been a feature of the Roman bath?

   a. a museum
   b. a tepidarium
   c. a swimming pool
   d. a ball court
   e. a market*

25. The columns of the Colosseum were arranged in the following order from the first to the third level:

    a. Doric, Corinthian, Ionic
    b. Ionic, Doric, Corinthian
    c. Doric, Ionic, Corinthian*
    d. Corinthian, Ionic, Doric
    e. Corinthian, Doric, Ionic

26. The most impressive Roman buildings were faced with

    a. marble*
    b. tufa
    c. concrete
    d. terracotta

27. The Roman circus was used primarily for

    a. animal performances
    b. libraries
    c. gladiatorial contests
    d. horse races
    e. chariot races*

28. The Colosseum was constructed during the reign of

    a. Nero
    b. Trajan
    c. Vespasian*
    d. Constantine
    e. Caracalla

29. The Roman Colosseum was built primarily of _____.

    a. concrete*
    b. brick
    c. sandstone
    d. iron

30. Which is true of Roman temples?

    a. they were peripteral
    b. they have a front and a back porch
    c. they have a double cella
    d. they are pseudo-peripteral*

31. Which is <u>not</u> a feature of the Pantheon?

     a. an oculus
     b. a rectangular cella*
     c. a rotunda
     d. a portico
     e. a curved entablature

32. An oculus is

     a. the opening at the center of a dome*
     b. a mystical doorway in a temple
     c. the portholes in a Roman galley
     d. the window in the wall above the main level of a temple which let light in

33. Coffering

     a. helped expand interior space
     b. lighten the weight of a dome or arch
     c. enhances the illusion of recession in the ceiling
     d. b and c*

34. The Pantheon included that included

     a. barrel vaults and groin vaults
     b. a central dome
     c. an eight-sided room
     d. all of the above*

35. Which is <u>not</u> a commemorative monument?

     a. Trajan's Column
     b. the Arch of Titus
     c. the Ara Pacis
     d. Colosseum*
     e. the Pantheon

36. The Ara Pacis was constructed under

     a. Augustus*
     b. Julius Caesar
     c. Trajan
     d. Nero
     e. Constantine

37. Trajan's most famous monument was

    a. the Baths of Trajan
    b. an Arch of Trajan
    c. the Ara Pacis of Trajan
    d. Trajan's Column*

38. The Column of Trajan is uniquely Roman because of

    a. its enormous height
    b. its narrative frieze*
    c. its setting
    d. its material

39. The reliefs of Trajan's column differ from classical Greek reliefs in the

    a. use of a spiral frieze
    b. realistic rather than idealized battle scene
    c. emphasis on historical facts
    d. a, b, and c*

40. Which is <u>not</u> a feature of Roman triumphal arches?

    a. relief sculptures
    b. an attic
    c. inscriptions
    d. the Composite Order
    e. a portico*

41. Which is incorrect?

    a. Juno is the wife of Jupiter
    b. Vulcan is the son of Juno
    c. Diana is the daughter of Juno*
    d. Minerva is the daughter of Jupiter
    e. Mercury is the god of speed

42. The Jewish Wars were chronicled by

    a. Josephus*
    b. Virgil
    c. Suetonius
    d. Julius Caesar
    e. Ovid

43. Trajan's purpose in declaring war on the Dacians was to obtain their

     a. territory
     b. women
     c. gold*
     d. works of sculpture
     e. weapons

44. Which was not a Roman funerary practice?

     a. the use of cinerary urns
     b. the necropolis*
     c. the sarcophagus
     d. burial in graves

45. Apotheosis refers to

     a. deification*
     b. abdication
     c. ascending to power
     d. election to office

46. Marcus Aurelius was

     a. an emperor and poet
     b. an emperor and Stoic philosopher*
     c. a poet and Platonic philosopher
     d. Hadrian's lover
     e. an equestrian monument

47. Roman's may well have developed it early, but they probably did not use

     a. formal linear perspective*
     b. aerial perspective
     c. architectural frames
     d. painterly technique

48. The Battle of Issos is a

     a. Roman fresco of the first century A.D.
     b. Roman frieze based on a Hellenistic fresco
     c. Roman relief on Trajan's Column
     d. Roman mosaic based on a Hellenistic fresco*
     e. Roman relief on the Arch of Constantine

49. The figures from the frieze of the Villa of the Mysteries are thought to depict an initiation into _____.

      a. the cult of Artemis
      b. Christianity
      c. the cult of Bacchus*
      d. the cult of Isis and Osiris

50. Which is not true of the Villa of the Mysteries frescoes?

      a. they represent an initiation rite
      b. they have erotic elements
      c. they have a red background
      d. the figures are naturalistic
      e. they include details of landscape*

51. The entry court of a Roman house was called the _____.

      a. aquarium
      b. atrium*
      c. bacterium
      d. oculus

52. In the Odyssey Landscape illustrated in this chapter

      a. cannibals are depicted*
      b. Laestrygonians are depicted helping Odysseus' men
      c. there is no landscape detail
      d. people are hunting animals

53. The Young Woman with a Stylus is an example of

      a. a relief
      b. a marble bust
      c. a tondo*
      d. a second style fresco

54. Hercules is the son of

      a. Juno and Jupiter
      b. Alkmene and Amphitryon
      c. Juno and Amphitryon
      d. Jupiter and Alkmene *

55. Which is <u>not</u> a characteristic of Roman frescoes?

    a. they are fresco secco*
    b. they are often found in private houses
    c. they are naturalistic
    d. they contain shading, cast shadows, and oblique viewpoints
    e. they contain the illusion of three-dimensional space

56. Faiyum painting was produced in

    a. Greece
    b. Egypt*
    c. Rome
    d. Nubia
    e. Carthage

57. The portrait of Artemidoros

    a. is an ancestor portrait
    b. is a fresco
    c. is encaustic*
    d. is a portrait bust

58. The Punic Wars were fought between

    a. Rome and Carthage*
    b. Rome and Greece
    c. Rome and Phoenicia
    d. Rome and Etruria

59. Dido was

    a. the deserted wife of Aeneas
    b. the queen of Carthage*
    c. the queen of Faiyum
    d. the heroine of Petrarch's Africa

60. The Tophet refers to

    a. a Punic shrine
    b. a temple
    c. a site of child sacrifice*
    d. a site of ritual suicide

CHAPTER 8:
Early Christian and Byzantine Art

Key Works

West wall of Dura Europos synagogue, c. 245

Moses Giving Water to the Twelve Tribes of Israel, detail of the west wall of the Dura Europos synagogue

Christ as the Good Shepherd, catacomb of Priscilla, Rome, 2nd – 3rd century

Jonah as an idealized Classical reclining nude, detail of an early Christian sarcophagus, Santa Maria Antiqua, Rome, 4th century

Christus-Sol, from the Christian Mausoleum of the Julii under Saint Peter's necropolis, Rome, mid-3rd century

Saint Paul outside the Walls, Rome, begun A.D. 385

Interior of Santa Costanza, Rome, c. 350

The ambulatory ceiling of Santa Costanza, Rome, c. 350

Exterior of the mausoleum of Galla Placidia, Ravenna, c. 425 – 426

Interior of the mausoleum of Galla Placidia showing niche with two apostles and the *Saint Lawrence* mosaic, Ravenna, c. 425 – 426

Christ as the Good Shepherd, the mausoleum of Galla Placidia, Ravenna, c. 425 – 426

Detail of a barrel vault from the mausoleum of Galla Placidia, Ravenna, c. 425 – 426

Detail of geometric border from the mausoleum of Galla Placidia, Ravenna, c. 425 – 426

Exterior of San Vitale, Ravenna, 540 – 547

Interior of San Vitale looking east toward the apse, Ravenna

Ceiling of the choir, San Vitale, c. 547

Detail of a capital, San Vitale, c. 540

Apse mosaic, San Vitale, c. 547

Court of Justinian, apse mosaic, San Vitale, c. 547

Court of Theodora, apse mosaic, San Vitale, c. 547

Theodora, detail of *Court of Theodora*, apse mosaic, San Vitale, c. 547

The throne of Maximian, 543 – 553, Ravenna (?)

Two Evangelists, from the front of the throne of Maximian

Exterior of Hagia Sophia, Constantinople, completed 537

Interior of Hagia Sophia

Detail of arcade spandrels and capital, Hagia Sophia

The Transfiguration, Church of Saint Catherine monastery, Mount Sinai, Egypt, c. 550 – 565

Joseph Interpreting Dreams in Prison, from the Vienna Genesis, early 6th century

Joseph and Potiphar's Wife, from the Vienna Genesis, early 6th century

Virgin and Child Enthroned with Saints Felix and Augustus, Commodilla catacomb, Rome, 528

Icon of *Saint Peter*, Saint Catherine monastery, Mount Sinai, Egypt

Monastery churches of Hosios Loukas, Greece, c. 1020

Virgin and Child Enthroned, church of Hosios Loukas, Greece, c. 1020

Crucifixion, Katholikon, church of Hosios Loukas, Greece, c. 1020
Harrowing of Hell, Katholikon, church of Hosios Loukas, Greece, c. 1020
Central dome and apse, Katholikon, Hosios Loukas, Greece, c. 1020
Incense burner in the shape of a domed building, 12th century
Pantokrator, from the abbey church of Monreale, Palermo, before 1183
Christ, detail of a *deësis* mosaic, Hagia Sophia, 13th century
Andrei Rublev, *Old Testament Trinity*, early 15th century
Barma and Postnik, Saint Basil's Cathedral, Moscow, 1554 – 1560

Maps, Diagrams, and Projections

Map of Byzantine Empire under Justinian I, A.D. 565
Plan of Old Saint Peter's basilica, Rome, 333 – 390
Reconstruction diagram of the nave of Old Saint Peter's basilica
Cross-section and plan of the martyrium of Santa Costanza, Rome, c. 350
Plan and section of San Vitale
Plan, section, and axonometric projection of Hagia Sophia
Domes, Pendentives, and Squinches
Plan of the monastery churches of Hosios Loukas (after Diehl), Greece, c. 1020

Key Terms

Aisle
ambulatory
axonometric projection
baptistry
blind niche
catacomb
clerestory
cloisonné
codex, codices
cruciform
decussis
deësis
diptych
gable
gallery
Greek cross
horror vacuui
icon
iconoclasm

iconography
Latin cross
mandorla
martyrium
minaret
mosque
narthex
nave
orant
parchment
pendentive
polyptych
repoussé
screen wall
squinch
tessera, tesserae
transept
vellum

Key Works

Chaitya hall, Karli, Maharashtra, India, c. 50 – 70 A.D.
Interior of Santa Sabina, Rome, 423 – 432
Mithuna from the façade of the *chaitya* hall, Karli, Maharashtra, India, c. 50 – 70 A.D.
Preaching Buddha, from Sarnath, Uttar Pradhesh, India, c. 475
The Ajanta Caves, Maharashtra, India, c. 450 – 500
Chaitya hall entrance, Ajanta Cave 19, Maharashtra, India, c. 450 – 500
Chaitya hall interior, Ajanta Cave 19, Maharashtra, India, c. 450 – 500
Prince Distributing Alms, Ajanta Cave 17, Maharashtra, India, c. 450 – 500
Padmapani, Ajanta Cave 1, Maharashtra, India, c. 450 – 500
Detail of *Padmapani*, Ajanta Cave 1, Maharashtra, India, c. 450 – 500
Worship of the Buddha, Ajanta Cave 10, Maharashtra, India, c. 450 – 500
Colossal Buddha, Cave 20, Yungang, Shaanxi Province, China, c. 460 – 490
Buddha with Disciples, Pinyang Cave, Longmen, Hunan Province, China, early 6ᵗʰ century
Vairochana Buddha, Longmen Caves, Hunan Province, China, 672 – 675

Maps, Diagrams, and Projections

Map of South Asia
Plan and section of the *chaitya* hall, Karli, Maharashtra, India
Plan of the Ajanta Cave complex, Maharashtra, India, c. 450 – 500
Map of China

Key Terms

abhaya mudrā   *mithuna*
bhūmisparsha mudrā   *tribhanga*
chaitya arch, *chaitya* hall   veranda
crypt   *vihāra*

Videos

Facade of Power (Russian architecture)
60 min. Home Vision

Medieval Manuscripts
30 min, 1989, FFTH

Tibet's Holy Mountain
52 min, 1994, VM

CD-ROMs

Medieval Realms, From the Collections of the British Museum
Windows, FFTH

Multiple-Choice Questions

1. Christianity was recognized by Constantine in

    a. the second century
    b. early fourth century*
    c. first century B.C.
    d. the fifth century

2. Christianity was legalized

    a. by the emperor Caracalla
    b. by the Edict of Milan*
    c. in the first century A.D.
    d. in Jerusalem

3. Christ was crucified around the year

    a. A.D. 30
    b. A.D. 35
    c. A.D. 32
    d. A.D. 33*

4. The most unusual feature of the Dura Europos synagogue is

    a. its Greek inscriptions
    b. its naturalistic images
    c. its figurative images*
    d. its Christian images

5. The Pentateuch refers to

    a. the Torah
    b. the first 5 books of the New Testament
    c. the Zoroastrian texts
    d. the first 5 books of the Old Testament*
    e. the 5 hymns to Mithras

6. The Holy Family refers to

    a. Mary, Christ, and God
    b. Christ, God, and the Holy Ghost
    c. Joseph, Mary, and the Holy Ghost
    d. God, Joseph, Mary, and Christ
    e. Christ, Mary, and Joseph*

7. The 12 followers of Christ are called the

    a. Evangelists
    b. Prophets
    c. Apostles*
    d. Disciples

8. Which does not match?

    a. The Baptism -- John baptizes Christ
    b. The Nativity -- Christ's birth
    c. The Transfiguration -- Christ is flanked by Moses and Elijah
    d. The Wedding at Cana -- Mary and Joseph are married*
    e. The Harrowing of Hell -- Christ descends to Limbo

9. The catacombs in Rome were primarily

    a. underground cemeteries*
    b. underground shrines
    c. underground meeting places
    d. underground sewers

10. Which is not a feature of the Early Christian basilica?

    a. nave
    b. apse
    c. aisle
    d. clerestory
    e. none of the above*

11. The first bishop of Rome was

    a. Constantine
    b. St. Paul
    c. St. Peter*
    d. Eusebius

12. Christ took on attributes of the emperor after the early 4th century. This meant Christ had (a)

    a. halo
    b. royal purple
    c. throne
    d. all of the above*

13. Which is <u>not</u> true of the Christian altar?

    a. it was originally a table
    b. in most churches it is in the western end*
    c. it is the site of the Eucharist in the Mass
    d. It often supports a Crucifix

14. A significant new architectural feature of Old Saint Peter's was

    a. the transept*
    b. the nave
    c. the atrium
    d. the clerestory

15. The Roman Basilica was entered from a door in its side but Old St. Peter's in Rome was entered

    a. through the atrium
    b. through its narthex*
    c. in the side of the nave
    d. behind the apse

16. The pagan god most often associated with Christ was

    a. Dionysos
    b. Apollo*
    c. Jupiter
    d. Hermes
    e. Zeus

17. Galla Placidia was

    a. an empress
    b. a mausoleum
    c. an Early Christian church
    d. all of the above
    e. a and b*

18. The components of Byzantine mosaics are

    a. pigments
    b. marble squares
    c. semi-precious jewels
    d. tesserae*
    e. polished stones

19. Which is <u>not</u> a feature of San Vitale?

    a. a transept*
    b. a narthex
    c. an ambulatory
    d. an apse

20 Which is <u>not</u> true of San Vitale?

    a. it is on the east coast of Italy
    b. it was the personal Church of Justinian*
    c. it is filled with mosaics
    d. its exterior is plain brick

21. The vaulted choir of San Vitale contains a representation of

    a. angels with Mary
    b. a bust of San Vitale
    c. Bishop Ecclesius
    d. angels with a lamb*
    e. Christ as a shepherd

22. The dome of the Hagia Sophia is supported by _____.

    a. squinches
    b. pendentives*
    c. vaults
    d. arches

23. A dome can be supported by

    a. a cylindrical drum
    b. pendentives
    c. squinches
    d. all of the above*

24. The main Byzantine contribution to monumental architecture was

       a. the pendentive*
       b. the Composite Order
       c. the dome
       d. the narthex
       e. the round arch

25. Compared with Roman frescoes and mosaics, Byzantine mosaics are

       a. more naturalistic
       b. more narrative
       c. more static*
       d. more three-dimensional

26. Which is least likely to be represented in a Byzantine mosaic?

       a. frontality
       b. contrapposto*
       c. outlined figures
       d. repeated poses
       e. flattened forms

27. In the apse mosaics of San Vitale

       a. Justinian is to the left of Christ
       b. Theodora is to the right of Christ
       c. Justinian is next to a baptismal font
       d. Theodora is in an abbreviated apse*

28. Justinian's mosaic in San Vitale depicts

       a. soldiers, senators, Maximian, and Justinian
       b. churchmen, senators, Maximian, and Justinian
       c. soldiers, churchmen, Maximian, and Justinian*
       d. Justinian, Theodora, Maximian, and churchmen

29. Compared to Justinian's mosaic at San Vitale, in Theodora's

       a. the figures are less colorful
       b. there is less architecture
       c. the figures are set back from the picture plane*
       d. the figures are all female

30. The ivory throne of Maximian was probably used for

    a. receiving dignitaries
    b. royal celebrations
    c. a reliquary casket
    d. a ritual chair*

31. Typology refers primarily to

    a. prefiguration and fulfillment*
    b. genealogical history
    c. Adam and Eve
    d. prophets and prophecy

32. Which feature of Hagia Sophia was not part of the original design?

    a. the dome
    b. the pendentives
    c. the minarets*
    d. the atrium
    e. the narthex

33. Dura Europos housed

    a. a synagogue
    b. a Christian house
    c. a catacombs
    d. a and b*

34. A mandorla is

    a. a Far Eastern chant
    b. an oval aureole*
    c. the plan of a Hindu temple
    d. a halo around the head of a saint

35. In Byzantine iconography, Christ is conventionally

    a. bearded*
    b. Apollonian
    c. shown in contrapposto
    d. shown holding a globe
    e. shown in a horizontal plane

36. St. Mark's in Venice shows its Byzantine influence in its

    a. elongated nave
    b. elaborate narthex
    c. insertion of a triple apse
    d. dome on a centralized building*

37. Byzantine art did not make a strong impact on

    a. Russia
    b. England*
    c. Turkey
    d. Greece

38. The "book with many folded skins" referred to a

    a. papyrus scroll
    b. tablet
    c. codex*
    d. spiral frieze
    e. rotulus

39. Which is least likely to have been illustrated in the Vienna Genesis?

    a. the story of Joseph and pharaoh
    b. the story of the tower of Babel
    c. the story of Moses on Mt. Sinai
    d. the story of the birth of Christ*
    e. the events in the Pentateuch

40. The narrative format of the Vienna Genesis has been compared to

    a. the Ara Pacis
    b. the Parthenon frieze
    c. the Column of Trajan*
    d. the Arch of Constantine
    e. the San Vitale mosaics

41. Which best defines an icon?

    a. a frontal image in a church
    b. an image on a wood panel
    c. an image of Christ
    d. any religious image
    e. a purely devotional image*

42. The Iconoclastic Controversy took place in the

    a. 6th century
    b. 7th century
    c. 8th century*
    d. 9th century

43. An iconoclast is literally

    a. one who breaks images*
    b. one who believes in icons
    c. one who worships icons
    d. one who worships the real person instead of the icon

44. The tradition that St. Luke painted the Virgin was used

    a. to define the features of Mary
    b. to support the iconophiles*
    c. to support the iconoclasts
    d. to defend religious portraiture

45. One result of the Iconoclastic Controversy was

    a. a decline in painted images
    b. a decline in mosaics
    c. a decline in architectural innovation
    d. a decline in sculpture*

46. A homunculus is

    a. an imp
    b. a devil
    c. an evil spirit
    d. a little man*
    e. a midget

47. Christ as Pantokrator represents Christ as

    a. ruler of everything*
    b. ruler of the world
    c. ruler of heaven
    d. ruler of the Church

48. Deësis refers to an image of

    a. the Holy Family
    b. the Holy Ghost
    c. God, Mary, and Christ
    d. Christ, Mary, and John the Baptist*
    e. God, Christ, and John the Baptist

49. *Ichthus* is an acronym for

    a. Jesus Christ Savior of the World
    b. Jesus Christ Son of God Savior*
    c. Jesus Christ Son of Man
    d. Jesus Christ Son of God and Ruler of the Universe

50. The most important late Byzantine Russian icon painter was

    a. Ivan
    b. Barma
    c. Postnik
    d. Basil
    e. Rublev*

Key Works

Dome of the Rock, Jerusalem, late 7th century
Page from the Kairouan manuscript of the Koran, written in Kufic, Tunisia, 9th – 10th centuries
Illuminated *tugra* of Sultan Suleyman, c. 1555 – 1560
Great Mosque, Samarra (Iraq), 847 – 852
Arches of the Great Mosque, Córdoba, c. 961 – 966
Mihrāb bay, the Great Mosque, Córdoba, c. 961 – 966
Dome in front of the *mihrāb*, the Great Mosque, Córdoba, c. 961 – 966
Sinan the Great, Mosque of Suleyman I, Istanbul, Turkey, begun 1550
Courtyard (*sahn*) of the Mosque of Suleyman I, Istanbul
Interior of the Mosque of Suleyman I
The Luftullah Mosque, Isfahan, Iran, 1602 – 1616
Sutton Hoo purse cover, East Anglia, England, c. 630
Animal headpost, Oseberg, Norway, 800 – 850
Lion-head finial, Kul Oba, Russia
Axe from Mammen, Jutland, Denmark, Late Viking, c. 950 – 975
The Rök stone, Östergötland, Sweden, early 9th century
Harald Bluetooth's rune stone, Jelling, Denmark, c. 965
Warrior Entering Valhalla, Tjangvide, Gotland, Sweden, 8th – 9th century
Celtic cross, Ahenny, Tipperary, Ireland, late 8th century
Lion Symbol of Saint John, from the Book of Durrow, c. 650 – 700
Tunc Crucifixerant XPI, from the Book of Kells, late 8th or early 9th century
Odo of Metz, Charlemagne's Palace Chapel, Aachen, 792 – 805
Court School of Charlemagne, *Christ Blessing*, from the Godescalc Gospels, 781 – 783
Saint John, from the Coronation Gospels, late 8th century
Four Evangelists, from a Carolingian Gospel book, palace chapel school, Aachen, early 9th
  century
Christ in Majesty, Vivian Bible frontispiece, c. 845 – 846
Reims school, illustration to Psalm 88, from the Utrecht Psalter, c. 825 – 850
Reconstructed model of the monastery of Saint Gall, Switzerland, c. 820
Restored abbey church of Saint Michael's, Hildesheim, c. 1001 – 1031
Restored interior of Saint Michael's, looking west, Hildesheim
Bronze doors, Saint Michael's, Hildesheim, completed 1015
Adam and Eve Reproached by God, detail of the bronze doors of Saint Michael's
Paschal candlestick, Saint Michael's, Hildesheim, c. 1022
Saint Luke, from the Gospel book of Otto III, c. 1000
Christ Enthroned with Saints and Emperor Otto I, Ottonian, 962 – 973, from Milan or Richenau

Maps, Diagrams, and Projections

The expansion of Islam, 622 – c. 750
Plan of the Great Mosque, Samarra, 847 – 852
Plan of the Great Mosque, Córdoba, Spain, originally built 786 – 787
Plan of the mosque of Suleyman I and the imperial complex, Istanbul
Map of Northern Europe in the Middle Ages
Map of Holy Roman Empire under Charlemagne, 814
Plan (restored) of Charlemagne's palace chapel, Aachen
Reconstruction drawing of Charlemagne's palace chapel, Aachen
Plan of the monastery of Saint Gall, Switzerland, c. 820
Reconstruction model of the monastery of Saint Gall, Switzerland, c. 820
Section and plan of Saint Michael's, Hildesheim

Key Terms

arabesque
calligraphy
cloisonné
enamel
gilding
imam
iwan
interlace
madrasah
manuscript
mihrāb

minbar
mosque
picture stone
polychrome
qibla
refectory
rune stone
sahn
scriptorium
westwork

Window on the World
Mesoamerica (1500 B.C. – A.D. 1500)

Key Works

Seated Jaguar, San Lorenzo, Veracruz, Mexico, Olmec, Early Preclassic, 1200 – 900 B.C.
Colossal head, from San Lorenzo, Veracruz, Mexico, Olmec, c. 1000 B.C.
View of Teotihuacán
Detail of heads from the façade of the Temple of Quetzalcoatl, Teotihuacán, before 300 A.D.
Detail of warrior in Teotihuacán costume, from side of stele 31, Tikal, Guatemala, Maya
The Leiden Plate
Maya Lord, Tabasco, Mexico, 6th century
Tatiana Proskouriakoff, reconstruction drawing of the site of Copán, Honduras, Maya, Late
    Classic
Ball court, Copán, Honduras, Maya, Late Classic, c. 800

Monkey-man scribal god, Copán, Honduras, Maya, Late Classic, c. 600 – 900
Temple I, Tikal, Guatemala, Maya, before A.D. 800
Reconstruction of mural painting, Bonampak, Chiapas, Mexico, Maya, Classic, c. 790
Detail of mural painting, Bonampak, Chiapas, Mexico, Maya, Classic, c. 790
Plan of the site of Chichén Itzá, Mexico
View of Chichén Itzá showing the *Caracol* with the Temple of the Warriors and the *Castillo* in the distance, c. 800 – 1000
Chacmool, Chichén Itzá, Mexico
Coyolxauhqui, Goddess of the Moon, Templo Mayor, Tenochtitlán, Mexico, 15ᵗʰ century
Eagle Warrior, Templo Mayor, Tenochtitlán, Mexico, 15ᵗʰ century
Roll-out drawing of the Lanzón, from the Old Temple at Chavín de Huántar, Late Initial, c. 900 – 500 B.C.
Textile with "impersonator" figures, Paracus, Peru, Early Intermediate, c. 100 – 200
Vessel depicting composite fish, feline, and human figure, Nazca, c. 50 – 200
Moche portrait vessel of ruler, Peru, 400 – 500
Earspool, from the Tomb of the Warrior Priest, Sipan, c. 300
The Sun Gate, Tiwanaku, Bolivia, 500 – 700
Detail of a Wari tunic, from Peru, 600 – 1000
Machu Picchu, Inka culture, near Cuzco, Peru, 15ᵗʰ – 16ᵗʰ centuries

Maps, Diagrams, and Projections

Map of Mesoamerica in relation to North and South America
Map of Mesoamerica
View of Teotihuacán
Plan of Teotihuacán, c. 350 – 650
Diagrams of *talud-tablero* platform
Tatiana Proskouriakoff, reconstruction drawing of the site of Copán, Honduras, Maya, Late Classic
Plan of site of Chichén Itzá, Mexico
Map of central Andes
Chavín de Huántar, Late Initial, c. 900 – 500 B.C.

Key Terms

roof comb
talud-tablero

Videos

Ancient America
60 min, 1995, VM

Civilisation, Volume 1
The Skin of Our Teeth & The Great Thaw
94 min.

History Through Art: The Middle Ages
34 min, Clearvue

Islamic Art
30 min, FFTH

Lost Kingdoms of the Maya
60 min, 1993, VM

Mayans: Apocalypse Then
27 min, 1991, VM

Medieval Art and Music
35 min, Clearvue

The World of Islam Series: Orient/Occident
30 min, FFTH

CD-ROMs

Exploring the Lost Maya
Mac/Windows, Sumeria

History Through Art: The Middle Ages
Mac/Windows, Clearvue

The Medieval Era
Mac/Windows, Clearvue

Multiple-Choice Questions

1. "Middle Ages" in western Europe includes which of the following time periods?

    a. the beginning of Early Christian through the 13th or 14th centuries*
    b. the end of the Roman Empire through the Byzantine period
    c. the beginning of Byzantine through the end of the Roman Empire
    d. A.D. 300 – A.D. 1600

2. The new religion that entered Europe in the 8th century was

    a. Buddhism
    b. Hinduism
    c. Islam*
    d. Judaism

3. Which of the following cultures influenced Islamic art?

    a. Byzantine
    b. Archaic Greek
    c. Early Christian
    d. a and c*

4. The Christian recovery of Moorish strongholds is called the

    a. Reformation
    b. Rebellion
    c. Revolution
    d. Reconquest*
    e. Renaissance

5. Which is true?

    a. Muhammad was born in Mecca in 622.
    b. Muhammad claimed to be the son of Allah.
    c. The *hijra* marks the beginning of the Islamic calendar.*
    d. Muslims are required to pray six times a day.

6. The *hadj* refers to

    a. the Islamic calendar
    b. a pilgrimage*
    c. a leader
    d. a mosque

7. Jihad is a _____.

    a. religious sentence
    b. priest
    c. holy book
    d. holy war against sin, in oneself and in the world*

8. Muslims must pray

    a. in a mosque
    b. facing west
    c. facing Mecca*
    d. facing a *qibla*

9. Which is <u>not</u> a tenet of Islam?

    a. daily prayer
    b. fasting during Ramadan
    c. the only God is Allah
    d. Muhammad is the son of God*
    e. almsgiving

10. Which is <u>not</u> true of the Dome of the Rock?

    a. it is centrally planned
    b. it is the site of Muhammad's ascent to heaven
    c. it is the site of the Sacrifice of Isaac
    d. it is the site of Solomon's Temple
    e. it is the site of Christ's ascension*

11. The Dome of the Rock is in _____.

    a. Jerusalem*
    b. Mecca
    c. Córdoba
    d. Damascus

12. Which is <u>not</u> an architectural feature of the mosque?

    a. a *sahn*
    b. a *qibla*
    c. an *immam**
    d. a *mihrab*
    e. a *minbar*

13. A mihrab is _____.

    a. a niche in a qibla wall*
    b. an entryway to a mosque
    c. a ceiling mosaic
    d. an official calligraphic document

14. Islamic artists use

   a. calligraphy
   b. mosaics
   c. weaving
   d. all the above*

15. The largest 9th century mosque was located in

   a. Samarra*
   b. Córdoba
   c. Granada
   d. Jerusalem
   e. Iran

16. The first Muslim ruler of Spain was

   a. Caliph Abd al-Malik
   b. Sultan Suleyman
   c. Sinan the Great
   d. Caliph al-Mutawakkil
   e. Abd ar-Rahman I*

17. The Court of the Lions is at the _____.

   a. Damascus
   b. Taj Mahal
   c. Dome of the Rock
   d. Alhambra*

18. "Architect in the Abode of Felicity" refers to

   a. Suleyman
   b. Koca*
   c. Justinian
   d. Muhammad

19. Which is not true of the Luftullah Mosque?

   a. it is in Iran
   b. it is covered with floral and calligraphic tiles
   c. it was built in the 16th century*
   d. there are no human figures on its exterior surface
   e. its predominate color on the exterior is blue

20. The purse cover from Sutton Hoo is an example of

     a. Islamic tracery
     b. Viking iconography
     c. Anglo-Saxon metalwork*
     d. a Neolithic artifact

21. Which of the following is <u>not</u> a feature of the Sutton Hoo purse cover?

     a. *cloisonné*, enamel
     b. red garnets
     c. symmetry
     d. Scythian influence
     e. Islamic influence*

22. The Vikings inhabited

     a. Sweden, Norway, and Denmark*
     b. Finland, Norway, Denmark, and Sweden
     c. Lapland, Finland, Norway, Denmark, and Sweden
     d. Lapland, Norway, Sweden, and Denmark

23. Which is <u>not</u> true of the Vikings

     a. they wrote sagas
     b. they were pagans
     c. they were ferocious warriors
     d. they were ship-builders
     e. they became Christians in the 8th century*

24. A rich sixth-century ship burial was found at _____.

     a. Centula
     b. Lindisfarne
     c. Sutton Hoo*
     d. Iona

25. The opening scene of Beowulf describes

     a. the defeat of the monster Grendel
     b. the death of Beowulf
     c. the arrival of Scyld Scefing in Denmark*
     d. the birth of Beowulf
     e. the arrival of Beowulf in Scandinavia

26. Which is not a pair?

    a. Thor -- Zeus
    b. Asgard -- Olympos
    c. Ragnarok -- the Apocalypse
    d. Jotun -- Titans
    e. Volur -- Vulcan*

27. The tree where the Norse gods held daily council was called

    a. Ymir
    b. Yggdrasil*
    c. Utgard
    d. Norn

28. Which is true?

    a. Snorri Sturlson wrote the Edda in Scaldic.*
    b. Saemund wrote the Edda in the 13th century.
    c. Harald Bluetooth wrote the Edda on a rune stone.
    d. Harald Fairhair is the main subject of the Edda.

29. Which is not a member of the Norse pantheon?

    a. Baldr
    b. Heimdall
    c. Ymir*
    d. Elves
    e. Vanir

30. The role of the Valkyries was

    a. to slay the enemies of the gods
    b. to select dead heroes for entry to Valhalla*
    c. to seduce the enemies of the gods
    d. to destroy the enemies of the Vikings

31. Which is not true of Harald Bluetooth's rune stone?

    a. it is in Jelling
    b. it was raised in the 10th century
    c. it has interlace designs
    d. it celebrates Harald's conversion
    e. it is Norwegian*

32. *Hibernia* means

    a. Scandinavia in Italian
    b. Ireland in Latin*
    c. Germany in Anglo-Saxon
    d. Scotland in Latin

33. Illuminated manuscripts were

    a. made in *scriptoria* by scribes*
    b. made of encaustic on vellum
    c. made of pigments mixed with water and egg yolk
    d. written in Gaelic in Irish monasteries

34. The Irish monks are most famous for their _____.

    a. sculptures
    b. splendid dwellings
    c. manuscript decoration*
    d. elaborate reliquaries

35. The Book of Kells is

    a. a 7th-century manuscript
    b. the text of the Acts of Paul
    c. late 8th or early 9th century*
    d. a text of the Edda

36. Celtic stone crosses have

    a. the figure of the crucified Christ
    b. Viking runes
    c. cross bars of equal length
    d. a circle intersecting the cross arms*

37. Which is <u>not</u> a feature of Hiberno-Saxon manuscripts?

    a. Latin text
    b. interlace
    c. stylization
    d. naturalism*
    e. monstrous details

38. Charlemagne was crowned Roman Emperor

    a. in the year 800*
    b. at Aachen, in Germany
    c. because he defeated the pope in Rome
    d. at Aix-la-Chapelle on December 25

39. Charlemagne's court scribe was

    a. Odo of Metz
    b. Godescalc*
    c. Hildegarde
    d. Charles Martel

40. Charlemagne revived an interest in the classical world in

    a. the sixth century
    b. the ninth century
    c. his seat at Aachen
    d. b and c*

41. Charlemagne's Chapel at Aachen is based on the church of _____.

    a. Old St. Peter's
    b. San Vitale*
    c. Hagia Sophia
    d. Santa Costanza

42. The Book of Revelation

    a. was written by John the Baptist on Patmos
    b. is the last book of the Old Testament
    c. was written by John the Divine on Patmos
    d. is the last book of the New Testament
    e. c and d*

43. The Coronation Gospels are _____ than the Godescalc Gospels. Fill in the blank.

    a. more naturalistic*
    b. more iconic
    c. more Byzantine
    d. more stylized
    e. less naturalistic

44. The images in the Utrecht Psalter differs from those in the Vienna Genesis because

    a. they have more variety of color
    b. they illustrate the Gospels
    c. they illustrate the Pentateuch
    d. they are metaphorical rather than narrative*
    e. they are straightforward narratives

45. The Utrecht Psalter is most closely related to the _____.

    a. Book of Lindisfarne
    b. Ebbo Gospels*
    c. The Book of Kells
    d. Las Siete Partidas of Alphonse the Wise

46. The monastery of Saint Gall

    a. dates to the early 9th century and was in Switzerland
    b. was in southern France
    c. followed the Rule of St. Benedict
    d. a and c*
    e. b and c

47. The basilica for the Monastery of St. Gall showed its early Christian pedigree by its

    a. transept
    b. choir before the altar
    c. towers
    d. all of the above*

48. St. Michael's at Hildesheim was

    a. Carolingian
    b. Ottonian*
    c. a monastery
    d. a palace chapel

49. Bernward was the tutor of

    a. Otto I
    b. Otto II
    c. Otto III*
    d. Charlemagne

CHAPTER 10:
Romanesque Art

Key Works

Aerial view of Sainte-Foy, Conques, Auvergne, France, c. 1050 – 1120

Reliquary statue of Sainte Foy, Conques, late 10th – 11th century

Tribune and nave vaults, Sainte-Foy, Conques, c. 1050 – 1120

West portal with tympanum, Sainte-Foy, Conques, c. 1130

Last Judgment, tympanum of west portal, Sainte-Foy, Conques, c. 1130

Christ the Judge, tympanum of west portal, Sainte-Foy, Conques, c. 1130

South porch, Saint-Pierre, Moissac, c. 1115 – 1135

Tympanum of south porch, Saint-Pierre, Moissac, c. 1115 – 1135

Christ, tympanum of south porch, Saint-Pierre, Moissac, c. 1115 – 1135

Christ in Majesty, from the Stavelot Bible, 1093 – 1197

The Stavelot Triptych, (open) Mosan, c. 1156 – 1158

Vision of Constantine, detail of the Stavelot Triptych, Mosan, c. 1156 – 1158

The elders, tympanum of south porch, Saint-Pierre, Moissac, c. 1115 – 1135

Detail of an elder, tympanum of south porch, Saint-Pierre, Moissac, c. 1115 – 1135

Saint Paul, trumeau of Saint-Pierre, Moissac

Cloister pier with relief of *Abbott Durand*, Saint-Pierre, Moissac, 1047 – 1072

Initial L and *Saint Matthew*, region of Agen-Moissac, c. 1100

Capital, north gallery of the cloister, Saint-Pierre, Moissac, c. 1100

Initial *T,* from the sacramentary of Saint-Sauveur de Figeac, 11th century

Gislebertus, capital depicting the *Flight into Egypt*, Cathedral of Saint-Lazare, Autun, Burgundy, France, c. 1130

Gislebertus, *Last Judgment*, tympanum of west portal, Cathedral of Saint-Lazare, Autun, Burgundy, c. 1120 – 1135

Gislebertus, *Last Judgment* (detail showing the weighing of souls)

Gislebertus, *Last Judgment* (detail showing two pilgrims)

Decorative detail of interlace sculpture, right jamb of west portal, Ål Cathedral, Norway, 12thc.

Borgund stave church, Sogne, Norway, second half of 12th century

View of the baptistry, cathedral, and campanile, Pisa, 1053 – 1272

Nave of Pisa Cathedral, 12th century

Campanile of Pisa Cathedral, 1174 – 1271

Apse of the chapel of Castel Appiano, Italy, c. 1200

Mary and Christ with Two Angels (detail from the Apse of the chapel of Castel Appiano), Italy, c. 1200

Detail of battle scene showing Bishop Odo with mace, from the Bayeux "Tapestry," c.1070 – 80

Detail of Viking Ships from the Bayeux "Tapestry"

Detail of craftsmen from the Bayeux "Tapestry"

West façade, Saint-Étienne, Caen, Normandy, France, 1067 – 1087

Nave, Saint-Étienne, Caen, 1067 – 1087

Exterior of Durham Cathedral, England, begun 1093

Nave, Durham Cathedral

Maps, Diagrams, and Projections

Map of Romanesque and Gothic sites in western Europe, including pilgrimage routes to Santiago
de Compostela
Plan of Sainte-Foy, Conques, c. 1050 – 1120
Diagram of the three main Romanesque vaulting systems
Diagram of a Romanesque portal
Plan of the abbey and church of Saint-Pierre, Moissac, France
Plan of Pisa Cathedral and the surrounding complex
Plan of Saint-Étienne, Caen
Plan of Durham Cathedral

Key Terms

abutment
bay
butress
campanile
cluster pier, compound pier
compound pier
crossing
jamb
mandorla
portal

program
quadrant vaulting, half-barrel vaulting
radiating chapels
reliquary
ribbed vault
transverse rib
tribune
trumeau(x)
tympanum(a)

Videos

Art of the Western World
Volume 1: A White Garment of Churches: Romanesque and Gothic
55 min, VM

First Crusade
54 min, 1994, VM

Italian Romanesque: Architecture - Sculpture - Painting
26 min, 1994, VM, RMI

Shadow of the Templars
50 min, 1995, VM

Multiple-Choice Questions

1. Romanesque refers to

    a. a distinctive style in western Europe from 1000 to 1400
    b. a period of western European art and history
    c. a range of styles with regional variations*
    d. Medieval sculpture and architecture, but not painting

2. Most innovative Romanesque works were created in

    a. France*
    b. Germany
    c. Italy
    d. Spain
    e. England

3. Romanesque buildings were supported by

    a. stylobates
    b. flying buttresses
    c. buttresses*
    d. podia

4. Romanesque architects used all of the following <u>except</u>

    a. ribbed vaults
    b. flying buttresses*
    c. towers
    d. clerestory windows

5. The three most popular pilgrimage sites were

    a. Rome, Paris, and Jerusalem
    b. Compostela, Paris, and Rome
    c. Rome, Compostela, and Jerusalem*
    d. Paris, Jerusalem, and Compostela

6. The Liber Sancti Jacobi was a

    a. 12th-century biography of St. Jacob
    b. 12th-century biography of St. James
    c. 12th-century guide for pilgrims*
    d. 12th-century guide to the pilgrimage roads

7. Sainte-Foy at Conques was dedicated to

    a. Saint Faith*
    b. Saint Frederic
    c. Saint Philobert
    d. Saint Francis

8. A reliquary is a

    a. cinerary urn
    b. medieval sarcophagus
    c. a container for relics*
    d. a jeweled container

9. Which is not part of the plan of Sainte-Foy at Conques?

    a. a narthex*
    b. a nave
    c. a transept
    d. a crossing
    e. an apse

10. Which is not a feature of the typical Romanesque portal?

    a. voussoir
    b. tympanum
    c. lintel
    d. door jamb
    e. transept*

11. A refectory is

    a. container for relics
    b. a monastery kitchen
    c. a monastery dining hall*
    d. a mirror image

12. Saint-Pierre at Moissac has a visionary character because

    a. it was inspired by a vision of St. Peter
    b. it was inspired by a dream of Clovis*
    c. it was inspired by a miracle of St. Peter
    d. it was inspired by an oracle

13. The traditional apocalyptic symbols of the Evangelists are

    a. a bull, an eagle, a serpent, a lion
    b. a bull, a serpent, an eagle, an angel
    c. a serpent, a lion, an angel, an eagle
    d. an angel, a bull, an eagle, a lion*

14. Which is <u>not</u> true of the Stavelot reliquary?

    a. it is a triptych
    b. it illustrates the Legend of the True Cross
    c. it is located in Holland*
    d. it attracted pilgrims to Belgium
    e. it was believed to contain a nail used in the Crucifixion

15. Which best describes the tympanum of Saint-Pierre at Moissac

    a. the figures are elongated and stylized*
    b. the figures are frontal and elongated
    c. the figures are naturalistic and patterned
    d. the figures are elongated and are made of marble

16. St.-Pierre, Moissac demonstrated a comprehensive sculptural program in its

    a. portal
    b. porch
    c. westwork
    d. a and b*

17. The tympanum at Moissac shows

    a. the Last Judgment*
    b. Christ in Glory with the Elders of the Apocalypse
    c. Crucifixion
    d. the Virgin and Child

18. The cleric who criticized the extravagant decoration of places like the cloister of St-Pierre, Moissac, was

    a. St. James of Compostela
    b. St. Bernard*
    c. St. Francis
    d. St. Benedict

19. Who was the sculptor at Autun?

    a. Durand
    b. Giselbertus*
    c. Jacobus
    d. no one knows

20. Examples of Romanesque style outside of France are found

    a. in Norway
    b. at Pisa
    c. in Belgium
    d. at Castel Appiano
    e. all of the above*

21. The Bayeux Tapestry is

    a. a tapestry
    b. an embroidery*
    c. a Viking work
    d. a parchment

22. The Bayeux Tapestry was probably commissioned by

    a. William the Conqueror
    b. Giselbertus
    c. Bishop Odo*
    d. the Norman Queen Mathilde
    e. Harold of Saxony

23. William the Conqueror encouraged

    a. the building of churches in Normandy
    b. the conquest of Anglo-Saxon England
    c. the building of churches in England
    d. all of the above*

24. Tall twin towers were integrated into the facades of Romanesque churches in _____.

    a. Italy
    b. England
    c. South of France
    d. Normandy*

25. Because the year 1000 suggested the end of time, Romanesque churches often showed the Last Judgment on

       a. the jambs
       b. the tribune
       c. the tympanum*
       d. the trumeau

26. The text on the Bayeux Tapestry is

       a. in French
       b. in English
       c. in Norwegian
       d. in Latin*
       e. in Anglo-Saxon

27. The subject of the Bayeux Tapestry is

       a. the construction of Bayeux Cathedral
       b. the Norman conquest*
       c. the Viking invasion of Europe
       d. the Saxon invasion of Normandy

Key Works

West façade, Saint-Denis, near Paris, dedicated 1140

Interior of Saint-Denis

View of piers in the nave arcade, Chartres Cathedral, France, 13th century

Jeroboam Worshiping Golden Calves, detail of a lancet under the north rose window, Chartres
    Cathedral, early 13th century

Carpenters' Guild signature window, detail of stained-glass window, Chartres Cathedral, early
    13th century

Geometric architectural diagrams from the sketchbook of Villard de Honnecourt, c. 1225

Geometric analysis of human and animal figures from the sketchbook of Villard de Honnecourt,
    c. 1225

West façade of Chartres Cathedral, c. 1140 – 1150

South wall of Chartres Cathedral, 13th century

Apse of Chartres Cathedral, with radiating chapels and flying buttresses, 13th century

The three portals of the west façade, Chartres Cathedral, c. 1140 – 1150

Tympanum, lintel, and archivolts of the central portal, west façade, Chartres Cathedral, c. 1145 –
    70

Doorjamb statues, west façade, Chartres Cathedral, c. 1145 – 1170

Stylized drapery, detail of doorjamb statues, south transept, Chartres Cathedral, c. 1145 – 1170

Saints Theodore, Stephen, Clement, and Lawrence, door jamb statues, south transept, Chartres
    Cathedral, 13th century

Teaching Christ, trumeau, south transept, Chartres Cathedral, 13th century

Antichrist as a Three-Headed Tyrant, from the Harley Manuscript, 1527

Hildegard of Bingen, *Antichrist's Birth and Destruction Liber scivias*, Eibington Abbey, late 12th
    century

Nave, Chartres Cathedral, looking east

Rose window and lancets, north transept, Chartres Cathedral, 13th century

West façade, Amiens Cathedral, France, 1220 – 1269

Nave, Amiens Cathedral, 1220 – 1269

Choir vaults, Amiens Cathedral, 1220 – 1269

Beau Dieu, central portal, west façade, Amiens Cathedral, c. 1225 – 1230

Vierge dorée, south portal, Amiens Cathedral, c. 1250

West façade, Reims Cathedral, France, begun 1211

Nave, Reims Cathedral, 1211 – c.1290

Annunciation and Visitation, doorjamb statues, Reims Cathedral, c. 1225 – 1245

Philip I of France granting privileges to the priory of Saint-Martin-des-Champs, France, c. 1250

Scene from the *Life of Saint Denis*, completed 1317

Nave, Saint-Chapelle, Paris, 1243 – 1248

Choir, Canterbury Cathedral, 1174 – 1184

View of Canterbury Cathedral

Vault, Corona Chapel, Canterbury Cathedral

The Return of the Messengers from the Promised Land, detail of window, Corona Chapel, Canterbury Cathedral, 13th century

Solomon and the Queen of Sheba, detail of window, Canterbury Cathedral, late 12th century

Salisbury Cathedral, England, begun 1220

Vault, chapter house, Salisbury Cathedral, 1263 – 1284

King's College Chapel, Cambridge, England, founded 1441, vaulting 1508 – 1515

Siena Cathedral, Tuscany, Italy, 1284 – 1299

Milan Cathedral, Milan, Italy, begun 1386

Southeast view of Palma de Mallorca Cathedral, island of Mallorca, begun 1306

Apse, Prague Cathedral, Czech Republic

Doges' Palace, Venice, Italy, façade, 1420s

Town Hall, Louvain, Belgium, 1448

Aerial view of Saint Patrick's Cathedral, New York, 1858 – 1879

Maps, Diagrams, and Projections

Plan of Saint-Denis, 1140 – 1144

Diagram of a ribbed vault.

Section diagram of a Gothic cathedral (after E. Viollet-lr-Duc)

Plan of Chartres Cathedral

Perspective diagram and cross section of Chartres Cathedral

Plan of Amiens Cathedral

Plan of Reims Cathedral (after W. Blaser)

View of Canterbury Cathedral

Plan of Canterbury Cathedral

Plan of Salisbury Cathedral

Salisbury Cathedral, England, begun, 1220

Key Terms

armature

chevet

choir

compound

crenellations

elevation

fan vault

flying buttresses

guilds

lancet

Pietà

ribbed vault

rose window

tracery

triforium

web

Key Works

Buddha (Shakyamuni or Amitabha) Preaching the Law, Cave 17, Dunhuang Province, China, early 8th century
Shakyamuni Buddha Preaching on Vulture Peak, Cave 17, Dunhuang Province, China, 8th century
Pagoda, Yunshusu, Mount Fang, Hopei, China, early 8th century
Pagoda, Kaifeng, Hunan Province, China, mid-11th century
Five-storied pagoda, *Goju-no-to*, monastery of Horyu-ji, Nara, Japan, late 7th century
View of the monastery of Horyu-ji, Nara, Japan, late 7th century
Kondō (Golden Hall), Horyu-ji, Nara, late 7th century
Temple of Vishnu, Deogarh, Uttar Pradesh, India, early 6th century
Vishnu Sleeping on Ananta, relief panel, south side, Temple of Vishnu, Deogarh, Uttar Pradesh, India, early 6th century
West doorway, Temple of Vishnu, Deogarh, Uttar Pradesh, India, 6th century
Mukteshvar temple of Shiva, Bhubaneshvar, Orissa, India, c. 950
Aerial view of Angkor Wat, Cambodia
Roadway approaching Angkor Wat, Cambodia
Army on the March, Angkor Wat, Cambodia, first half of 12th century
Apsaras, exterior wall of a gallery, Angkor Wat, Cambodia
"*Water Nymph*," detail of frieze, Angkor Wat, Cambodia
Bayon temple, Angkor Thom, Cambodia, c. 1200
Towers with monumental faces of Devaraja, Bayon, Angkor Thom, Cambodia

Maps, Diagrams, and Projections

Map of East Asia
Diagram section of the Horyu-ji *kondo*
Drawing of part of the Horyu-ji *kondo*
Plan of the Temple of Vishnu, Deogarh, Uttar Pradesh, India, early 6th century
Elevation of a typical Orissan temple
Plan of Mukteshvar Temple of Shiva, Bhubaneshvar, Orissa, India, c. 950
Plan of the central complex at Angkor Wat, Cambodia, c. 1113 – 1150

Key Terms

Āmalaka	*garbha griha*
bhūmi	*mandapa*
kondō	pagoda

Videos

French Gothic Architecture: Cathedrals
25 min, 1995, VM

Gothic Cathedrals
50 min, 1996, VM

CD-ROMs

Great Works of Art Explained Part 1
Mac/Windows, Clearvue

Multiple-Choice Questions

1. The Gothic style originated

        a. on the Ile Saint Louis
        b. on the Ile-de-France*
        c. at Chartres
        d. at Amiens

2. Abbot Suger is credited with creating the first truly Gothic building near Paris. It was

        a. Chartres Cathedral
        b. St.-Denis*
        c. St.-Chapelle
        d. St.-Pierre, Moissac

3. Saint-Denis was dedicated in

        a. 1140*
        b. 1200
        c. 1100
        d. 1210
        e. 1194

4. Which is <u>not</u> an element of Gothic architecture?

        a. rib vaults
        b. flying buttresses
        c. round arches*
        d. stained glass windows

5. In a Gothic cathedral, a bay consists of

    a. an arch and a triforium
    b. the space between two piers*
    c. clerestory windows and a section of the nave arcade
    d. the space in the crossing

6. Which is <u>not</u> used in making stained glass windows?

    a. an iron armature
    b. clear glass
    c. pigments
    d. metallic oxides
    e. tesserae*

7. A cathedral is

    a. the seat of a bishop*
    b. a large church
    c. a Gothic church
    d. the center of an ecclesiastical hierarchy

8. Most great French Gothic cathedrals were dedicated to

    a. Christ
    b. God
    c. the Virgin*
    d. St. Joseph
    e. St. Peter

9. A signature window is

    a. one that has been signed by the artist
    b. one that has been signed by the patron
    c. one that has an image of the artist and patron
    d. one that has an image of the work done by a guild*

10. In the Middle Ages, the function of the guilds was

    a. to protect workers and establish standards of work*
    b. to permit strikes if workers were dissatisfied
    c. to exclude craftsmen from professional organizations
    d. to influence patrons

11. Which is not a pair?

    a. Villard De Honnecourt -- sketchbooks
    b. Augustine -- the City of God
    c. Panofsky -- Gothic Architecture and Scholasticism
    d. Suger -- The Life of Saint-Denis*

12. A winch is a

    a. seductive female
    b. small crane*
    c. pulley system
    d. template

13. Which of the following is true?

    a. Over 80 cathedrals and large abbeys were built around Paris in the 13th century.*
    b. More Gothic cathedrals were built in England than in France.
    c. Gothic builders used power tools to construct more complex buildings than Romanesque builders had.
    d. Master builders were not very well paid.

14. Which of the following in true?

    a. Stones for Gothic cathedrals were cut with power tools.
    b. Master builders used geometric principles to organize their templates.*
    c. Gothic tools were technologically advanced.
    d. Only one master builder supervised each cathedral.

15. Which is not a pair?

    a. rose window -- circle
    b. towers -- vertical
    c. gable -- rectangle*
    d. apse -- semicircle

16. Compared to the Romanesque tower of Chartres, the Gothic tower is

    a. more elaborate*
    b. shorter
    c. less detailed
    d. less vertical

17. A gargoyle is a

    a. monster
    b. finial
    c. capital sculpture
    d. waterspout*

18. The text on which the sculptures above the center west portal at Chartres are based is from

    a. the City of God
    b. the Gospel of John
    c. Revelation*
    d. the Gospel of Matthew

19. The Central West Portal of Chartres was

    a. Late Romanesque
    b. Early Gothic*
    c. High Gothic
    d. Late Gothic

20. In the tympanum of the center west door at Chartres

    a. The eagle is John, the bull is Luke, the lion is Mark.*
    b. The eagle is Matthew, the bull is Luke, the lion is John.
    c. The eagle is Luke, the bull is Matthew, the lion is Mark.
    d. The lion is John, the bull is Luke, the angel is Matthew.

21. The door jamb statues on the center west door of Chartres

    a. are frontal, naturalistic, and represent French royalty
    b. are frontal, stylized, and represent Old Testament royalty*
    c. are frontal, have contrapposto, and are prophets
    d. represent prophets, are frontal, and stylized

22. Compared to the west door jambs of Chartres, those on the south

    a. are more two-dimensional
    b. are more three-dimensional*
    c. are frontal
    d. are elderly
    e. are more static

23. At Chartres, the trumeau represents

   a. St. Stephen
   b. an Old Testament prophet
   c. an apostle
   d. Christ*
   e. the Virgin

24. The Antichrist was

   a. a legendary monster
   b. an incarnation of Satan
   c. an incarnation of evil*
   d. Frederick II

25. Compared to the west facade of Reims, the west facade at Amiens

   a. is symmetrical
   b. has glass tympanums
   c. is proportionally taller and thinner
   d. has a smaller rose window*

26. The west portal of _____ has an important sculptural program.

   a. Salisbury Cathedral
   b. Florence Cathedral
   c. Reims Cathedral*
   d. Cologne Cathedral

27. The Beau Dieu refers to

   a. a book by Augustine
   b. a statue at Amiens*
   c. a statue at Reims
   d. a book by Hildegarde of Bingen

28. The Visitation is when

   a. Gabriel visits Mary
   b. Christ visits Joseph
   c. Mary visits Elizabeth*
   d. the angel visits Constantine

29. The church that contains segments built in the Early Gothic as well as the High Gothic is
_____.

    a. Beauvais Cathedral
    b. Amiens Cathedral
    c. Notre-Dame, Paris*
    d. St.-Maclou, Rouen

30. Sainte-Chapelle in Paris was commissioned by

    a. Louis IX*
    b. Suger
    c. Louis VI
    d. Louis VII

31. English Gothic begins

    a. with the facade of Salisbury Cathedral
    b. with the fan vaults of Kings College, Cambridge
    c. with the choir of Canterbury Cathedral*
    d. with the Norman tower of Canterbury

32. The Corona Chapel was built

    a. as a reliquary*
    b. as a shrine of Henry II
    c. by Thomas á Becket
    d. by William of Sens

33. The Canterbury Tales were written by

    a. William the Englishman
    b. the monk Gervase
    c. Augustine
    d. Thomas á Becket
    e. Geoffrey Chaucer*

34. The Bell Harry Tower was added to Canterbury cathedral in

    a. the 15th century
    b. the 16th century*
    c. the 14th century
    d. the 13th century

35. In contrast to French Gothic cathedrals, Salisbury has

    a. a triple transept
    b. a square apse*
    c. clerestory windows
    d. a vaulted nave

36. Which is <u>not</u> true of English cathedrals?

    a. They are set in a cathedral close.
    b. They have more varied stone than French cathedrals.
    c. They have fan vaults.
    d. They usually rise directly from the high point of a city.*

CHAPTER 12:
Precursors of the Renaissance

Key Works

Nicola Pisano, pulpit, Pisa Baptistry, 1259 – 1260

Nicola Pisano, relief of the *Nativity*, also showing the *Annunciation*, the *Annunciation to the Shepherds*, and the *Washing of the Infant Christ*, pulpit, Pisa Baptistry, 1259 – 1260

Cimabue, *Madonna Enthroned*, c. 1280 – 1290

Giotto, *Madonna Enthroned* (Ognissanti Madonna), c. 1310

Interior view, looking east, Arena Chapel, Padua, c. 1305

Giotto, *Annunciation*, Arena Chapel, Padua, c. 1305

Giotto, *Nativity*, Arena Chapel, Padua, c. 1305

Giotto, *Crucifixion*, Arena Chapel, Padua, c. 1305

Giotto, *Last Judgment*, Arena Chapel, Padua, c. 1305

Giotto, *Last Judgment*, detail, Arena Chapel, Padua, c. 1305

Giotto, *Justice*, Arena Chapel, Padua, c. 1305

Giotto, *Stigmatization of Saint Francis*, exterior of the Bardi Chapel, Santa Croce, Florence, after 1317

John White, photo montage of Duccio's *Maestà* (front), 1308 – 1311

Duccio, *Maestà*, from Siena Cathedral, 1308 – 1311

John White, photo montage of Duccio's *Maestà* (back), 1308 – 1311

Kiss of Judas, Sant'Apollinare Nuovo, Ravenna, early 6th century

Duccio, *Kiss of Judas*, from the *Maestà*, Siena Cathedral, 1308 – 1311

Giotto, *Kiss of Judas*, Arena Chapel, Padua, c. 1305

Ambrogio Lorenzetti, *Effects of Good Government in the City and the Country*, from the *Allegory of Good Government*, Sala della Pace, Palazzo Pubblico, Siena, 1338 – 1339

Ambrogio Lorenzetti, detail showing attacking a woman, from the *Allegory of Bad Government*, Palazzo Pubblico, Siena, 1338 – 1339

Andrea Orcagna, detail showing figures invoking Death, from the *Triumph of Death*, c. 1360

Andrea Orcagna, detail showing two men watching an eclipse of the sun, from the *Triumph of Death*, c. 1360

Simone Martini, Saint Louis altarpiece, c. 1317

Claus Sluter, Portal, Chartreuse de Champmol, Dijon, 1385 – 1393

Claus Sluter, *Virgin Mary and Christ*, central trumeau of portal, Chartreuse de Champmol, Dijon, 1385 – 1393

Claus Sluter, Well of Moses, Chartreuse de Champmol, Dijon, begun 1395

Limbourg Brothers, *Annunciation*, from the *Très Riches Heures du Duc de Berry*, 1413 – 1416

Limbourg Brothers, *January*, from the *Très Riches Heures du Duc de Berry*, 1413 – 1416

Maps, Diagrams, and Projections

Map of leading art centers during the Renaissance in western Europe

Key Terms

Apocrypha
arriccio
gesso
predella
stigmata

Videos

Birth of the Renaissance: Giotto to Masaccio
58 min, 1991, Facets

Giotto and the Pre-Renaissance
47 min, VM, Crystal

Masters of Illusion: The Birth of Special Effects
30 min, 1992, Clearvue

Trecento: Italian Art and Architecture in the Fourteenth Century
26 min, 1992, VM

CD-ROMs

Great Paintings: Renaissance to Impressionism
Mac/Windows, Clearvue

Multiple-Choice Questions

1. Which of the following was <u>not</u> a 14th-century humanist?

      a. Boccaccio
      b. Petrarch
      c. Giotto
      d. Dante*

2. Which of the following was <u>not</u> part of the Classical revival?

    a. anecdotes about artists
    b. comparisons with antiquity
    c. three-dimensional form
    d. translating Latin texts
    e. a rejection of Italian history*

3. Which is <u>not</u> a feature of the Divine Comedy?

    a. it was written in Latin*
    b. Virgil is Dante's guide through the Inferno
    c. it is divided into three parts
    d. it is a source for Italian history

4. The painter Cimabue was deeply influenced by _____.

    a. The court of Charlemagne
    b. Byzantine icons*
    c. Giotto
    d. Claus Sluter

5. The monastic order that put an emphasis on nature and the individual was

    a. Cistercian
    b. Benedictine
    c. Dominican
    d. Franciscan*

6. The Arena Chapel in Padua

    a. is part of a larger church
    b. is Gothic in style
    c. illustrates Dante's Divine Comedy
    d. represents three sets of lives*

7. In the Arena Chapel, the Virtues and Vices

    a. are in the top row of scenes
    b. are in between the narrative scenes
    c. are between panels of imitation marble*
    d. are on the ceiling

8. In the scene of the Annunciation

      a. Gabriel tells Mary she will be the mother of Christ*
      b. God tells Mary she will be the mother of Christ
      c. Mary tells Joseph she will be the mother of Christ
      d. Mary has a dream telling her she will be the mother of Christ

9. Giotto's Nativity differs from that of Nicola Pisano in that

      a. it combines two scenes in one space
      b. it is more sculpturesque
      c. it is later
      d. it is more dramatic*

10. Which is not true of Giotto's Crucifixion?

      a. it refers to typology
      b. it takes place in Jerusalem*
      c. it depicts the effects of gravity
      d. Christ's form is elongated
      e. it emphasizes the distinction between the Romans and Christ's followers

11. The length of Mary Magdalen's hair is an example of

      a. a Renaissance coiffure
      b. her seductive nature
      c. an iconographic convention*
      d. a typological symbol

12. The Roman soldiers in the foreground of Giotto's Crucifixion

      a. are torturing Christ
      b. are arguing over possession of his cloak*
      c. are repenting their sins
      d. are leaving the scene

13. Which is not true of Giotto's Last Judgment?

      a. Christ is seated in a mandorla
      b. Enrico Scrovegni's portrait is included
      c. Christ faces the Saved
      d. only the figures in Hell are nude*
      e. the angels above Christ are in military dress

14. Giotto's Virtue of Justice

    a. reflects emerging ideas about good and bad government*
    b. is represented as blind
    c. is seated in a Renaissance building
    d. has no relationship to Classical antiquity

15. Giotto was important because he

    a. went back to nature as his guide as had the Greeks and Romans
    b. used direct experience to judge truth
    c. believed that what we see is the basis of art
    d. a, b, and c*

16. Which of the following had the least influence on Giotto?

    a. International style*
    b. Cimabue
    c. Gothic French sculpture
    d. art of ancient Rome

17. Which is not true of St. Francis of Assisi?

    a. he wrote *The Canticle of Brother Sun*
    b. he came from a wealthy family
    c. he received the *stigmata* as punishment for his sins*
    d. he established the Friars Minor

18. In contrast to Duccio's *Maestà*, Lorenzetti's *Effects of Good Government* is

    a. secular*
    b. more Byzantine in style
    c. more Christian in its iconography
    d. was commissioned by the Nine
    e. a reflection of the influence of International Gothic

19. Ambrogio Lorenzetti's *Good Government* was commissioned for the Palazzo Pubblico of
_____.

    a. Siena*
    b. Urbino
    c. Florence
    d. Rome

20. "The mortal pestilence" described by Boccaccio refers to

    a. the sinfulness of Florence
    b. the failure of the Bardi and Peruzzi banks
    c. the Triumph of Death
    d. the Black Death*

21. Which is <u>not</u> an example of royal patronage?

    a. Simone Martini's Saint Louis Altarpiece
    b. the Very Rich Hours of the Duke of Berry
    c. the Well of Moses
    d. the *Maestà* *

22. Burgundy

    a. was a tributary of the French crown
    b. was ruled by relatives of French kings
    c. independent of the French throne
    d. all of the above*

23. Who is the sculptor of the *Well of Moses*?

    a. Giotto
    b. Claus Sluter*
    c. Tilman Riemenschneider
    d. Cimabue

24. Claus Sluter's work was like

    a.   Simone for its lightness
    b.   Giotto's for its massiveness*
    c.   Cimbue's for its Byzantine finish
    d.   Michelangelo's for its Greek classicism

25. Philip the Bold's court was located in

    a. Siena
    b. Berry
    c. Dijon*
    d. Flanders

26. Philip the Bold of Burgundy built the

    a. Chartreuse de Champmol*
    b. Hospital des Invalides

c. Palazzo Pubblico of Siena

d. Town Hall of Ghent

27. Books of Hours were made for

a. the clergy

b. the peasants

c. the artists

d. the aristocracy*

28. The patron of *Les Trés Riches Heures* was

a. John, duke of Berry*

b. Giovanni Arnolfini

c. Tommaso Portinari

d. Philip the Bold

29. Which of these does not match?

a. Limbourg Brothers -- Very Rich Hours

b. Dante -- Life of Saint Francis*

c. Orcagna -- Triumph of Death

d. Boccaccio -- The Decameron

CHAPTER 13:
The Early Renaissance

Key Works

Bernardo Rossellino, Tomb of Leonardo Bruni, Santa Croce, Florence, 1444

Filippo Brunelleschi, *Sacrifice of Isaac*, competition panel for the east doors of the Florence Baptistry, 1401 – 1402

Lorenzo Ghiberti, *Sacrifice of Isaac*, competition panel for the east doors of the Florence Baptistry, 1401 – 1402

Exterior of Florence Cathedral

Filippo Brunelleschi, Hospital of the Innocents, Piazza de Santissima Annunziata, Florence, begun 1419

Filippo Brunelleschi, plan of Santo Spirito, Florence (after R. Sturgis)

Filippo Brunelleschi, interior of Santo Spirito, Florence, planned 1434

Piero della Francesca, *Flagellation*, c. 1460

Reconstructed plan and elevation of the foreground and praetorium in Piero della Francesca's *The Flagellation*; drawing by Thomas Czarnowski

Reconstructed plan and elevation of Piero della Francesca's *The Flagellation*; drawing by Thomas Czarnowski

Leonardo da Vinci, perspective study for the *Adoration of the Magi*, c. 1481

Paolo Uccello, perspective drawing of a chalice, c. 1430 – 1440

Andrea Mantegna, *Dead Christ*, c. 1500

Lorenzo Ghiberti, *The Meeting of Solomon and Sheba*, detail of the east door of the Baptistry (showing perspective lines), 1450 – 1452

Lorenzo Ghiberti, *Self-Portrait*, from the east door of the Florence Baptistry, 1424 – 1452

Lorenzo Ghiberti, *The Gates of Paradise*, east door, Florence Baptistry, 1424 – 1452

Pisanello, medal of John VIII Paleologus (obverse and reverse), 1438 – 1439

Masaccio, *The Holy Trinity*, Santa Maria Novella, Florence, c. 1425

Masaccio, *The Holy Trinity*, c. 1425, showing perspective lines

View of the Brancacci Chapel (after restoration), looking toward the altar, Santa Maria del Carmine, Florence, 15th century

Left side of the Brancacci Chapel, Santa Maria del Carmine, Florence (after restoration, 1989)

Masaccio, *The Expulsion of Adam and Eve*, detail of the Brancacci Chapel, left pilaster

The Medici Venus, 1st century A.D.

Masaccio, *Saint Peter*, detail of *The Tribute Money* from the left side of the Brancacci Chapel

Gentile da Fabriano, *Adoration of the Magi*, altarpiece, 1423

Donatello, *Saint Mark*, shown in its original Gothic niche on the outside wall of Or San Michele, Florence, with a teaching Christ above and the Evangelist's lion symbol below, 1411 – 1415

Donatello, *David*, c. 1430 – 1440

Donatello, detail of *David* showing *putti* relief on Goliath's helmet, c. 1430 – 1440

Leon Battista Alberti, Rucellai Palace, Florence, c. 1446 – 1450

Leon Battista Alberti, exterior of the Tempio Malatestiano, Rimini, designed 1450

Matteo de' Pasti, foundation medal of the Tempio Malatestiano, Rimini, 1450

Leon Battista Alberti, Sant'Andrea, Mantua, 1470 – 1493

Nave of Sant'Andrea, Mantua, 1470 – 1493

Andrea del Castagno, *The Youthful David*, c. 1450

Andrea del Verrocchio, *David*, early 1470s

Andrea del Castagno, *Famous Men and Women*, Villa Carducci at Legnaia, 1450

Andrea del Castagno, *Dante*, detail of *Famous Men and Women*, Villa Carducci at Legnaia, 1450

Paolo Uccello, *Sir John Hawkwood*, Florence Cathedral, 1436

Andrea del Castagno, *Niccolò da Tolentino*, Florence Cathedral, 1455 – 1456

Donatello, *Gattamelata*, 1445 – 1450

Donatello, detail of *Gattamelata*, 1445 – 1450

Piero della Francesca, *Battista Sforza, Duchess of Urbino* and *Federico da Montefeltro, Duke of Urbino* (after cleaning), after 1475

Piero della Francesca, *Annunciation* (after cleaning), c. 1450

Fra Angelico, *Annunciation*, c. 1440

Filippo Lippi, *Madonna and Child with Scenes from the Life of Saint Anne (Pitti Tondo)*, 1450

Filippo Lippi, *Head of a Woman*, study for *Madonna and Child*, c. 1449 – 1450

Piero della Francesca, left wall of the Bacci Chapel, San Francesco, Arezzo, 1450s

Piero della Francesca, right wall of the Bacci Chapel, San Francesco, Arezzo, 1450s

Piero della Francesca, *Dream of Constantine* (after cleaning), Bacci Chapel, San Francesco, Arezzo, 1450s

Andrea Mantegna, Camera Picta (also known as the Camera degli Sposi), Ducal Palace, Mantua, finished 1474

Andrea Mantegna, Camera Picta (detail showing the view over the fireplace, including the Duke and Duchess of Mantua, their family, dwarf, nursemaid, and courtiers)

Andrea Mantegna, ceiling oculus of the Camera Picta, Ducal Palace, Mantua, finished 1474

Andrea Mantegna, *Parnassus*, c. 1497

Sandro Botticelli, *Mars and Venus*, c. 1475

Sandro Botticelli, *Birth of Venus*, c. 1480

Donatello, *Mary Magdalen*, c. 1455

Sandro Botticelli, *Mystical Nativity*, 1500 or 1501

Robert Campin (Master of Flémalle), Mérode Altarpiece (open), c. 1425 – 1430

Detail of the central panel of the Mérode Altarpiece

Jan van Eyck, Ghent Altarpiece (open), completed 1432

Jan van Eyck, Ghent Altarpiece, detail showing the Cathedral of Saint Bavon

Jan van Eyck, Ghent Altarpiece, detail of God's crown

Jan van Eyck, Ghent Altarpiece (closed)

Jan van Eyck, *Man in a Red Turban (Self-Portrait ?)*, 1433

Jan van Eyck, *Arnolfini Portrait*, 1434

Jan van Eyck, *Arnolfini Portrait*, detail of the convex mirror

Rogier van der Weyden, *Descent from the Cross*, c. 1435 – 1438

Rogier van der Weyden, *Saint Luke Depicting the Virgin*, c. 1435 – 1440

Hans Memling, *Tomasso Portinari*, c. 1470

Hans Memling, *Maria Baroncelli Portinari*, c. 1470

Hugo van der Goes, Portinari Altarpiece (open), c. 1470s

Domenico del Ghirlandaio, *Adoration of the Shepherds*, 1485

Maps, Diagrams, and Projections

Map of leading art centers in Renaissance Italy

Plan of Florence Cathedral (after W. Blaser)

Axonometric section of the dome of Florence Cathedral

Filippo Brunelleschi, plan of Santo Spirito, Florence (after R. Sturgis)

Reconstructed plan and elevation of the foreground and praetorium in Piero della Francesca's *Flagellation*; drawing by Thomas Czarnowski

Reconstructed plan and elevation of Piero della Francesca's *Flagellation*; drawing by Thomas Czarnowski

Leonardo da Vinci, perspective study for the *Adoration of the Magi*, c. 1481

Paolo Uccello, perspective drawing of a chalice, c. 1430 – 1440

Masaccio, *The Holy Trinity*, c. 1425, showing perspective lines

Plan of Sant'Andrea, Mantua

Map of northern and central Europe in the Renaissance

Key Terms

aerial (or atmospheric) perspective

aisle

ambulatory

arcade

architrave

basilica

bay

bistre

bust

caryatid

centering

chiaroscuro

choir

coffer, coffering

colonnade

column

contrapposto

convention

corbelling

Corinthian

cornice

Deësis

dome

drum

engaged (half-) column

entasis

Eucharist

façade

flutes, fluting

foreground

frieze

gilding

Gospel

grisaille

guild

isocephaly, isocephalic

lantern

Latin cross

linear (or scientific) perspective

loggia

lunette

Magus, Magi

manuscript

memento mori

module

monastery

nave

niche

Nike

obverse

oculus

oil paint

orthogonals

patron
pedestal
pediment
pilaster
polyptych
proportion
putto, putti
quatrefoil
reverse
rib
sarcophagus

sibyl
stained glass
symmetry
tempera
tondo
transept
trefoil
triptych
type
vanishing point

Videos

Art of Asia: India, Southeast Asia, China, Korea and Japan
66 min, Clearvue

Art of the Western World
Volume 2: The Early Renaissance
55 min, VM

Beaune, Rogier van der Weyden
14 min, 1987, TRC

Botticelli's *Calumny of Apelles*
12 min, 1987, TRC

Botticelli's *Venus* in the Uffizi
30 min, 1991, Applause Productions

Civilisation, Volume 2
Romance and Reality & Man-The Measure of All Things
94 min, 1970, VM

Donatello: The First Modern Sculptor
1991, 60 min, MFA, HVC, Facets

Early Italian Renaissance: Brunelleschi - Donatello - Masaccio
27 min, 1994, VM

Exploring the Renaissance (1350 – 1650)
20 min, 1994, UL

15th Century: Renaissance in Full Bloom
59 min, 1991, Facets

The Flagellation of Christ by Piero della Francesca
30 min, 1993, Britannica

Florence: Cradle of the Renaissance
30 min, 1992, PBS

Great Masters Series: Botticelli
52 min, 1993, NDM

History Through Art: The Renaissance
33 min, Clearvue

Masaccio: A View of Mankind
40 min, 1983, MFA

Portrait of An Artist: Donatello
60 min, 1991, Clearvue

CD-ROMs

History Through Art: The Renaissance
Mac/Windows, Clearvue

The Renaissance
Mac/Windows, Clearvue

Multiple-Choice Questions

1. Which best describes Renaissance humanism?

      a. study of human nature
      b. human-based culture
      c. revival of Classical texts*
      d. a Christian bias

2. Leonardo Bruni was

      a. a humanist
      b. chancellor of Florence
      c. a historian
      d. none of the above
      e. all of the above*

3. Which two cities were most at the forefront of early humanism?

    a. Venice and Rome
    b. Florence and Padua*
    c. Rome and Florence
    d. Siena and Florence
    e. Siena and Padua

4. In the 15th century the _____ of Florence were the great patrons.

    a. Urbini
    b. Innocenti
    c. Popes
    d. Medici*

5. Which is not a feature of Bruni's tomb?

    a. its sculptor was Marzocco*
    b. lions are a part of its iconography
    c. it merges Christian and Classical motifs
    d. the effigy of Bruni lies on a bier

6. Who of the following was not a *condottiere*?

    a. Federico da Montefeltro
    b. Sir John Hawkwood
    c. Erasmo da Narni
    d. Niccolo da Tolentino
    e. Leon Battista Alberti*

7. Which text goes with which author?

    a. Dante -- the *Decameron*
    b. Brunelleschi -- the *Commentarii*
    c. Alberti -- *Oration on the Dignity of Man*
    d. Masaccio -- *On Painting*
    e. Bruni -- *Praise of the City of Florence*

8. Which are some of the reasons for Ghiberti's victory in the competition of 1401?

    a. his relief was less expensive to cast and more monumental than Brunelleschi's
    b. his relief was less expensive and more graceful*
    c. his relief was more expensive, but also more elegant
    d. his relief was more monumental, more original, and he had political connections

9. Ghiberti's style is

    a. aligned by orthogonals of true perspective
    b. realistic
    c. classically inspired
    d. all of the above*

10. Which best defines "foreshortening?"

    a. reduction in scale
    b. placing a smaller object in front of a larger object
    c. a twist at the waist
    d. depicting a form in perspective*

11. Which is <u>not</u> a feature of the Hospital of the Innocents?

    a. arcades
    b. round arches
    c. Doric colonnettes*
    d. pediments
    e. bays

12. _____ was able to combine Neo-Platonic ideals and mainline religiosity.

    a. Fra Filippo Lippi
    b. Mantegna
    c. Leonardo
    d. Fra Angelico*

13. The Pazzi Chapel is the gem of the Early Renaissance because it sums up its principles. It is by

    a. Brunelleschi*
    b. Alberti
    c. Michelozzo
    d. Bramante

14. Brunelleschi did many things, but he did not

    a. design the dome of Florence Cathedral.
    b. take measured drawings of the Roman Forum and develop a theory of perspective
    c. work in Florence.
    d. use the Colosseum as his model for the Ospedale degle Innocenti*

15. Which is least a feature of Brunelleschi's design for the Church of Santo Spirito?

   a. Latin cross plan
   b. a flat ceiling
   c. chapels on three sides
   d. stained-glass windows*
   e. round arches

16. The re-discovery of linear perspective was made by

   a. Ghiberti
   b. Brunelleschi*
   c. Uccello
   d. Leonardo

17. Which of the following is true of one-point perspective?

   a. orthogonals converge at the vanishing point*
   b. orthogonals run from right to left on the picture plane
   c. orthogonals are at right angles to the floor of the painted space
   d. orthogonals are not used

18. The artist whom Vasari accused of being too obsessed with perspective was

   a. Piero della Francesca
   b. Mantegno
   c. Uccello*
   d. Masaccio
   e. Brunelleschi

19. The term *paradiso* as used in reference to Ghiberti's doors means

   a. the Garden of Eden
   b. the illustration of Dante
   c. the space between a cathedral and its baptistry*
   d. the dome of the cathedral
   e. the dome of the baptistry

20. The medal of John VIII Paleologus was cast by

   a. Alberti
   b. Matteo de' Pasti
   c. the Byzantine emperor
   d. Pisanello*

21. Which is not a new, Renaissance feature of Masaccio's Trinity?

    a. a barrel-vault with coffers
    b. Classical Orders
    c. donors
    d. a *memento mori**
    e. one-point perspective

22. Masaccio

    a. maintained strict monochrome paintings and avoided contrast in light and dark
    b. used complex, dramatic settings
    c. embellished his scenes with sumptuous drapery
    d. clearly defined his light sources so that shadows were logical and realistic*

23. Masaccio created the barrel vault in the *Trinity* by using _____ perspective.

    a. atmospheric
    b. linear*
    c. intuitive
    d. herringbone

24. The nearest sense of chiaroscuro would be

    a. gradual shading*
    b. high contrast of light and dark
    c. shadow
    d. silhouetting

25. Atmospheric perspective depicts near and far according to

    a. diminution in size
    b. increase in size
    c. degrees of clarity*
    d. haziness in the sky

26. Which of the following match?

    a. Masaccio -- *Famous Men and Women*
    b. Brunelleschi -- one-point perspective*
    c. Castagno -- *Holy Trinity*
    d. Alberti -- medal of John VIII Paleologus
    e. Mantegna -- Rucellai Palace

27. Which do not match?

    a. Rimini -- Tempio Malatestiano
    b. Brancacci Chapel -- Florence
    c. Sant'Andrea -- Mantua
    d. Gattamelata -- Ravenna*
    e. Sir John Hawkwood -- Florence Cathedral

28. Which is not a 15th-century development?

    a. illusionism
    b. mythological subject matter
    c. one-point perspective
    d. an increase in literacy
    e. stained-glass windows*

29. The *Camera degli Sposi* refers to

    a. a state bedroom*
    b. a marriage ceremony
    c. a room for a wedding
    d. Mantegna's studio

30. The frescoes of the *Camera degli Sposi* were painted by

    a. Fra Filippo Lippi
    b. Andrea Mantegna*
    c. Leonardo
    d. Sandro Botticelli

31. The frescoes of the *Camera degli Sposi* were painted for

    a. theDuke of Manua*
    b. the Duke of Urbino
    c. the Medici
    d. the Pope

32. In Mantegna's *Parnassus*, which god does not appear?

    a. Apollo
    b. Vulcan
    c. Mars
    d. Juno*
    e. Venus

33. Who of the following did <u>not</u> have a *studiolo*?

    a. Federigo Gonzaga*
    b. Isabella d'Este
    c. Federico da Montefeltro
    d. Leonello d'Este

34. The artist who painted portraits of real people was

    a. Jan van Eyck*
    b. Hieronymous Bosch
    c. Rogier van der Weyden
    d. Cimabue

35. Burgundy

    a. Was a tributary of the French crown
    b. Was ruled by relatives of French kings
    c. Independent of the French throne
    d. All of the above*

36. Dirk Bouts

    a. was an artist in the employ of the Church
    b. sculpted in the style of Claus Sluter
    c. understood perspective intuitively*
    d. rivaled Giotto in 15th-century Italy

37. _____ was not included in Jan van Eyck's Ghent Altarpiece?

    a. Adoration of the Mystic Lamb
    b. God the Father*
    c. Christ crucified
    d. Adam and Eve

38. The Guild of _____ had St. Luke as its patron saint.

    a. painters*
    b. book binders
    c. weavers
    d. stonemasons

39. Hugo van der Goes's Portinari Altarpiece has

    a. rich colors and a somber mood*
    b. a confined sense of space
    c. a flat, gold background worked with a pattern punch
    d. dim colors and a somber mood

40. The Ghent Altarpiece is a _____.

    a. diptych
    b. panel
    c. polyptych*
    d. triptych

41. The subject of *Man in the Red Turban* is believed to be:

    a. Cosimo de Medici
    b. Jan van Eyck*
    c. Philip the Bold
    d. Rogier van der Weyden

42. The most outstanding examples of the new Flemish style of painting included all of the following except:

    a. Giovanni Bellini*
    b. Jan Van Eyck
    c. Hans Memmling
    d. Rogier van der Weyden

43. Match the artist with the work

    a. Robert Campin -- *The Ghent Altarpiece*
    b. Botticelli -- *The Mérode Altarpiece*
    c. Rogier van der Weyden -- *St. Luke Painting the Virgin**
    d. Ghirlandaio -- *The Portinari Altarpiece*

44. Which figure or figures do <u>not</u> appear in the *Ghent Altarpiece*?

    a. crusaders
    b. angels
    c. Joseph*
    d. John the Baptist
    e. Mary

45. *Grisaille* means

    a. imitation sculpture*
    b. gesso
    c. foreshortening
    d. contrapposto
    e. imitation architecture

46. Which does <u>not</u> appear in the *Arnolfini Wedding*?

    a. a dog
    b. a mirror
    c. sandals
    d. fruit
    e. a vase of lilies*

47. Botticelli was influenced by

    a. Marsilio Ficino
    b. Neo-Platonism
    c. The Medici Circle
    d. all of the above*

48. Which does <u>not</u> appear in Botticelli's *Birth of Venus*?

    a. a scallop shell
    b. the mother of Venus*
    c. waves
    d. a nymph
    e. flowers

CHAPTER 14:
The High Renaissance in Italy

Key Works

Leonardo da Vinci, *Vitruvian Man*, c. 1485 – 1490

Leonardo da Vinci, church resembling the Holy Sepulcher in Milan

Donato Bramante, Tempietto, c. 1502 – 1503

Donato Bramante, Plan of the Tempietto with projected courtyard, after 16th-century engraving by Sebastiano Serlio

Anonymous, *An Ideal City*, mid-15th century

Raphael, *Betrothal of the Virgin*, 1504

Donato Bramante, plan for the New Saint Peter's, Vatican, Rome, c. 1505

Christoforo Caradosso Foppa, medal showing Bramante's design for the New Saint Peter's, Vatican, Rome, 1506

Michelangelo, plan for the New Saint Peter's, Vatican, Rome, c. 1546

Plan for the New Saint Peter's as built to Michelangelo's design with additions by Carlo Maderno, 1606 – 1615

New Saint Peter's, Vatican, Rome

Leonardo da Vinci, *Embryo in the Womb*, c. 1510

Andrea Verrocchio, *The Baptism of Christ*, c. 1470

Leonardo da Vinci, *The Last Supper*, refectory of Santa Maria delle Grazie, Milan, c. 1495 – 1498

Leonardo da Vinci, *Madonna and Child with Saint Anne*, 1503 – 1506

Leonardo da Vinci, *Mona Lisa*, c. 1503 – 1505

Michelangelo, copy of Masaccio's Saint Peter in the *Tribute Money*, 1489 – 1490

Michelangelo, *Pietà*, 1498/99 – 1500

Michelangelo, *David*, 1501 – 1504

Michelangelo, *Moses*, c. 1513 – 1515

Michelangelo, *Sistine Chapel*, Vatican, Rome, 1508 – 1512

Michelangelo, ceiling of the Sistine Chapel, Vatican, Rome (after cleaning), 1508 – 1512

Michelangelo, *Creation of Adam* (before cleaning), c. 1510, detail of the ceiling of the Sistine Chapel

Michelangelo, *Creation of Adam* (after cleaning), c. 1510, detail of the ceiling of the Sistine Chapel

Michelangelo, *The Fall of Man*, 1510, detail of the ceiling of the Sistine Chapel

Michelangelo, *Jeremiah*, detail of the ceiling of the Sistine Chapel

Michelangelo, *Last Judgment* (after cleaning), altar wall of the Sistine Chapel, 1534 – 1541

Michelangelo, Saint Bartholomew with flayed skin, detail of *The Last Judgment*, 1534 – 1541

Michelangelo, *Rondanini Pietà*, c. 1555 – 1564

Raphael, *Madonna of the Meadow*, 1505

Raphael, *Portrait of Pope Julius II*, 1511 – 1512

Raphael, *Galatea*, Villa Farnesina, Rome, c. 1512

Galatea in situ, Grand Salon, Villa Farnesina, Rome

Raphael, *Disputation over the Sacrament*, Stanza della Segnatura, Vatican, Rome, 1509 – 1511

Raphael, *School of Athens*, Stanza della Segnatura, Vatican, Rome, 1509 – 1511
Raphael, Plato and Aristotle, detail of *School of Athens*
Leonardo da Vinci, *Self-Portrait, after 1500*
Raphael's self-portrait, detail of *School of Athens*
Jacopo Bellini, *Christ Before Pilate*, Louvre sketchbook, 1503
Gentile Bellini, *Sultan Mehmet II*, c. 1480
Gentile Bellini, *Procession of the Reliquary of the Cross in Piazza San Marco*, 1496
Gentile Bellini, detail of *Procession of the Reliquary of the Cross in Piazza San Marco*
Giovanni Bellini, San Giobbe Altarpiece, 1480s
Giovanni Bellini, *Doge Leonardo Loredan*, soon after 1501
Giovanni Bellini, *Saint Francis in Ecstasy*, c. 1485
Giorgione, *Tempest*, c. 1505 – 1510
Giorgione, *Old Woman (Col Tempo)*, early 16th century
Giorgione, *Sleeping Venus*, c. 1509
Giorgione, *Fête Champêtre*, c. 1510
Titian, *Assumption of the Virgin*, 1516 – 1518
Titian, *Pesaro Madonna*, 1519 – 1526
Titian, *Venus of Urbino*, c. 1538
Titian, *Rape of Europa*, 1559 – 1562

Maps, Diagrams, and Projections

Map of leading art centers in Renaissance Italy
Leonardo da Vinci, *Vitruvian Man*, c. 1485 – 1490
Leonardo da Vinci, church resembling the Holy Sepulcher in Milan
Donato Bramante, plan of the Tempietto with a projected courtyard, after a 16th-century
    engraving by Sebastiano Serlio
Anonymous, *An Ideal City*, mid-15th century
Donato Brmante, plan for the New Saint Peter's, Vatican, Rome, c. 1505
Michelangelo, plan for the New Saint Peter's, Vatican, Rome, c. 1546
Plan for the New Saint Peter's as built to Michelangelo's design with additions by Carlo
    Maderno, 1606 – 1615
Diagram of scenes from the ceiling of the Sistine Chapel

Key Terms

balustrade	*ignudi*
buttress	jeremiad
cella	*martyrium*
chiaroscuro	painterly
cromlech	pastel
Doric	peristyle
entablature	*poesia*
glaze	pyramidal composition

red-figure
rose window
reliquary
sculptured wall motif

sfumato
spandrel
tholos

Videos

Art & Splendor: Michelangelo and the Sistine Chapel
35 min, VM

Art of the Western World
Volume 2: "The High Renaissance"
55 min, VM

Civilisation, Volume 3
The Hero as Artist & Protest and Communication
94 min, 1970, VM

Bellini: The Feast of the Gods
27 min, 1990, HVC, Crystal Productions

Giorgione: Poet of Vision
199?, 24 min, VM, RMI

Great Masters Series: Leonardo da Vinci
52 min, 1993, NDM

Leonardo da Vinci: The Visionary Intellect
30 min, 1992, RMI

Leonardo, Michelangelo, Raphael & Titian
56 min, 1991, Facets

Michelangelo and the Sistine Chapel
35 min, MFA

Michelangelo: The Early Years
AIMS
1992, 29 min.

Michelangelo: The Later Years
AIMS
1992, 29 min.

Raphael
60 min, 1983, MFA

Renaissance Art and Music
54 min, Clearvue

Titian
57 min, MFA

Titian: Venetian Colorist
27 min, 1991, VM

CD-ROMs

Art of the Renaissance, 4 CD-ROMs
Raphael, Michelangelo, Leonardo da Vinci, Botticelli
Windows, Clearvue

Leonardo: The Paintings
Windows, MFA

Michelangelo
Windows, MFA

The Renaissance of Florence
Windows, MFA

The Sistine Chapel
Windows, Clearvue

Multiple-Choice Questions

1. The Tempietto was a

      a. martyrium*
      b. little temple
      c. baptistry
      d. mausoleum

2. Which is not a feature of the Tempietto?

      a. a Doric peristyle
      b. a balustrade
      c. a dome
      d. an Ionic frieze*
      e. a cella

3. Raphael learned at the elbow of

    a. Leonardo
    b. Perugino*
    c. Fra Angelico
    d. Michelangelo

4. Which is <u>not</u> a feature of Raphael's *Betrothal of the Virgin*?

    a. round arches
    b. an angry suitor
    c. a bearded priest
    d. a pseudo-peripteral temple*
    e. a pediment

5. Who were two important figures in Raphael's *School of Athens*?

    a. David and Goliath
    b. Venus and Adonis
    c. Plato and Aristotle*
    d. Alexander the Great and Socrates

6. Which is <u>not</u> true of Leonardo da Vinci?

    a. he made anatomical drawings
    b. he was a *uomo universale*
    c. he wrote backwards
    d. he made more paintings than drawings*
    e. he made more paintings than sculptures

7. Who advertised his services by saying: "In time of peace I believe I can give perfect satisfaction and to the equal of any other in architecture and the composition of buildings."?

    a. Bramante
    b. El Greco
    c. Michelangelo
    d. Leonardo da Vinci*

8. Leonardo was apprenticed to

    a. Bramante
    b. Verrocchio*
    c. Donatello
    d. Botticelli
    e. Raphael

9. Some experts say that the pyramidal style of the High Renaissance first emerges in the cartoon of _____.

     a. Raphael's *Galatea*
     b. Michelanglo's *Sybils*
     c. Leonardo's *Virgin and Child with Saint Anne**
     d. Masaccio's *Trinity*

10. Which of the following is the best match?

     a. Leonardo's *Last Supper* -- Milan*
     b. Bramante's *Tempietto* -- Florence
     c. The Sistine Chapel -- Siena
     d. The *Mona Lisa* -- Rome

11. Which is <u>not</u> by Leonardo?

     a. *Madonna and Child with Saint Anne*
     b. *Mona Lisa*
     c. *Moses**
     d. *Vitruvian Man*

12. The term *sfumato* refers to:

     a. the fashion of smoking while painting adopted soon after the discovery of America
     b. a smoky haze to convey depth and distance*
     c. aerial perspective
     d. the style in imitation of the candle-smoke darkened walls of Roman churches

13. Which was completed earliest?

     a. Raphael's *School of Athens*
     b. Michelangelo's Sistine ceiling
     c. Michelangelo's *Last Judgment*
     d. Leonardo's *Last Supper**

14. The pyramid was

     a. the echo of ancient Egypt in the piazzas of Rome
     b. a compositional arrangement much favored by High Renaissance artists
     c. a stable, hierarchical structure for arranging figures in a composition
     d. b and c*

15. Which is the correct chronological sequence of works by Michelangelo?

    a. *Moses*, the Rome *Pietà*, *David*, the Sistine Ceiling
    b. *David*, the Rome *Pietà*, the Sistine Ceiling, *Moses*
    c. the Rome *Pietà*, *David*, the Sistine Ceiling, *Moses**
    d. *David*, *Moses*, Saint Peter's, the Sistine Ceiling

16. *Terribilità* refers to

    a. Leonardo's painting style
    b. traits of stubbornness and firmness Michelangelo shared with pope Julius*
    c. Fra Angelico's subtle messages
    d. Raphael's violent imagery in his *Stanza della Segnatura*

17. Michelangelo approached the stone he was to carve

    a. looking to bring out the forms hidden within*
    b. with great fasting and prayer
    c. imposing his will on it from all sides in a demonstration of *terribilità*
    d. trying to get inspiration from the stone's outward shape

18. Which does <u>not</u> appear in the Sistine Ceiling frescoes?

    a. Prophets
    b. Christ*
    c. Sibyls
    d. Jeremiah
    e. Adam

19. _____ commissioned Michelangelo to create his most famous works.

    a. Lorenzo de' Medici
    b. the Duke of Mantua
    c. Julius II*
    d. Francis I of France

20. Michelangelo was inspired by

    a. Leonardo da Vinci's single-minded dedication to sculpture
    b. Classical mythology
    c. Neo-Platonic idea of the Medici Circle
    d. The rough and tumble life he found in Renaissance Rome

21. The Campidoglio

    a. was a piazza based on an ancient Roman space
    c. illustrated Michelangelo's interest in urban planning
    c. demonstrated the Popes' ambitious plans for making Rome beautiful
    d. all of the above*

22. Who was <u>not</u> a Renaissance pope?

    a. Julius II
    b. Paul III
    c. John Paul II*
    d. Clement X

23. The High Renaissance is usually dated

    a. 1495 – 1527*
    b. 1460 – 1564
    c. 1500 – 1535
    d. 1500 – 1600

24. The High Renaissance was centered in

    a. Rome*
    b. Paris
    c. Florence
    d. Urbino

25. Which work matches the correct patron?

    a. Sistine Chapel Ceiling -- Sixtux IV
    b. Tempietto -- Ferdinand and Isabella*
    c. *School of Athens* -- Agostino Chigi
    d. *Mehmet II* -- Giovanni Bellini
    e. *Venus of Urbino* -- Philip II of Spain

26. The patron saint of Venice is

    a. Saint Mark*
    b. Saint Peter
    c. Saint Matthew
    d. Saint Sebastian
    e. Saint John the Evangelist

27. Which best describes the *stigmata*?

    a. an outcast
    b. the Flagellation
    c. the arrows of Saint Sebastian
    d. the wounds of Christ*
    e. a painting by Giotto

28. Match the artist with his place of birth

    a. Giorgione -- Castelfranco*
    b. Michelangelo -- Siena
    c. Leonardo -- Padua
    d. Raphael -- Milan
    e. Bramante -- Venice

29. Titian's self-portrait appears in

    a. the *Rape of Europa*
    b. the *Pesaro Madonna*
    c. the *Galatea*
    d. the *Allegory of Prudence**
    e. the *Tempest*

30. Michelangelo's self-portrait appears in

    a. the *Moses*
    b. the *Last Judgment**
    c. the *Last Supper*
    d. the *Creation of Adam*
    e. the *Flood*

31. Which is true?

    a. Gentile Bellini had two sons, Jacopo and Giovanni
    b. Giovanni Bellini had two sons, Gentile and Jacopo
    c. Jacopo Bellini was the father of Gentile, Giovanni, and Mantegna
    d. Jacopo Bellini had two sons and one daughter*

32. Jacopo Bellini's style is best known today from his

    a. drawings*
    b. paintings
    c. autobiography
    d. etchings
    e. biography

33. Gentile Bellini's rich textures and ability to convey character appealed to

    a. the ruler of Venice
    b. the Sultan in Constantinople*
    c. the Byzantine Patriarch
    d. the Pesaro family

34. The Venetian artist who most influenced Giorgione and Titian was

    a. Jacopo Bellini
    b. Andrea Mantegna
    c. Genitle Bellini
    d. Giovanni Bellini*

35. Giorgione demonstrated the superiority of painting over sculpture by

    a. a description in his autobiography
    b. painting a nude man with reflections from two sides*
    c. making a sculpture and a painting of a man
    d. dictating a comparison to Vasari

36. The surface details in 16th-century Venetian painting show influence from

    a. Flanders*
    b. Naples
    c. the International Style
    d. Byzantium

37. Which is true?

    a. Titian painted the *Tempesta*
    b. There are crowds of figures in the *Tempesta*
    c. The main colors of the *Tempesta* are gray and black
    d. The subject of the *Tempesta* is a matter of debate*

38. *Col Tempo* refers to

    a. an Italian proverb
    b. a book by Aretino
    c. a painting by Giorgione*
    d. a painting by Titian

39. The two Venetian artists who painted reclining nudes are

    a. Giovanni and Gentile Bellini
    b. Titian and Giovanni Bellini
    c. Giorgione and Gentile Bellini
    d. Titian and Giorgione*

40. The vernacular refers to

    a. Italian*
    b. Latin
    c. Greek
    d. the *Dialogues* of Plato

41. Which are by Titian?

    a. *Charles V at Mühlberg*, the *Rape of Europa*, and *Saint Francis in Ecstasy*
    b. *The Tempesta*, the *Allegory of Prudence*, and the *Sleeping Venus*
    c. the *Allegory of Prudence*, the *Venus of Urbino*, and the *Pesaro Madonna**
    d. *The Tempesta*, the *Rape of Europa*, and the *Venus of Urbino*

42. The theme of the *Allegory of Prudence* is

    a. the relationship of humans to animals
    b. time*
    c. portraiture
    d. history

43. Which painting is based on Ovid's *Metamorphoses*?

    a. the *Rape of Europa**
    b. the *Allegory of Prudence*
    c. the *Venus of Urbino*
    d. the *Sleeping Venus*

CHAPTER 15:
Mannerism and the Later Sixteenth Century in Italy

Key Works

Jacopo da Pontormo, *Entombment*, Capponi Chapel, Santa Felicità, Florence, 1525 – 1528

Parmigianino, *Self-Portrait in a Convex Mirror*, 1524

Parmigianino, *Madonna and Child with Angels (Madonna of the Long Neck)*, c. 1535

Agnolo Bronzino, allegory called *Venus, Cupid, Folly, and Time*, c. 1545

Agnolo Bronzino, *Eleonora of Toledo and her Son Don Giovanni*, 1545 – 1546

Paolo Veronese, *The Last Supper*, renamed *Christ in the House of Levi*, 1573

Benvenuto Cellini, saltcellar of Francis I, finished 1543

Benvenuto Cellini, *Narcissus*, c. 1548

Giambologna, *Mercury* (front and side views), c. 1576

Properzia de' Rossi (attrib.), *Joseph and Potiphar's Wife*, c. 1520

Sofonisba Anguissola, *The Artist's Sister Minerva*, c. 1559

Giulio Romano, Palazzo de Tè, plan, Mantua, 1525 – 1535

Giulio Romano, courtyard façade of the Palazzo de Tè, Mantua, 1525 – 1535

Giulio Romano, Sala dei Giganti ceiling, Palazzo de Tè, 1530 – 1532

Giulio Romano, Sala dei Giganti wall view showing the *Fall of the Giants*, Palazzo de Tè, 1530 – 1532

Jacopo Tintoretto, *Last Supper*, 1592 – 1594

El Greco, *Resurrection of Christ*, c. 1597 – 1610

Section of the *Villa Rotonda* (from the *Quattro libri dell'architettura*, 1570). 18th-century engraving

Andrea Palladio, Villa Rotonda, Vicenza, begun 1567 – 1569

Andrea Palladio, San Giorgio Maggiore, Venice, begun 1565

Giacomo da Vignola and Giacomo della Porta, plan of the Church of Il Gesù, 1565 – 1573, Rome

Engraving of Vignola's design for the façade of Church of Il Gesù, Rome, late 16th century

Giacomo da Vignola and Giacomo della Porta, façade of the Church of Il Gesù, Rome, c. 1575 – 1584

Maps, Diagrams, and Projections

Giulio Romano, plan of the Palazzo de Tè, Mantua

Section of the *Villa Rotonda* (from the *Quattro libri dell'architettura*, 1570). 18th-century engraving

Plan of the Villa Rotunda, Vicenza

Plan of San Giorgio Maggiore, Venice

Giacomo da Vignola, plan of the Church of Il Gesù, Rome, 1565 – 1573

Engraving of Vignola's design for the façade of Church of Il Gesù, Rome, late 16th century

Key Terms

broken pediment
cross-section
crossing
figura serpentinata
keystone
rustication
triglyph
volute
voussoir

Videos

Civilisation, Volume 4
Grandeur and Obedience & The Light of Experience
94 min, 1970, VM

El Greco
31 min, 1987, HVC, Crystal Productions

El Greco
57 min, 198?, Films for the Humanities

Paolo Veronese: Between Art and Inquisition
60 min, MFA

Portrait of an Artist: El Greco
31 min, 1987, Clearvue

CD-ROMs

Great Works of Art Explained Part 2 CD-ROM
Mac/Windows, Clearvue

Multiple-Choice Questions

1. Mannerism involved

   a. twisted forms
   b. stange colors
   c. ambiguous space
   d. all of the above*

2. _____ was not a Mannerist painter.

    a. Pontormo
    b. Parmigianino
    c. Correggio
    d. Michelangelo*

3. Which is not a meaning related to the Mannerist style?

    a. affectation
    b. mannered
    c. to the manner born*
    d. stylized
    e. bizarre

4. Indulgences refer to

    a. liberal child-rearing practices
    b. credits against one's sins*
    c. the 95 theses of Martin Luther
    d. the rules of the Council of Trent

5. Match the work with its artist

    a. Parmigianino -- the *Allegory*
    b. Bronzino -- *Saltcellar*
    c. Cellini -- *Narcissus**
    d. Giambologna -- Palazzo del Tè

6. Who wrote "Self-Portrait in a Convex Mirror?"

    a. Parmigianino
    b. Ashbery*
    c. Clement VII
    d. Carlo Ridolfi

7. The patron of the *Saltcellar* was

    a. Francis I*
    b. Cosimo I de' Medici
    c. Eleonora of Toledo
    d. Federigo Gonzaga

8. *Serpentinata* refers to

    a. Cellini's lizard
    b. the salamander of Francis I
    c. a Mannerist pose*
    d. Bronzino's iconography

9. Vasari's account of women artists is a reflection of

    a. his feminism
    b. his humanism*
    c. his patriarchal view of art
    c. his political correctness

10. Autobiographies were written in 16th-century Italy by

    a. Tintoretto and Cellini
    b. Vasari and Ridolfi
    c. Aretino and Giorgione
    d. Vasari and Cellini*

11. Tintoretto painted

    a. dynamic compositions
    b. strong diagonals
    c. serpentine curves
    d. all of the above*

12. One of the great ceiling painters of Mannerism

    a. Tintoretto
    b. Correggio*
    c. Michelangelo
    d. El Greco

13. Giambologna was born in

    a. Italy
    b. Germany
    c. Flanders*
    d. France

14. The exterior of the Palazzo del Tè contains

    a. triglyphs
    b. metopes

c. keystones

d. rustication

e. all of the above*

15. Veronese satisfied the Inquisition by

   a. repainting his picture

   b. renaming his picture*

   c. putting his picture in storage

   d. destroying his picture

   e. sending his picture out of the country

16. A significant influence on the development of El Greco's style was

   a. Tintoretto

   b. Titian

   c. Byzantine style*

   d. High Renaissance style

17. Martin Luther was

   a. an American civil rights leader

   b. a 16th-century monk*

   c. an artist

   d. a member of the Council of Trent

18. Important Counter-Reformation authors include

   a. Ridolfi, Teresa, and Ignatius

   b. Luther, Clement VII, and Teresa

   c. Teresa, John of the Cross, and Clement VII

   d. John of the Cross, Teresa, and Ignatius*

19. El Greco was born

   a. in the Greek mainland

   b. in Venice

   c. in Constantinople

   d. in Toledo

   e. in Crete*

20. Palladio used the ancient texts of

    a. Vitruvius*
    b. Plato
    c. Aristotle
    d. Suetonius

21. The first Italian guidebook was written by

    a. Vasari
    b. Cellini
    c. Palladio*
    d. Vitruvius
    e. Ridolfi

22. What problem did Palladio solve in the façade of San Giorgio Maggiore?

    a. how to deal with the fact that it is on an island
    b. how to reconcile a high nave with lower side aisles*
    c. how to combine a dome with a Greek portico
    d. how to relate the building to its environment

23. The design of the Gesù was planned to

    a. accommodate large congregations*
    b. satisfy the humanist tastes of the patron
    c. reflect the Greek cross plan
    d. show the importance of Alberti's churches

24. Match the work with the patron

    a. the Gesù -- Palladio
    b. Bronzino's *Eleonora of Toledo* -- the king of Spain
    c. Palazzo del Tè -- Federigo Gonzaga*
    d. Villa Rotonda -- Pythagoras

CHAPTER 16:
Sixteenth-Century Painting in the Northern Europe

Key Works

Attributed to Hieronymus Bosch, *Seven Deadly Sins and the Four Last Things,* painted table top, poss. c. 1475, or as late as 1505 – 1515

Attributed to Hieronymus Bosch, *Superbia*, detail of *The Seven Deadly Sins and the Four Last Things*, painted table top

Hieronymus Bosch, *Garden of Earthly Delights*, c. 1510 – 1515

Hieronymus Bosch, couple in the transparent globe, detail of *The Garden of Earthly Delights*

Hieronymus Bosch, monster with an egglike body, detail of *The Garden of Earthly Delights*

Pieter Bruegel the Elder, *Landscape with the Fall of Icarus*, c. 1554 – 1555

Pieter Bruegel the Elder, *The Alchemist*, drawing, 1558

Pieter Bruegel the Elder, *Netherlandish Proverbs*, 1559

Pieter Bruegel the Elder, detail of *Netherlandish Proverbs*

Pieter Bruegel the Elder, *Peasant Dance*, c. 1567

Albrecht Dürer, *Self-Portrait*, 1498

Attributed to Albrecht Dürer, *Folly of Astrology*, from Sebastian Brant, *The Ship of Fools*

Albrecht Dürer, *Four Horsemen of the Apocalypse*, c. 1497 – 1498

Albrecht Dürer, *Melencolia I*, 1514

Albrecht Dürer, *Erasmus*, 1526

Matthias Grünewald, *Crucifixion with Saint Sebastian*, *Saint Anthony*, and *Lamentation*, the Isenheim Altarpiece (closed), c. 1510 – 1515

Matthias Grünewald, *Annunciation*, *Virgin and Child with Angels*, and *Resurrection*, the Isenheim Altarpiece (opened), c. 1510 – 1515

Nicholas von Hagenau, central corpus and base of the Isenheim Altarpiece, early 16th century

Lucas Cranach the Elder, *The Judgment of Paris*, 1530

The Three Graces, from Pompeii, 1st century A.D.

Lucas Cranach the Elder, *Martin Luther*, 1533

Hans Holbein the Younger, *Erasmus of Rotterdam*, c. 1523

Hans Holbein the Younger, *Henry VIII*, c. 1540

Maps, Diagrams, and Projections

Map of northern and central Europe in the Renaissance

Key Terms

burin
edition
engraving
intaglio

plate
print
print matrix

Videos

Art of Claude Lorrain
25 min, 1970, MOMA

Peter Breughel the Elder
90 min, Crystal

Multiple-Choice Questions

1. The *Adagia* was written by

      a. Martin Luther
      b. Bosch
      c. van Mander
      d. Erasmus*

2. Kramer and Sprenger were the authors of

      a. "Sermon on Indulgences"
      b. "The Garden of Earthly Delights"
      c. *The Witches' Hammer**
      d. *The Praise of Folly*

3. The ideas of the Counter Reformation encouragd the Baroque. They were arrived at in the

      a. Diet of Worms
      b. Convocation of Rome
      c. Council of Nicea
      d. Council of Trent*

4. Match the region, city, or country with the personages

      a. Erasmus -- Amsterdam
      b. Luther -- Germany*
      c. Bosch -- Belgium
      d. Dürer -- Dresden

5. Printmaking refers to

      a. woodcuts, engravings, and editions*
      b. woodcuts, drawings, and painting
      c. engravings, editions, and painting
      d. woodcuts, intaglio, and drawings

6. _____ created the Woodcut of the *Four Horsemen of the Apocalypse*

  a. Dürer*
  b. Cranach the Elder
  c. Holbein
  d. Vermeer

7. Which of the following artists was most famous for his woodcuts?

  a. Grünewald
  b. Bruegel
  c. Holbein
  d. Dürer*

8. The textual source of Dürer's *Four Horsemen* is the

  a. *Metamorphoses*
  b. the *Moriae encomium*
  c. Revelation*
  d. the *Ship of Fools*

9. *Knight, Death, and the Devil* is Dürer's picture of

  a. the Christian armed in faith
  b. the devil
  c. the image of Virtue
  d. a and b*

10. The closest northern equivalent of Vasari in the 16th century was

  a. Erasmus
  b. van Mander*
  c. Luther
  d. Sprenger and Kramer
  e. Tetzel

11. Match the work with the correct artist

  a. Bosch -- *Netherlandish Proverbs*
  b. Bruegel -- *The Table Top of the Seven Deadly Sins*
  c. Holbein -- *Henry VIII*
  d. Dürer -- the *Peasant Dance*
  e. Cranach -- *Melencolia I*

12. The artist who specialized in portraiture was _____.

    a. Grünewald
    b. Hans Holbein*
    c. Albrecht Dürer
    d. Pieter Bruegel

13. Grünewald's *Crucifixion* has two saints in the side panels. They are

    a. Sebastian and John the Evangelist
    b. Anthony and Mary Magdelene
    c. John the Baptist and John the Evangelist
    d. Anthony and Sebastian*
    e. Sebastian and Jerome

14. Grünewald's *Isenheim Altarpiece* shows

    a. musical angels
    b. various depictions of martyrdom
    c. profound religious emotion
    d. all of the above*

15. *The Isenheim Altarpiece* is a _____.

    a. diptych
    b. panel
    c. polyptych*
    d. triptych

16. Cranach's *Judgment of Paris* is set in

    a. Saxony*
    b. Troy
    c. Mycenae
    d. Italy
    e. France

17. "P.M." in Erasmus's satire on Julius II refers to

    a. Prime Minister
    b. *Pontifex Maximus*
    c. Saint Peter
    d. Prime Mover

18. *Het Schilderboeck* is

    a. the title of a painting
    b. the title of a book*
    c. the title of an etching
    d. the title of a poem

19. Astrology is best described as

    a. a form of black magic
    b. a heresy
    c. a pseudo-science*
    d. a moral philosophy

20. _____ was one of the first painters to show people working out in the countryside

    a. Bellini
    b. Grünewald
    c. Pieter Bruegel*
    d. Holbein

21. _____ is thought to have visited Italy.

    a. Pieter Bruegel
    b. Hans Holbein
    c. Albrecht Dürer
    d. a and c*

22. *The Peasant Dance* must have been done in Northern Europe because of

    a. the happiness
    b. the hidden symbolism*
    c. the fact that there are peasants
    d. the energy

23. In the myth of Icarus, who made the wings?

    a. Icarus
    b. Zeus
    c. Breugel
    d. Daedalos*
    e. the plowman

24. Which is the best match?

    a. Hubris -- folly*
    b. alchemy -- melancholy
    c. etching -- painting
    d. proverbs -- myths

25. In which work is there a Pool of Lust?

    a. *Landscape with the Fall of Icarus*
    b. *The Alchemist*
    c. *The Judgment of Paris*
    d. the *Garden of Earthly Delights**
    e. *Netherlandish Proverbs*

26. What carries the inscription "Melencolia" in Dürer's engraving?

    a. a mouse
    b. an angel
    c. a dog
    d. a toad
    e. a bat*

27. The word "melancholy" is derived from which two Greek words?

    a. *choleros* meaning "anger" and *bilas* meaning "bile"
    b. *melas* meaning "black" and *ira* meaning "anger"
    c. *chola* meaning "depression" and *melas* meaning "bile"
    d. *cholas* meaning "bile" and *melas* meaning "black"*

28. Erasmus compared Dürer to

    a. Apelles*
    b. Leonardo
    c. Zeuxis
    d. Giotto
    e. Raphael

29. Holbein was born in

    a. England
    b. Antwerp
    c. Augsberg*
    d. Nüremburg
    e. Rotterdam

30. Holbein obtained a letter of introduction to Sir Thomas More from _____.

    a. Martin Luther
    b. Henry VIII
    c. Albrecht Dürer
    d. Erasmus*

31. Holbein's *Erasmus* rests his hands on a book of

    a. the Bible
    b. the *Moriae encomium*
    c. the *Adagia*
    d. the *Metamorphoses*
    e. the *Labors of Herakles**

CHAPTER 17:
The Baroque Style in Western Europe

Key Works

Gianlorenzo Bernini, baldacchino, Saint Peter's, Rome, 1624 – 1633

Gianlorenzo Bernini, Aerial view of colonnade and Piazza of Saint Peter's, Rome, begun 1656

Francesco Borromini, façade of San Carlo alle Quattro Fontane, Rome, 1665 – 1667

Francesco Borromini, plan of San Carlo alle Quattro Fontane, Rome, 1638 – 1641

Francesco Borromini, view toward the high altar, San Carlo alle Quattro Fontane, Rome, 1638 – 1641

Francesco Borromini, interior dome of San Carlo alle Quattro Fontane, Rome, 1665 – 1667

Francesco Borromini, Collegiate Church of Sant' Ivo della Sapienza, Rome, 1642 – 1660

Francesco Borromini, plan of Collegiate Church of Sant' Ivo della Sapienza

Francesco Borromini, interior of dome, Collegiate Church of Sant' Ivo della Sapienza, 1642 – 1660

Claude Perrault, Louis le Vau, and Charles Le Brun, east façade of the Louvre, Paris, 1667 – 1670

Aerial view of the park, palace, and town of Versailles, after a 17th-century engraving by G. Pérelle

Charles Le Brun and Jean-Baptiste Tuby, Fountain of Apollo, Versailles, 1668 – 1670

Jules Hardouin-Mansart and Charles Le Brun, Galerie des Glaces (Hall of Mirrors), Palace of Versailles, c. 1680

Gianlorenzo Bernini, *Louis XIV*, 1665

Christopher Wren, Saint Paul's Cathedral, London, western façade, 1675 – 1710

Gianlorenzo Bernini, *Pluto and Proserpina*, 1621 – 1622

Gianlorenzo Bernini, *David*, 1623

Anonymous, *Cornaro Chapel*, Santa Maria della Vittoria, Rome, oil on canvas, 1645 – 1652

Gianlorenzo Bernini, *Ecstasy of Saint Teresa*, Cornaro Chapel, Santa Maria della Vittoria, Rome, 1645 – 1652

Annibale Carracci, ceiling frescoes in the Grand Gallery, Farnese Palace, Rome, 1597 – 1601

Annibale Carracci, *Venus and Anchises*, detail of ceiling frescos in the Grand Gallery, Farnese Palace, Rome, 1597 – 1601

Pietro da Cortona, *Glorification of the Reign of Urban VIII*, 1633 – 1639

Giovanni Battista Gaulli, *Triumph of the Name of Jesus*, 1676-1679

Caravaggio (Michelangelo Merisi), *Boy with a Basket of Fruit*, c. 1594

Caravaggio, *Medusa*, c. 1597

Caravaggio, *The Calling of Saint Matthew*, Contarelli Chapel, San Luigi dei Francesi, Rome, 1599 – 1600

Caravaggio, *Conversion of Saint Paul*, 1601

Artemisia Gentileschi, *Judith Slaying Holofernes*, c. 1614 – 1620

Artemisia Gentileschi, *Judith and Her Maidservant with the Head of Holofernes*, c. 1625

Peter Paul Rubens, *Venus and Adonis*, c. 1635

Peter Paul Rubens, *Straw Hat* (Susanna Fourment), c. 1620 – 1625

Peter Paul Rubens, *Raising of the Cross*, Antwerp Cathedral, 1609

Anthony van Dyck, *Charles I on Horseback*, c. 1638

Rembrandt van Rijn, *Blinding of Samson (The Triumph of Delilah)*, 1636

Rembrandt van Rijn, *Belshazzar's Feast*, c. 1635

Rembrandt van Rijn, *Militia Company of Captain Frans Banning Cocq* (known as *The Night Watch*), 1642

Rembrandt van Rijn, *Self-Portrait, Leaning on a Sill* (aged thirty-four), 1640

Rembrandt van Rijn, *Self-Portrait as Saint Paul* (aged fifty-five), 1661

Rembrandt van Rijn, *Self-Portrait in a Cap, Openmouthed and Staring*, 1630

Rembrandt van Rijn, *Self-Portrait Grimacing*, 1630

Rembrandt van Rijn, *Self-Portrait, Leaning on a Stone Sill*, 1639

Frans Hals, *The Laughing Cavalier*, 1624

Judith Leyster, *The Last Drop (Gay Cavalier)*, c. 1628 – 1629

Johannes Vermeer, *Geographer*, c. 1668

Johannes Vermeer, *View of Delft* (after restoration), c. 1660 – 1661

Jacob van Ruisdael, *Extensive Landscape with Ruins, c. 1670*

Maria van Oosterwyck, *Vanitas Still Life*, 1668

Diego Velázquez, *Crucifixion*, 1630s

Diego Velázquez, *Philip IV on Horseback*, 1629 – 1630

Diego Velázquez, *Surrender of Breda*, c. 1635

Diego Velázquez, *Venus with a Mirror (Rokeby Venus)*, c. 1648

Diego Velázquez, *Las Meninas* (after cleaning), 1656

Nicolas Poussin, *Assumption of the Virgin*, c. 1626

Nicolas Poussin, *The Ashes of Phokion*, 1648

Nicolas Poussin, *The Dance of Human Life*, c. 1638 – 1640

Maps, Diagrams, and Projections

Map of Europe during the Baroque period

Plan of St. Peter's and the piazza

Francesco Borromini, plan of San Carlo alle Quattro Fontane, Rome, 1638 – 1641

Francesco Borromini, plan of Collegiate Church of Sant' Ivo della Sapienza

Aerial view of the park, palace, and town of Versailles, after a 17th-century engraving by G. Pérelle

Longitudinal section and plan of Saint Paul's Cathedral, London

Key Terms

Academy	gable (or pitched) roof
aedicule	illusionismimpasto
baldacchino	naturalism
burr	pendentive
camera obscura	podium
cantilever construction	rectilinear
château	section

clerestory
etching
etching ground
foreshortening
drypoint
vanitas

silhouette
state
stylus
tenebrism
travertine

Window on the World
Mughal Art and the Baroque

Key Works

Lal and Sanwah, *Akbar Viewing a Wild Elephant Captured near Malwa*, 1600
Bichtir, *Allegorical Representation of the Emperor Jahangir Seated on an Hourglass Throne*,
    early 17th century
Taj Mahal, Agra, India, 1634

Maps, Diagrams, and Projections

Map of India in the 17th century

Key Terms

calligraphy
chattra
minaret
miniature
mausoleum, mausolea
stupa

Videos

Art of the Western World, 4-Pack
Volume 2: Realms of Light: The Baroque
55 min, VM

Baroque Art and Music
37 min, Clearvue

Buried Mirror - Program III: The Age of Gold
59 min, 1991, VM

Caravaggio
30 min, 1991, VM
Caravaggio and the Baroque
53 min, 19??, Facets Mutimedia

History Through Art: The Baroque
43 min, Clearvue

Portrait of An Artist: Velázquez
56 min, 1992, Clearvue

Rembrandt: Painter of Man and the Restoration of "The Night Watch"
56 min, MFA

Two Faces of the 17th Century: Rembrandt and Velázquez
28 min, 1987, MFA

Velázquez: The Nobleman of Painting
60 min, MFA

CD-ROMs

History Through Art: The Baroque
Mac/Windows, Clearvue

The Baroque
Mac/Windows, Clearvue

Multiple-Choice Questions

1. Which is the best match?

     a. Hobbes -- astronomy
     b. Copernicus -- political philosophy
     c. Galileo -- biology
     d. Kepler -- heliocentrism*

2. Which is the best match?

     a. Philip IV -- Habsburg*
     b. Charles I -- Protector
     c. Louis XIII -- the Sun King
     d. Cromwell -- Stuart

3. High Baroque style is

    a. dynamic
    b. sensual
    c. theatrical
    d. all of the above*

4. Baroque intellectuals and artists were interested in

    a. showing the hand of God at work in an orderly the world
    b. demonstrating the laws of creation in action
    c. illustrating the hierarchy of authority in society and religion
    d. all of the above*

5. Which is the most characteristic feature of Baroque style?

    a. elongation
    b. violent action*
    c. restraint
    d. flat spaces
    e. frontal figures

6. _____ was the place Baroque art was born.

    a. London
    b. Rome*
    c. Versailles
    d. Florence

7. Which gained new status in the 17th century?

    a. landscape, mythology, genre
    b. portraiture, mythology, still life
    c. landscape, portraiture, mythology
    d. landscape, genre, still life*

8. The "Throne of Saint Peter" is

    a. an elaborate chair in St. Peter's cathedral
    b. a baldacchino
    c. a reliquary*
    d. a triptych
    e. an altarpiece

9. The two main shapes used by Bernini in front of Saint Peter's are

    a. a square and a circle
    b. a trapezoid and an oval*
    c. a rectangle and an oval
    d. a trapezoid and a circle

10. A piazza is

    a. an Italian pie
    b. an Italian villa
    c. an Italian costume
    d. an Italian square*
    e. an Italian palace

11. Bernini's colonnades outside St. Peter's are made of

    a. marble
    b. travertine*
    c. tufa
    d. concrete
    e. stucco

12. Which is by Borromini?

    a. San Carlo alle Quattro Fontane
    b. the facade of the Louvre
    c. Saint'Ivo della Sapienza
    d. a, b, and c
    e. a and d*

13. Borromini's used

    a. dramatic frontality and heightened proportion
    b. curved movement fromspace to space
    c. contrasting concave and convex forms
    d. b and c*

14. The Collegiate Church of St. Ivo della Sapienza was Baroque because of its

    a. centralized, but asymmetrical plan*
    b. all-embracing arms as at St. Peter's
    c. remarkably classical façade
    d. orderly, symmetrical floor plan

15. Which is true of the interior dome of San Carlo alle Quattro Fontane?

    a. it has square coffers only
    b. it has square, hexagonal, and octagonal coffers
    c. it has hexagonal, square, and cross-shaped coffers
    d. it has hexagonal, octagonal, and cross-shaped coffers*

16. The purpose of Louis XIV's Academy was to

    a. educate artists in humanism
    b. establish a national style*
    c. have a school for the court painters
    d. teach the principles of Baroque style
    e. revive the Socratic method

17. _____ worked for Louis XIV in a style called the Classical Baroque

    a. Poussin*
    b. Cravaggio
    c. Bernini
    d. Rubens

18. Nicolas Poussin was a Classical Baroque painter because we can see _____ in his work.

    a. restraint
    b. passion
    c. moderation
    d. a and c*

19. Louis XIV moved the court to Versailles in

    a. 1665
    b. 1660
    c. 1667*
    d. 1650

20. Which is the best match?

    a. Poussin -- color -- Apollo -- Moderns
    b. Rubens -- color -- Apollo -- Ancients
    c. Poussin -- line -- Dionysos -- Moderns
    d. Rubens -- color -- Moderns -- Dionysos*
    e. Poussin -- line -- Dionysos -- Ancients

21. The landscape architect at Versailles was

   a. Le Brun
   b. Le Nôtre*
   c. Le Vau
   d. Hardouin-Mansart
   e. Colbert

22. The Greek god most closely associated with Louis XIV was

   a. Zeus
   b. Ares
   c. Dionysos
   d. Apollo*
   e. Poseidon

23. Which is not a feature of Wren's facade of St. Paul's?

   a. pediment
   b. columns
   c. entablature
   d. towers
   e. pointed arches*

24. When Christopher Wren designed St. Paul's Cathedral in London he was influenced by

   a. Borromini
   b. Bernini
   c. the architecture of Louis XIV
   d. a synthesis of all the above*

25. The Great Fire of London occurred in

   a. 1666*
   b. 1677
   c. 1688
   d. 1655

26. Which does not appear in Bernini's *Pluto and Proserpina*?

   a. contrapposto
   b. Cerberus
   c. *figura serpentinata*
   d. Ceres*
   e. Pluto

27. Which is <u>not</u> true of Bernini's *Saint Teresa*?

    a. she has erotic quality
    b. she is on a horizontal plane*
    c. she is in the process of levitating
    d. she is both relaxed and aroused
    e. she synthesizes emotion with mysticism

28. The Farnese Grand Gallery ceiling frescoes illustrate

    a. Christian scenes
    b. scenes of the Farnese family
    c. mythological scenes*
    d. scenes of Roman history

29. The Italian Baroque equivalent of Vasari was

    a. van Mander
    b. Carracci
    c. Cortona
    d. Bellori*

30. Anchises was

    a. the lover of Ceres
    b. the lover of Juno
    c. the father of Aeneas
    d. a and b
    e. c and d*

31. Which is <u>not</u> true of Pietro da Cortona's *Reign of Urban VIII*

    a. it is on a ceiling in the Palazzo Barbarini
    b. it depicts three huge bees
    c. it exalts the Catholic Church
    d. it is organized like a Last Judgment*
    e. it contains mythological figures

32. Gaulli's *Triumph of the Name of Jesus*

    a. is in the vault of Saint Peter's
    b. is in the vault of the Gesú*
    c. is a collaboration between Gaulli and Bernini
    d. was commissioned by the pope

33. Caravaggio was described by van Mander as

    a. combining the qualities of Mars and Minerva*
    b. violent but charming
    c. a realist and a Neoplatonist
    d. a good tennis player

34. Caravaggio's *Medusa*

    a. was based on the features of his lover
    b. was a wedding present*
    c. is oil on wood
    d. is the same figure as the boy in the *Boy with a Basket of Fruit.*

35. Caravaggio's *Calling of Matthew* quotes visually from

    a. the gospel of Matthew
    b. the *Amor Vincit Omnia*
    c. Gaulli's ceiling
    d. Michelangelo's Sistine Ceiling*

36. *Tenebrism* refers to

    a. *chiaroscuro*
    b. a preponderance of cast shadows
    c. a preponderance of darkness*
    d. the tenets of shading

37. Artemisia Gentileschi was influenced by

    a. Rubens
    b. El Greco
    c. Tintoretto
    d. Caravaggio*

38. Artemisia Gentileschi's *Judith Slaying Holofernes* is based on

    a. the Bible
    b. the Old Testament Apocrypha*
    c. the *Metamorphoses*
    d. the New Testament Apocrypha

39. Which is the best match?

    a. Catholic -- Holland
    b. Catholic -- Switzerland

c. Protestant -- Holland*

d. Protestant -- France

40. Rubens's paintings are characterized by

    a. strong angular compositions
    b. brilliant colors and textures
    c. the human body in motion
    d. all of the above*

41. Rubens synthesized the ideas

    a. Caravaggio
    b. Michelangelo
    c. Titian
    d. all of the above*

42. The figure in Rubens's *The Straw Hat* was

    a. a wealthy patron
    b. the artist's sister
    c. the artist's wife
    d. the artist's future sister-in-law*
    e. the artist's future mother-in-law

43. Which best describes Rubens's women?

    a. they are overweight
    b. they are voluptuous*
    c. they are pious
    d. they are mythological
    e. they are peasants

44. The court portrait painter to Charles I of England was

    a. Anthony van Dyck*
    b. Christopher Wren
    c. Hans Holbein
    d. Oliver Cromwell

45. The Dutch East India Company secured a monopoly on

    a. textiles
    b. slaves
    c. spices*

d. tulips

e. porcelain

46. Three emperors who patronized Mughal painting in India were

    a. Genghis Khan, Akbar, and Shah Jehan

    b. Genghis Khan, Akbar, and Jahangir

    c. Mumtaz, Jahangir, and Akbar

    d. Akbar, Jahangir, and Shah Jehan*

47. The Taj Mahal was a memorial to

    a. Akbar

    b. Mumtaz*

    c. Shah Jehan

    d. Jahangir

48. Rembrandt's painted light is typically

    a. yellow*

    b. white

    c. light blue

    d. gray

    e. light green

49. The "writing on the wall" appears in

    a. *The Blinding of Samson*

    b. *The Night Watch*

    c. *Belshazzar's Feast*

    d. *The Assumption of the Virgin*

50. _____ was one of the "Little Dutch Masters.

    a. Holbein

    b. Anthony Van Dyck

    c. Velázquez

    d. Jan Vermeer*

51. The seventeenth-century artist most interested in the science of optics was _____.

    a. Spinoza

    b. Rubens

    c. Vermeer*

    d. Ucello

52. Jacob van Ruisdael specialized in _____.

    a. landscape*
    b. moralizing pictures
    c. *vanitas*
    d. portraits

53. The predominant planes in Baroque painting are

    a. horizontal
    b. vertical
    c. curvilinear
    d. spiral
    e. diagonal*

54. The Baroque artist best known for self-portraits is

    a. Poussin
    b. Rubens
    c. Rembrandt*
    d. Vermeer
    e. Bernini

55. Rembrandt's religious work was

    a. contemplative
    b. spiritual
    c. heated and exotic
    d. a and b but not c*

56. The Baroque artist known to have used the *camera obscura* was

    a. Vermeer*
    b. Rubens
    c. Leyster
    d. Rembrandt
    e. Hals

57. Which artist is matched with the incorrect city of origin?

    a. Hals -- Haarlem
    b. Rembrandt -- Leiden
    c. Vermeer -- Delft
    d. Leyster -- Amsterdam*

58. *Vanitas* is the Latin word for

    a. emptiness*
    b. vanity
    c. vainglory
    d. lies

59. Which is least likely to appear as *vanitas* iconography?

    a. a skull
    b. a windmill*
    c. a watch
    d. a candle
    e. a shell

60. Diego de Velázquez was strongly influenced by

    a. Annibale Carracci
    b. Caravaggio*
    c. Tintoretto
    d. El Greco

61. Velázquez's main patron was

    a. Philip II
    b. Louis XIV
    c. Philip IV*
    d. Charles V

62. Which is <u>not</u> by Velázquez?

    a. *The Nightwatch*￼*
    b. *The Surrender of Breda*
    c. *The Rokeby Venus*
    d. *Las Meninas*

63. The most "classical" of the following Baroque artists was

    a. Bernini
    b. Caravaggio
    c. Poussin*
    d. Rubens
    e. Rembrandt

CHAPTER 18:
Rococo and the Eighteenth Century

Key Works

Sir William Chambers, *Pagoda*, Kew Gardens, England, 1761; engraving by William Woollett after J. Kirby, hand-colored by Heath

Germain Boffrand, Salon de la Princess, Hôtel de Soubise, Paris, c. 1740

Joseph Wright, *An Experiment on a Bird in the Air Pump*, 1768

Antoine Watteau, *Pilgrimage to Cythera*, 1717

Antoine Watteau, *Gilles*, undated

François Boucher, *Venus Consoling Love*, 1751

Jean-Honoré Fragonard, *The Swing*, 1766

Hyacinthe Rigaud, *Louis XIV*, 1701

Rosalba Carriera, *Louis XV*, 1751

Élisabeth Vigée-Lebrun, *Marie Antoinette and her Children*, 1788

Thomas Gainsborough, *Mrs. Richard Brinsley Sheridan*, 1785 – 1787

William Hogarth, *Marriage à la Mode II*, 1745; engraving by B. Baron after an oil painting of 1743

William Hogarth, *Time Smoking a Picture*, 1761

Balthasar Neumann, the Residenz, Würzburg, Germany, 1719 – 1753

Staircase of the Residenz showing the ceiling fresco of Giovanni Battista Tiepolo, Würzburg, Germany, 1752 – 1753

Giovanni Battista Tiepolo, *The Investiture of Bishop Harold*, a detail of the ceiling frescoes in the Kaisersaal, the Residenz, Würzburg, Germany, 1751 – 1752

Matthäus Daniel Pöppelmann, Wallpavillon, the Zwinger, Dresden, Germany, 1711 – 1722

Dominikus Zimmermann, Wieskirche, Bavaria, 1745 – 1754

Richard Boyle (Earl of Burlington), Chiswick House, near London, begun 1725

Robert Adam, fireplace niche, Osterley Park House, Middlesex, England, begun 1761

Horace Walpole, Strawberry Hill, Twickenham, near London, 1749 – 1777

Jean-Baptiste Siméon Chardin, *La Fontaine*, first exhibited 1733

Jean-Baptiste Siméon Chardin, *Pipe and Jug*, undated

Angelica Kauffmann, *Amor and Psyche*

John Singleton Copley, *Paul Revere*, c. 1768 – 1770

Benjamin West, *The Death of General Wolfe*, c. 1770

Maps, Diagrams, and Projections

Map of Western Europe, c. 1740

Plan of the Weiskirche

Plan of Cheswick House

Map of North American settlements in the 18th century

Key Terms

chancel
chinoiserie
fleur-de-lys
krater
hôtel
impasto
molding
pagoda
stucco
trompe l'oeil

Videos

Art of the Western World, 4-Pack
Volume 3: An age of Reason
55 min, VM

Civilisation, Volume 5
The Pursuit of Happiness & The Smile of Reason
94 min, 1970, VM

Colonial American History Through Art
18 min, Clearvue

Eighteenth-Century Art and Music
35 min, Clearvue

Fragonard
7 min, 1975, Britannica

History Through Art: The Enlightenment
42 min, Clearvue

John Singleton Copley
6 min, 197?, Britannica

The London of William Hogarth (B&W)
27 min, 1956, IFB

Antoine Watteau
18 min, 1991, AP

CD-ROMs

History Through Art: The Enlightenment
Mac/Windows, Clearvue

The Eighteenth Century
Mac/Windows, Clearvue

Multiple-Choice Questions

1. Which are the most characteristic features of Rococo?

    a. fussiness
    b. frivolity
    c. elegance
    d. irony
    e. all of the above*

2. The Rococo style is most closely related to

    a. Classical Baroque
    b. Mannerism
    c. Renaissance style
    d. Late Baroque style*

3. The Rococo style started in _____.

    a. America
    b. Germany
    c. Italy
    d. France*

4. The Rococo style is characterized by _____.

    a. pastel colors
    b. a spirit of play
    c. minimized human figures
    d. all of the above*

5. The aristocracy _____ French Rococo art.

    a. patronized
    b. had their sensibilities reflected in
    c. criticized
    d. a and b*

6. A *salonnière* is a

    a. hostess*
    b. waitress
    c. countess
    d. princess

7. Winckelmann is known primarily for

    a. German painting
    b. a historical approach to studying Greek and Roman art*
    c. a historical approach to artists' biographies
    d. German philosophy of art

8. Which does <u>not</u> match?

    a. Vivaldi -- music
    b. Priestly -- oxygen
    c. Halley -- biology*
    d. Swift -- satire
    e. Watt -- steam engine

9. The Seven Years' War was fought between

    a. England and France
    b. Prussia, France and Austria*
    c. England and Prussia
    d. France, Prussia, and England

10. Match the philosopher with his ideas or work

    a. Locke -- empiricism*
    b. Diderot -- social contract
    c. Rousseau -- encyclopedia
    d. Jefferson -- *Two Treatises of Civil Government*

11. Who is not a Rococo painter?

    a. Watteau
    b. Boucher
    c. Fragonard
    d. Chambers*

12. *Gilles* refers to

    a. a painting by Boucher
    b. a French philosopher
    c. a French novelist
    d. a painting by Watteau*
    e. a painting by Fragonard

13. Chardin

    a. painted still-lifes
    b. painted the common folk at their humble tasks
    c. painted "fêtes galantes"
    d. a and b but not c*

14. *L'Etat c'est moi* is

    a. the title of a painting
    b. an autobiography
    c. an expression of absolutism*
    d. the title of a philosophical treatise
    e. a work by Descartes

15. Which is <u>not</u> a texture depicted in Rigaud's *Louis XIV*?

    a. silk
    b. ermine
    c. velvet
    d. gold
    e. marble*

16. Pastels are

    a. waterpaints
    b. chalky crayons*
    c. tempera paints
    d. light-colored pencils

17. July 14, 1789 is

    a. the day that the American Revolution began
    b. the day that the Declaration of Independence was signed
    c. Bastille Day*
    d. the day that Louis XVI was executed

18. The artist who painted important personages in England in the end of the 18th century was

    a. Gainsborough*
    b. Stubbs
    c. Wright of Derby
    d. Thomas de Quincy

19. The Enlightenment

    a. started in 1650
    b. was the entire 18th century*
    c. was limited to the first half of the 19th century
    d. dates from the early nineteenth century

20. Who is <u>not</u> an 18th-century portraitist?

    a. Gainsborough
    b. Rigaud
    c. Vigée-Lebrun
    d. Carriera
    e. Boyle*

21. *Time Smoking a Picture* satirizes

    a. artists
    b. art dealers*
    c. art collectors
    d. art museums

22. The Kaisersaal refers to

    a. a palace
    b. a ruler
    c. a room*
    d. a stairway

23. Which is <u>not</u> a feature of *Tiepolo's Investiture of Bishop Harold*?

    a. trompe l'oeil
    b. stucco
    c. oval windows
    d. pastel colors
    e. velvet curtains*

24. The Zwinger is

    a. a German rock group
    b. a palace of the Polish king
    c. a courtyard*
    d. an elaborate wall

25. Which is not true of Zimmermann's Weiskirche?

    a. it is near Oberammergau
    b. it is influenced by a Classical revival in Germany*
    c. it is influenced by Borromini
    d. it has a longitudinal axis

26. _____ dominated the architectural style of the 18th century

    a. Boromini
    b. Michelangelo
    c. Bramante
    d. Palladio*

27. Which is true of Chiswick House?

    a. it was designed by Palladio
    b. it is in northern England
    c. it was originally a library and place of entertainment*
    d. it is based on San Giorgio Maggiore

28. Chiswick House was influenced by

    a. Palladio
    b. Inigo Jones
    c. Vitruvius
    d. all of the above*

29. Which is true of Osterley Park House?

    a. it was designed by Lord Burlington
    b. it was inspired by Palladian design
    c. it was built in East Anglia
    d. it was inspired by Classical precedents*

30. Strawberry Hill refers to

    a. a garden of roses in England designed by Boyle
    b. an English landscape painting
    c. a Gothic Revival villa*
    d. a medieval castle known as Otranto

31. Strawberry Hill was built in the style of the

    a. Oriental Revival
    b. Baroque Revival style
    c. Neoclassic Revival
    d. "Gothick" Revival*

32. The term Bourgeois Realism is applied to the work of

    a. Chardin*
    b. Hogarth
    c. Wright of Derby
    d. Copley

33. Paul Revere was

    a. a goldsmith
    b. a silversmith*
    c. an equestrian champion
    d. a British sympathizer

CHAPTER 19:
Neoclassicism: The Late Eighteenth and Early Nineteenth Centuries

Key Works

Clodion (Claude Michel), *The Intoxication of Wine*, c. 1775
Antonio Canova, *Cupid and Psyche*, 1787 – 1793
Jacques-Louis David, *The Oath of the Horatii*, 1784 – 1785
Jacques-Louis David, *The Death of Socrates*, 1787
Jacques-Louis David, *The Death of Marat*, 1793
Jacques-Louis David, *Napoleon at Saint Bernard Pass*, 1800
Jean-François-Thérèse Chalgrin et al., Arc de Triomphe, Paris, 1806 – 1836
Charles Percier and Pierre F.L. Fontaine, Place Vendôme column, Paris, 1810
Antonio Canova, *Maria Paolina Borghese as Venus*, 1808
Marie-Guillemine Benoist, *Portrait of a Negress*, 1800
Jean-Auguste-Dominique Ingres, *Madame Rivière*, 1805
Jean-Auguste-Dominique Ingres, *Napoleon Enthroned*, 1806
Jean-Auguste-Dominique Ingres, *Oedipus and the Sphinx*, 1808
Jean-Auguste-Dominique Ingres, *Grande Odalisque*, 1814
Jean-Antoine Houdon, *Thomas Jefferson*, 1789
Thomas Jefferson, Monticello, near Charlottesville, Virginia, 1769 – 84 (rebuilt 1794 – 1809)
Thomas Jefferson, State Capitol, Richmond, Virginia, 1785 – 1789
Thomas Jefferson, plan and section of the Rotunda, University of Virginia, Charlottesville (from
    W. Blaser)
Thomas Jefferson, Rotunda, University of Virginia, Charlottesville, 1817 – 1826
Horatio Greenough, *George Washington*, 1832 – 1841

Maps, Diagrams, and Projections

Map of the Napoleonic Empire, 1812
Map of the United States during Jefferson's presidency, c. 1803
Plan and elevation of Monticello (from W. Blaser)
Thomas Jefferson, plan and section of the Rotunda, University of Virginia, Charlottesville.
    (From W. Blaser)

Key Terms

metope
portico
satyr
terracotta
triglyph

Videos

Ingres: Slaves of Fashion
52 min, 1987, HVC

Jacques Louis David: The Passing Show
53 min, 1987, MFA, HVC, Crystal

Thomas Jefferson, two-tape set
92 min, 1996, VM

Multiple-Choice Questions

1. Neo-Classicism seemed to convey

      a. democratic ideals
      b. broad, enlightened culture
      c. civil virtue
      d. all of the above*

2. 1793 is the year that

      a. the French Revolution began
      b. the Directory began
      c. Louis XVI was guillotined*
      d. Napoleon became First Consul
      e. Napoleon lost the Battle of Waterloo

3. Bacchantes are

      a. wine gods
      b. priestesses of Dionysos*
      c. wine goddesses
      d. priests of Dionysos

4. Psyche is

      a. the lover of Cupid
      b. the Greek word for "soul"
      c. the goddess of love
      d. all of the above
      e. a and b*

5. The artist of the French Revolution was

    a. Jacques-Louis David*
    b. Angelica Kauffmann
    c. Antoine Watteau
    d. Chardin

6. The *Oath of the Horatii*

    a. is by Ingres
    b. is an event from Roman tradition*
    c. is described in Classical texts
    d. is the subject of a tragedy by Racine

7. The *Oath of the Horatii* was commissioned by

    a. Louis XIV
    b. Napoleon
    c. Louis XVI*
    d. Marie Antoinette

8. Plato's defense of Socrates is

    a. the *Death of Socrates*
    b. the *Apology**
    c. not recorded
    d. a treatise on political philosophy used by Napoleon

9. The architectural style of Ancient Greece was resurrected in the late 18th century because

    a. it was believed to inspire citizenship
    b. it seemed to encourage heroic sacrifice
    c. its crystalline lines seemed to reject the decadence of the Rococo
    d. all of the above*

10. Marat's assassin was

    a. Napoleon's messenger
    b. Colbert
    c. Richelieu
    d. Corday*
    e. never identified

11. *L'An Deux* refers to

    a. 2 B.C.
    b. 2 A.D.
    c. 1793*
    d. 1776

12. In *Napoleon at Saint Bernard Pass*, Napoleon is compared to

    a. Charlemagne and Caesar
    b. Hannibal and Scipio
    c. Caesar and Scipio
    d. Hannibal and Charlemagne*

13. Who of the following did <u>not</u> work for Napoleon?

    a. David
    b. Ingres
    c. Vigée-Lebrun*
    d. Benoist
    e. Canova

14. 1787 is the year that

    a. the U.S. Constitution was signed*
    b. George Washington became president
    c. Thomas Jefferson became president
    d. The American Revolution broke out

15. As depicted in *The Declaration of Independence*, the U.S. Capitol Rotunda has a (an) _____ frieze on the upper part of the walls. (Fill in the blank)

    a. Ionic
    b. Corinthian
    c. Tuscan
    d. Federal
    e. Doric*

16. Jefferson based his design for Monticello on the architecture of

    a. Christopher Wren
    b. Michelangelo
    c. Palladio*
    d. Borromini

17. Which <u>least</u> inspired Jefferson's architectural style?

    a. Palladio's *Four Books on Architecture*
    b. Gothic Revival*
    c. Chiswick House
    d. the Pantheon
    e. Neoclassicism

18. Which was <u>not</u> designed by Jefferson?

    a. the University of Virginia
    b. Monticello
    c. the U.S. Capitol Building*
    d. the Richmond Capitol Building

19. Greenough's *George Washington* was based on

    a. Napoleonic iconography
    b. Pharaonic iconography
    c. Jeffersonian iconography
    d. Phidian iconography*

20. *Place Charles de Gaulle* was formerly called

    a. Place de l'Etoile*
    b. Place Vendôme
    c. Place Napoléon
    d. Place Richelieu

CHAPTER 20:
Romanticism: The Late Eighteenth and Early Nineteenth Centuries

Key Works

Sir Charles Barry and Augustus W. N. Pugin, Houses of Parliament, London, 1836 – 1870

Richard Upjohn, Trinity Church, New York, 1841 – 1852

John Nash, Royal Pavilion, Brighton, England, 1815 – 1818

François Rude, *The Departure of the Volunteers of 1792* (La Marseillaise), 1833 – 1836

William Blake, *God Creating the Universe (Ancient of Days)*, frontispiece of *Europe: A Prophecy*, 1794

Théodore Géricault, *Mounted Officer of the Imperial Guard*, 1812

Théodore Géricault, *Mad Woman with a Mania of Envy*, 1822 – 1823

Théodore Géricault, *The Raft of the "Medusa,"* 1819

Eugène Delacroix, *The Bark of Dante*, 1822

Eugène Delacroix, *The Massacre at Chios*, 1822 – 1824

Eugène Delacroix, *Death of Sardanapalus*, 1827 – 1828

Eugène Delacroix, *Liberty Leading the People*, 1830

Eugène Delacroix, *Women of Algiers*, 1834

Eugène Delacroix, *Medea*, 1862

Francisco de Goya y Lucientes, *Los Caprichos*, Plate 3, published 1799

Francisco de Goya y Lucientes, *Witches' Sabbath*, 1798 – 1799

Francisco de Goya y Lucientes, *Family of Charles IV*, 1800

Francisco de Goya y Lucientes, *Executions of the Third of May, 1808*, 1814

Francisco de Goya y Lucientes, *Chronos Devouring One of His Children*, c. 1820 – 1822

Casper David Friedrich, *Moonrise over the Sea*, 1817

John Constable, *Salisbury Cathedral from the Bishop's Garden*, 1820

Joseph Mallord William Turner, *The Burning of the Houses of Lords and Commons, October 16, 1834*, 1835

Thomas Cole, *View from Mount Holyoke, Northampton, Massachusetts, after a Thunderstorm (The Oxbow)*, 1836

George Caleb Bingham, *The Squatters*, 1850

Edward Hicks, *Peaceable Kingdom*, c. 1834

Key Terms

aquatint

binder, binding medium

gouache

ground

monolith

wash

watercolor

Videos

American Light: The Luminist Movement, 1850–1875
32 min, 1989, National Gallery of Art

Art of the Western World, 4-Pack
Volume 3: An Age of Passion
55 min, VM

The Boundaries of Time: Caspar David Friedrich
39 min, 1991, HVC

Civilisation, Volume 6
The Worship of Nature & The Fallacies of Hope
94 min, 1970, VM

Civilisation, Volume 7
Heroic Materialism
94 min, 1970, VM

Caspar David Friedrich: Landscape as Language
18 min, 197?, TRC

Eugene Delacroix: The Restless Eye
62 min, 1987, HVC

Gericault: The Raft of the Medusa
21 min, 1987, TRC

Goya: His Life & Art
44 min, 1980, FFTH

Goya
54 min, VM, Crystal

History Through Art: Romanticism
24 min, Clearvue

Horace Pippen: There Will be Peace
28 min, Crystal

The Hudson River & Its Painters
58 min, 1990, HVC, Crystal

Joseph Mallord William Turner

8 min, 197?, Britannica

Landscapes of Frederich Edwin Church
29 min, 1990, HVC, Crystal

Portrait of An Artist: Turner at the Tate
55 min, 1991, MFA, Clearvue

Romanticism in Art and Music
38 min, Clearvue

CD-ROMs

History Through Art: Romanticism
Mac/Windows, Clearvue

The Romantic Era
Mac/Windows, Clearvue

Multiple-Choice Questions

1. Romanticism

    a. was interested in the wild and ghostly
    b. yearned for the past or a golden future
    c. loved wild landscapes
    d. all of the above*

2. 1830 is the date of

    a. the Restoration of the Bourbon monarchy
    b. the July Revolution in France*
    c. the attack on Fort Sumter
    d. the Spanish-American War

3. Which is not a tenet of Romanticism?

    a. nostalgia
    b. exoticism
    c. chivalric tales
    d. the sublime
    e. social realism*

4. The Houses of Parliament are examples of

       a. Classical revival architecture
       b. Palladian architecture
       c. Gothic revival architecture*
       d. Islamic revival architecture

5. *La Marseillaise* is

       a. a French city
       b. a French building
       c. a French song*
       d. a French epic

6. François Rude's sculpture *La Marseillaise* represents

       a. a parade in Paris
       b. Liberty leading France to protect the motherland*
       c. the French Revolution led by Louis XVI
       d. the battle of the Centaurs

7. The Brighton Pavilion is an example of

       a. Gothic revival
       b. Islamic Gothic
       c. Classical revival
       d. Indian Gothic*

8. Gouache is a kind of

       a. etching
       b. paint*
       c. woodcut
       d. pigment

9. Which best describes the work of William Blake?

       a. Classical
       b. Gothic
       c. down-to-earth
       d. military
       e. visionary*

10. Géricault's paintings reflect his interest in

   a. combating social injustice
   b. horsemanship
   c. psychology
   a. all of the above*
   e. a and c only

11. In the *Raft of the Medusa*, "Medusa" refers to

   a. a jellyfish
   b. a life raft
   c. a ship*
   d. a hospital
   e. a painting by Caravaggio

12. Géricault's *Raft of the Medusa* was based on

   a. a Romantic concoction under the influence of opium
   b. an event taken from the newspapers of the day*
   c. a scene from the French Revolution
   d. a mythological scene

13. The Salon refers to

   a. an official art exhibition*
   b. a room in a château
   c. a room in a private Paris apartment
   d. an art gallery

14. The Romantic movement in French literature was led by

   a. Voltaire
   b. Rousseau
   c. Descartes
   d. Hugo*
   e. Delacroix

15. The war depicted in the *Massacre at Chios* was between

   a. America and England
   b. France and Italy
   c. Greece and Turkey*
   d. Greece and Italy

16. The *Massacre at Chios* is sympathetic to

    a. Greece*
    b. Turkey
    c. Italy
    d. France
    e. England

17. In *Liberty Leading the People*, the figure of Liberty is an example of

    a. irony
    b. allegory*
    c. satire
    d. metonymy
    e. realism

18. Aquatint combines

    a. watercolor and drawing
    b. engraving and oil
    c. watercolor and silverpoint
    d. watercolor and engraving*

19. Which is <u>not</u> a theme in Goya's painting?

    a. social injustice
    b. child psychology
    c. irrational thinking
    d. frivolity*

20. Kronos was

    a. a bad Spanish father
    b. the father of the Olympians*
    c. the father of Goya
    d. the father of Hermes

21. Which does <u>not</u> match?

    a. Burke -- the sublime
    b. Goethe -- *Sturm und Drang*
    c. Freud -- *the Uncanny*
    d. Rousseau -- *Les Misérables**

22. Constable's painting of Salisbury Cathedral is an example of

    a. Gothic revival
    b. Realism
    c. Romanticism*
    d. watercolor

23. Towards the end of his career, Turner painted

    a. carefully delineated scenes of upper class virtue
    b. realistic landscapes
    c. broadly imagined, expressionistically colored landscapes*
    d. photographic-quality portraits

24. Who is not an American Romantic writer?

    a. Coleridge*
    b. Thoreau
    c. Emerson
    d. Cooper
    e. Poe

25. Pippin's *Holy Mountain* quotes from which of the following?

    a. Cole
    b. Hicks*
    c. Bingham
    d. Turner

26. Who wrote *The Seven Lamps of Architecture*?

    a. Nash
    b. Jefferson
    c. Ruskin*
    d. Upjohn

27. Match the author with his work

    a. Coleridge -- *The Solitary Reaper*
    b. Shelley -- *Kubla Khan*
    c. Byron -- *Don Juan*
    d. Keats – *Ozymandias*

CHAPTER 21:
Nineteenth-Century Realism

Key Works

Jean-François Millet, *Gleaners*, 1857
Rosa Bonheur, *Horse Fair*, 1853
Gustave Courbet, *Stone Breakers*, 1849
Gustave Courbet, *The Interior of My Studio: A Real Allegory Summing up Seven Years of My Life as an Artist from 1848 to 1855*, 1855
Honoré Daumier, *Third-Class Carriage*, c. 1862
Honoré Daumier, *Interior of a First-Class Carriage*, 1864
Honoré Daumier, *Freedom of the Press: Don't Meddle with It (Ne Vous y Frottez Pas)*, 1834
Honoré Daumier, *Louis-Philippe as Gargantua*, 1831
Joseph Nicéphore Niépce, *View from His Window at Gras*, 1826
Unknown photographer, daguerreotype, c. 1845
Gaspard-Félix Tournachon (Nadar), *Sarah Bernhardt*, c. 1864
Honoré Daumier, *Nadar Elevating Photography to the Height of Art*, 1862
Julia Margaret Cameron, *Mrs. Herbert Duckworth*, 1867
Matthew B. Brady, *Lincoln "Cooper Union" Portrait*, 1860
Matthew B. Brady, *Robert E. Lee*, 1865
Studio of Matthew B. Brady, *Ruins of Gallego Flour Mills, Richmond*, 1863 – 1865
Dante Gabriel Rossetti, *Ecce Ancilla Domini (The Annunciation)*, 1850
John Everett Millais, *John Ruskin*, 1854
Thomas Cowperthwait Eakins, *Gross Clinic*, 1875 – 1876
Thomas Cowperthwait Eakins, *John Biglen in a Single Scull*, 1873
Henry Ossawa Tanner, *Annunciation*, 1898
Edouard Manet, *Le Déjeuner sur l'Herbe*, 1863
Edouard Manet, *Olympia*, 1865
Gustave Courbet, *Woman with a Parrot*, 1866
Joseph Paxton, Crystal Palace, London, 1850 – 1851
John A. and W. A. Roebling, Brooklyn Bridge, New York, 1869 – 1883
Auguste Bartholdi and Alexandre-Gustave Eiffel, Statue of Liberty, New York, 1875 – 1884
Alexandre-Gustav Eiffel, diagram of the construction of the Statue of Liberty
Alexandre-Gustave Eiffel, Eiffel Tower, Paris, 1887 – 1889
Louis Sullivan, Wainwright Building, St. Louis, Missouri, 1890 – 1891

Maps, Diagrams, and Projections

Map of Industrialized Europe in the 19th century
Alexandre-Gustave Eiffel, diagram of the construction of the Statue of Liberty

Key Terms

avant-garde
camera obscura
caricature
cartoon
daguerreotype
fixing
lithography
palette
palette knife
truss construction
steel-frame construction
suspension bridge

Videos

Corot (1796–1875)
18 MIN, 19??, TRC, Applause

Daumier's France
60 min, 1989, Films for the Humanities and Sciences

Eiffel Tower
50 min, 1995, VM

An Illustrated Guide to Caricature
60 min, HVC

Edouard Manet: Painter of Modern Life
27 min, 1983, HVC

Portrait of An Artist: Thomas Eakins
55 min, 1987, Clearvue

Statue of Liberty
60 min, 1985, Direct Cinema

Multiple-Choice Questions

1. Millet's *The Gleaners* combines

   a. social observation with Neoclassicism
   b. Renaissance monumentality with Romanticism
   c. Medieval feudalism with Romanticism
   d. social observation with Romanticism*

2. Which author and work do <u>not</u> match?

   a. Baudelaire -- *Les Fleurs de Mal*
   b. Zola -- *Madame Bovary**
   c. Dickens -- *A Tale of Two Cities*
   d. Balzac -- *La Comédie Humaine*
   e. Marx -- *Introduction to the Critique of Political Economy*

3. Rosa Bonheur was particularly drawn to images of

   a. lions
   b. athletes
   c. horses*
   d. city life

4. Courbet's patron, who financed the Realist Exhibition was

   a. Baudelaire
   b. Zola
   c. Flaubert
   d. Bruyas*

5. Courbet was an anarchist, so he painted

   a. mythological scenes
   b. the "beautiful" as defined by the Academy
   c. heightened emotional states not encountered in the real world
   d. scenes of people and settings in the real world*

6. _____ painted realistic scenes of poor and oppressed peoples

   a. Courbet
   b. Millet
   c. Daumier
   d. all of the above*

7. The central group of Courbet's *My Studio* includes

    a. a boy, a cat, a painter, a woman, and a landscape*
    b. a juggler, a crucifix, a cat, and a painter
    c. a painter, a woman, a boy, and a journalist
    d. a painter, a woman, a boy, and a peddler

8. For most of his life Daumier made a living

    a. as a painter
    b. as a caricaturist*
    c. as a cartoonist
    d. as a photographer

9. Gargantua is a (an)

    a. tyrant
    b. greedy king
    c. good-natured giant*
    d. gargoyle
    e. ogre from French folklore

10. Daumier was sentenced to jail for

    a. fraud
    b. satirizing the king*
    c. revolutionary activities
    d. defending freedom of the press
    e. forgery

11. Nadar's *Giant* refers to

    a. a French painting
    b. a French photograph
    c. a French balloon*
    d. a French folktale

12. Who of the following was <u>not</u> a nineteenth-century photographer?

    a. Cameron
    b. Nadar
    c. Brady
    d. Duckworth*

13. Which is not a feature of the Pre-Raphaelites' style?

    a. pastel colors*
    b. clear edges
    c. erotic subtexts
    d. figuration

14. In *Modern Painters*, Ruskin wrote a defense of

    a. Constable
    b. Turner*
    c. Cole
    d. Nash
    e. Millais

15. The figures in Manet's *Déjeuner sur l'Herbe* are identified as

    a. Manet's sister, brother-in-law, and Victorine
    b. Manet's model, brother-in-law, and sister
    c. Manet's model, Gustave Manet, and Ferdinand Leenhoff*
    d. Manet, his model, and his brother

16. Critics objected to *Déjeuner sur l'Herbe* because

    a. it was not sufficiently Classical*
    b. it was not colorful enough
    c. it contained the artist's self-portrait
    d. it was too much like a Renaissance painting

17. Manet's *Olympia* was inspired by

    a. *The Rokeby Venus*
    b. *The Venus of Urbino**
    c. Ingres' *Grande Odalisque*
    d. Canova's *Pauline*

18. Courbet objected to the *Olympia* because

    a. it was not realistic enough
    b. it was too Classical
    c. it was based on Renaissance prototypes
    d. it was too flat*

19. Manet objected to Courbet's *Woman with a Parrot* because

    a. it was too realistic
    b. it was too voluptuous*
    c. it was not Classical enough
    d. the parrot was a Romantic element

20. Which were <u>not</u> among the advantages of the Crystal Palace?

    a. it was fireproof*
    b. it was prefabricated
    c. it was relatively inexpensive
    d. it was constructed quickly

21. Until the middle of the nineteenth century, bridges were designed according to what method?

    a. suspension
    b. cantilever
    c. truss*
    d. post-and-lintel

22. Which is <u>not</u> true of the Brooklyn Bridge?

    a. it was designed by the Roeblings
    b. it has Gothic arches
    c. it has four huge parallel cables
    d. it was the first use of steel wire in a bridge
    e. it connects Brooklyn with the Bronx*

23. Sullivan's Prudential Building was new because

    a.   its outer layer did not hide the logic of its inner structure*
    b.   it used cast iron
    c.   it was built of brick
    d.   it avoided references to old architectural styles

24. Which is <u>not</u> true of the Statue of Liberty?

    a. it was sculpted by Bartholdi
    b. its frame was wrought by Eiffel
    c. it is on Ellis Island*
    d. it was constructed from 1875 to 1884

25. Which was <u>not</u> a new feature in the development of nineteenth-century skyscrapers?

     a. masonry and brick construction*
     b. power-driven elevators
     c. steel frames
     d. concrete reinforced with steel wire

26. Match the writer with the correct work

     a. Melville -- *Uncle Tom's Cabin*
     b. Alcott -- *Far From the Madding Crowd*
     c. Thoreau -- *Leaves of Grass*
     d. Darwin -- *Origin of Species**

27. The leading American Civil War photographer was

     a. Robert E. Lee
     b. Matthew Brady*
     c. Nadar
     d. Fox Talbot

CHAPTER 22:
Nineteenth-Century Impressionism

Key Works

Aerial view of the Place de l'Étoile, Paris, seen from the west
Aerial view of the Place de l'Opéra, Paris
Jean-Louis-Charles Garnier, façade of the Opéra, Paris, 1862 – 1875
Grand Staircase of the Opéra, Paris, engraving, 1880
Edouard Manet, *Zola*, exhibited 1868
Edouard Manet, *A Bar at the Folies-Bergère*, 1881 – 1882
Pierre-Auguste Renoir, *Moulin de la Galette*, 1876
Hilaire-Germain-Edgar Degas, *Absinthe*, 1876
Hilaire-Germain-Edgar Degas, *Visit to a Museum*, c. 1885
Hilaire-Germain-Edgar Degas, *Dancing Lesson*, 1883 – 1885
Hilaire-Germain-Edgar Degas, *At the Races*, 1886 – 1887
Eadweard Muybridge, *Galloping Horse*, 1878
Mary Cassatt, *The Boating Party*, 1893 – 1894
Mary Cassatt, *The Letter*, 1891
Berthe Morisot, *The Cradle*, 1873
Claude Monet, *Terrace at Sainte-Adresse*, c. 1866 – 1867
Claude Monet, *Bassin des Nymphéas (Waterlily Pond)*, 1904
Claude Monet, *Rouen Cathedral, West Façade, Sunlight*, 1894
Claude Monet, *Rouen Cathedral, the Portal and the Tower of Albane, the Morning*, 1894
Pierre-Auguste Renoir, *Pont-Neuf*, 1872
Camille Pissarro, *Place du Théâtre Français*, 1898
Hilaire-Germain-Edgar Degas, *Fourth Position Front, on the Left Leg*, c. 1880s
Auguste Rodin, *The Thinker*, 1879 – 1889
Edward Steichen, *Rodin – The Thinker*, 1902
Auguste Rodin, *Balzac*, 1892 – 1897
Auguste Rodin, *Balzac*, after 1917
Beauford Delaney, *Balzac by Rodin*, 1960s
Winslow Homer, *Breezing Up (A Fair Wind)*, 1873 – 1876
John Singer Sargent, *The Daughters of Edward Darley Boit*, 1882
James Abbott McNeill Whistler, *Nocturne in Black and Gold (The Falling Rocket)*, c. 1875
Whistler versus Ruskin: An Appeal to the Law, from *Punch*, December 7, 1878, p. 254

Maps, Diagrams, and Projections

Aerial view of the Place de l'Étoile, Paris, seen from the west
Aerial view of the Place de l'Opéra, Paris
Plan of the Opéra, Paris

Key Terms

casting
impasto
plein-air
naturalism
salon
japonisme

Window on the World
Japanese Woodblock Prints

Key Works

Utagawa Kunisada, *The Actor Seki Sanjuro in the Role of the Kiogoku Takumi*, 1860
Utagawa Kunisada, *Scene from Sukeroku*, c. 1835
Utagawa Toyokuni, *Portrait of the Actor Onoe Matsusuke as the Villain Kudo Suketsune*, 1800
Kitagawa Utamaro, *Young Woman with Blackened Teeth Examining her Features in a Mirror*,
    from the series *Ten Facial Types of Women*, c. 1792 – 1793
Keisei Eisen, *Oiran on Parade*, c. 1830
Utagawa Kuniyoshi, *Tairano Koremochi Waking up from a Drunken Sleep*, 1843
Katsushika Hokusai, *The Great Wave of Kanagawa*, from the series *Thirty-six Views of Mt. Fuji*,
    1831
Katsushika Hokusai, *The Horsetail Gatherer*, c. 1840
Utagawa Hiroshige, *Travelers in the Snow at Oi*, late 1830s
Utagawa Hiroshige, *Saruwaka-cho Theater*, 1856

Maps, Diagrams, and Projections

Map of Japan in the 19th century

Key Term

cartouche

Videos

Art of the Western World, 4-Pack
Volume 3: A Fresh View: Impressionism and Post-Impressionism
55 min, VM

Art Nouveau
14 min, 197?, TRC

Berthe Morisot: The Forgotten Impressionist
32 min, 1990, EFPS

Claude Monet: Legacy of Light
34 min, 1990, AA

Day in the Country: Impressionism & the French Landscape
57 min, 1989, VM

Degas, Erte and Chagall
110 min, 1977, VM

Degas in New Orleans
13 min, 1977, Phoenix

French Impressionism: A School for Happiness
60 min, 1990, MMA

Impressionism & Pre-Impressionism in France
12 min, 1991, Green Acre Video

Impressionism: Shimmering Visions
23 min, Clearvue

Impressionism in Art and Music
34 min, Clearvue

Impressionists on the Seine
30 min, Clearvue, Crystal

In Open Air: A Portrait of the American Impressionists
1983, 30 min, Phoenix, Phoenix, Smithsonian

Living Treasures of Japan
60 min, 1980, VM

Oriental Art
30 min, 1990, Clearvue

Portrait of An Artist: Degas
58 min, 198?, Clearvue

Portrait of An Artist: Mary Cassatt

30 min, 1977, Clearvue

Portrait of An Artist: Monet
27 min, 1990, Clearvue, HVC, Crystal

Seminars in Modern Art: Part 1: The Break with Tradition
15 min, Clearvue

Winslow Homer: An American Painter
15 min, Clearvue

CD-ROMs

A Passion for Art: Renoir, Cézanne, Matisse and Dr. Barnes
Mac/Windows, MFA

Impressionism
Mac/Windows, Clearvue

Multiple-Choice Questions

1. The Café Guerbois was

      a. a nightclub in Paris
      b. a meeting place for artists*
      c. a bourgeois coffee shop
      d. the title of an Impressionist painting

2. The Second Empire refers to

      a. Napoleon I's Empire
      b. Napoleon II's Empire
      c. the period in which Napoleon I's nephew ruled France*
      d. the period in which Napoleon II's son ruled France

3. The façade of the Paris Opéra is

      a. Classical in style
      b. Realist in style
      c. Impressionist in style
      d. Baroque in style*

4. Which is the <u>least</u> typical subject in Impressionism?

    a. café scenes
    b. military scenes*
    c. circus scenes
    d. landscapes
    e. theaters and concerts

5. Which is <u>not</u> a feature of Manet's *Zola*?

    a. *Olympia*
    b. a Japanese print
    c. a Chinese screen*
    d. Velázquez's *The Drinkers*

6. The expedition that forced Japan to end its isolation policy was
    led by

    a. Charles Darwin
    b. Vasco da Gama
    c. Henry Hudson
    d. Matthew Perry*

7. Edo refers to

    a. Eisenhower's World War II command
    b. a Chinese painter
    c. the former name of Tokyo*
    d. the former name of Shanghai
    e. a kind of Japanese theater

8. *Ukiyo-e* refers to

    a. a transient world*
    b. a Japanese play
    c. a Japanese courtesan
    d. a kind of kimono

9. *Kabuki* and *Noh* are

    a. characters in a Japanese play
    b. Japanese playwrights
    c. types of Japanese theater*
    d. types of Japanese actors

10. The two greatest woodblock artists who emphasized landscape were

    a. Hiroshige and Hokusai*
    b. Utagawa and Utamaro
    c. Kuniyoshi and Kinisada
    d. Utamaro and Kuniyoshi

11. Manet's *A Bar at the Folies-Bergères* is an example of

    a. Realism
    b. a still life
    c. a portrait
    d. a cropped view*

12. The tilted viewpoint of Degas' *Absinthe* suggests

    a. a child's perspective
    b. an inability to depict three-dimensional space
    c. a candid photograph*
    d. that the figures are drunk

13. Which artist sketched ballerinas from the wings of the stage?

    a. Monet
    b. Manet
    c. Renoir
    d. Degas*

14. An example of a silhouette can be found in

    a. Manet's chandelier in *A Bar at the Folies-Bergères*
    b. The rower in Cassatt's *The Boating Party**
    c. The flags in Monet's *Terrace at Sainte-Adresse*
    d. The vases in *The Daughters of Edward Darley Boit*

15. Berthe Morisot was

    a. Manet's sister
    b. Manet's wife
    c. Manet's mother
    d. Manet's sister-in-law*
    e. Manet's daughter

16. The water in the *Terrace at Sainte-Adresse* is an example of

   a. broken color*
   b. silhouetting
   c. flat color
   d. a pure hue

17. The artist most known for his "waterscapes" was

   a. Manet
   b. Monet*
   c. Renoir
   d. Degas

18. The artist who painted the same scene under different conditions
       of lighting was

   a. Manet
   b. Monet*
   c. Renoir
   d. Degas

19. "A heap of decomposing flesh" refers to

   a. Manet's *Olympia*
   b. Courbet's *Woman with a Parrot*
   c. Degas' Absinthe drinker
   d. Renoir's woman in the sun*

20. A particular aspect of Haussmann's renovations of Paris that
       appealed to Impressionist painters were

   a. the slums
   b. the department stores
   c. the boulevards*
   d. the restaurants
   e. the Opéra

21. Which is <u>not</u> an example of photographic influence on the
       Impressionist style?

   a. the cropped viewpoint
   b. the slanted floor
   c. the silhouette
   d. blurring
   e. a preference for black and white over color*

22. "It was the very embodiment of a tribute to genius" refers to

    a. Steichen's *Rodin--the Thinker*
    b. Rodin's *The Thinker*
    c. Manet's *Zola*
    d. Garnier's Opera
    e. Rodin's *Balzac**

23. Balzac was

    a. an Impressionist sculptor
    b. a French novelist*
    c. a French photographer
    d. a French actor

24. Which is not a feature of Sargent's Impressionism?

    a. the dissolution of form*
    b. the "slice of life" view
    c. the oblique view
    d. the use of *japonisme*

25. The dates of the American Civil War are

    a. 1860 to 1867
    b. 1850 to 1854
    c. 1860 to 1864*
    d. 1800 to 1804

26. The author of *The Gentle Art of Making Enemies* was

    a. Ruskin
    b. Prendergast
    c. Sargent
    d. Whistler*

27. The philosophy of "Art for Art's Sake" is basically

    a. formalist*
    b. iconographic
    c. feminist
    d. Marxist
    e. semiotic

28. The "pot of paint" refers to

   a. Monet's palette
   b. *The Falling Rocket**
   c. Renoir's thick brush strokes
   d. Degas' broken color

29. For Whistler

   a. color was probity and drawing was vice
   b. etching was superior to painting
   c. drawing was masculine and color was feminine*
   d. color was vice and drawing was musical

30. The trial between Whistler and Ruskin exemplified

   a. the rise of the art critic as a force in the art world*
   b. the insanity of misjudging art
   c. the conflict between the Rubenists and the Poussinists
   d. the new role of the art galleries and dealers
   e. the mishandling of a jury

CHAPTER 23:
Post-Impressionism and the Late Nineteenth Century

Key Works

Henri de Toulouse-Lautrec, *Quadrille at the Moulin Rouge*, 1892

Henri de Toulouse-Lautrec, *La Goulue at the Moulin Rouge*, 1891

Paul Cézanne, *Temptation of Saint Anthony*, c. 1870

Paul Cézanne, *Self-Portrait*, c. 1872

Paul Cézanne, *Still Life with Apples*, c. 1875 – 1877

Paul Cézanne, *Great Bathers*, 1898 – 1905

Paul Cézanne, *Mont Sainte-Victoire*, c. 1900

Georges Seurat, *Sunday Afternoon on the Island of La Grande Jatte*, 1884 – 1886

Georges Seurat, *Monkey*, 1884

Georges Seurat, detail, *Sunday Afternoon on the Island of La Grande Jatte*, 1884 – 1886

Vincent van Gogh, *Potato Eaters*, 1885

Vincent van Gogh, *Japonaiserie: Bridge in the Rain (after Hiroshige)*, 1887

Utagawa Hiroshige, *Sudden Shower at Ohashi Bridge at Ataka*, from the series *One Hundred Views of Edo*, 1857

Vincent van Gogh, *Bedroom at Arles*, 1889

Vincent van Gogh, sketch for *Bedroom at Arles*, 1888

Vincent van Gogh, *Wheatfield with Reaper*, 1889

Vincent van Gogh, *Starry Night*, 1889

Vincent van Gogh, studies for *Self-Portrait*, 1889

Vincent van Gogh, *Self-Portrait*, 1889

Paul Gauguin, *Self-Portrait with Halo*, 1889

Paul Gauguin, *Nevermore*, 1897

Stone Heads, Easter Island, 5th – 17th century

Paul Gauguin, *Idol with the Seashell*, c. 1893

Bob Thompson, *Crucifixion*, 1963 – 1964

Paul Gauguin, *Yellow Christ*, 1889

Lucas Cranach the Elder, *Crucifixion*, 1503

Gustave Moreau, *Orpheus*, 1865

Gustave Moreau, *Galatea*, 1880 – 1881

Edvard Munch, *The Scream*, 1893

Edvard Munch, *Anixety*, 1894

Aubrey Beardsley, *Salomé with the Head of John the Baptist*, 1893

Victor Horta, staircase of the Maison Tassel, Brussels, 1892

Hector Guimard, entrance to a Métro station, Paris, 1900

Gustav Klimt, *Ver Sacrum*, poster for the first Secession exhibition depicting Theseus and the Minotaur, c. 1898

Gustav Klimt, *Kiss*, 1908

Henri Rousseau, *Dream*, 1910

Key Terms

Pointillism
Poster art
Premixed color

Key Works

Stone heads, Easter Island, 5th – 17th century
Paul Gauguin, *Idol with the Seashell*, c. 1893

Maps, Diagrams, and Projections

Map of Oceania

Videos

Cézanne: The Man and His Mountain
60 min, 1987, HVC

Georges Seurat: Point, Counterpoint
75 min, 1987, HVC, Crystal

Great Masters Series: Toulouse-Lautrec
52 min, 1993, NDM

Henri de Toulouse-Lautrec
55 min, 1991, HVC

History Through Art: The Pre-Modern Era
40 min, Clearvue

Munch and Ensor: Fathers of Expressionism
23 min, 1994, VM

Portrait of An Artist: Gauguin
45 min, 1990, Clearvue

Portrait of An Artist: Toulouse-Lautrec
60 min, 1988, Clearvue

Portrait of An Artist: Van Gogh in Arles
58 min, 1996, Clearvue

Seminars in Modern Art: Part 2: Reconstruction of Space
15 min, Clearvue

Vanished Culture – Easter Island
44 min, 1994, VM, Facets

Van Gogh
6 min, Phoenix

CD-ROMs

History Through Art: The Pre-Modern Era
Mac/Windows
Clearvue

Masterworks of Japanese Painting
Mac/Windows, MFA

Musee D'Orsay: A Post Impressionist Perspective
Videodisk, Mac , MFA

Van Gogh: Starry Night – A Matter of History, A History of Matter
Mac/Windows, MFA

Multiple-Choice Questions

1. Two important Post-Impressionist trends were

    a. emotion and realism
    b. formalism and figuration
    c. structure and emotion*
    d. figuration and abstraction

2. The Post-Impressionist most known for his posters was

    a. Gauguin
    b. Cézanne
    c. Van Gogh
    d. Seurat
    e. Toulouse-Lautrec*

3. Generally the French posters of the 19th century were

    a. woodblock prints

b. engravings
c. etchings
d. lithographs*
e. photographs

4. La Goulue was a

   a. circus performer
   b. waitress
   c. dancer*
   d. restaurant
   e. café

5. The artist best known for his apples was

   a. Van Gogh
   b. Cézanne*
   c. Cranach
   d. Seurat

6. The artist known for his crystalline, structured brushstrokes is

   a. Van Gogh
   b. Gauguin
   c. Munch
   d. Cézanne*
   e. Rousseau

7. The two Post-Impressionist artists who had a stormy friendship were

   a. Van Gogh and Cézanne
   b. Cézanne and Zola
   c. Seurat and Munch
   d. Gauguin and Van Gogh*

8. La Grande Jatte refers to

   a. an island in the Seine*
   b. a restaurant in Paris
   c. a large dance-hall in Paris
   d. an overweight French dancer

9. Which term best describes Seurat's brushstrokes?

   a. blurred
   b. divisionist*

c. spiraling

d. smooth

10. "Potato Eaters" refers to

    a. beggars
    b. homeless people
    c. farmers
    d. miners*
    e. ministers

11. Georges Seurat was not an Impressionist because he

    a. used broad brushstrokes that conveyed how the world looked to him
    b. used a scientific technique to convey how light was perceived by the eye*
    c. embraced the spontaneity of nature and the outdoors
    d. relied on the teachings of Jung to comment on the human condition

12. Père Tanguy was

    a. Van Gogh's father
    b. Gauguin's father
    c. a priest
    d. an art dealer*
    e. a French philosopher

13. The artist who copied Hiroshige's *Sudden Shower at Ohahsi Bridge at Ataka* was

    a. Van Gogh*
    b. Cézanne
    c. Seurat
    d. Manet
    e. Monet

14. "Theo" refers to

    a. a book by Van Gogh
    b. Van Gogh's brother*
    c. Van Gogh's father
    d. Van Gogh's son
    e. Van Gogh's art teacher

15. The Post-Impressionist who painted the most self-portraits was
    a. Cézanne
    b. Toulouse-Lautrec
    c. Munch

d. Van Gogh*

e. Seurat

16. The Post-Impressionist who began as an Impressionist, then identified with the Symbolists and the Nabis was

    a. Cézanne

    b. Toulouse-Lautrec

    c. Munch

    d. Gauguin*

    e. Van Gogh

17. The Post-Impressionist known for his paintings of Tahiti was

    a. Cézanne

    b. Toulouse-Lautrec

    c. Munch

    d. Gauguin*

    e. Van Gogh

18. Oceania includes which of the following?

    a. Micronesia, Polynesia, Melanesia, and New Guinea*

    b. Easter Island, Australia, New Zealand, and Hawaii

    c. Samoa, Tonga, New Guinea, and Easter Island

    d. South Island, Arnhem Land, Asmat, and Hawaii

19. Symbolists conveyed

    a. heightened emotion

    b. subjective reality

    c. references to Greek mythological stories, avoiding commentary on modern life

    d. a and b but not c*

20. Which is true of Symbolism?

    a. it was concerned with realistic social issues

    b. it was heroic in character

    c. it was preoccupied with the irrational*

    d. its colors tend to be the primary hues

21. A maenad is a

    a. follower of Medea

    b. follower of Dionysos*

c. follower of Orpheus

d. follower of Hermes

22. Polyphemos was

a. a musician

b. a satyr

c. an Olympian

d. a Cyclops*

e. a dwarf

23. Redon created

a. with pastels

b. his own landscapes of gentle wildness

c. closely observed interiors of Victorian houses

d. a and b but no c*

24. The English word "symbol" is from the Greek, meaning

a. token*

b. sign

c. allegory

d. metaphor

e. simile

25. Symbolist paintings are most likely to have jarring

a. brushstrokes

b. color*

c. lines

d. spatial arrangements

e. formal distortion

26. Oscar Wilde was a spokesman for

a. Symbolism

b. Post-Impressionism

c. Abstraction

d. Aestheticism*

e. Art Nouveau

27. Beardsley's pictorial style can be described as

a. perverse and macabre*

b. elegant and courtly

c. Post-Impressionist

d. colorful

28. Art Nouveau was a European response against

    a. Abstraction

    b. Impressionism

    c. Aestheticism

    d. Industrialization*

    e. Symbolism

29. Art Nouveau artists used

    a.   geometry

    b.   photographic reality to show the grace in the everyday

    c.   organic forms like vines drawn from nature*

    d.   modern technological marvels to convey progress

30. Métropolitain refers to

    a. French cities

    b. French subways*

    c. French night clubs

    d. French urban planning

31. The purpose of the Vienna Secession was

    a. to establish an international style of painting

    b. to withdraw from the establishment

    c. to establish a forum of diverse styles*

    d. to support Academic naturalism

32. For Klimt, the Minotaur represented

    a. tyranny

    b. Impressionism

    c. Industrialization

    d. conservatism*

33. In Klimt's poster for the first Secession exhibition, the Gorgon head is

    a. naturalistic

    b. frontal*

    c. horned and fanged

    e.   Symbolist

34. "Le Douanier" refer to

    a. Beardsley
    b. Monet
    c. Seurat
    d. Rousseau*
    e. Gauguin

35. Yadwigha most likely refers to

    a. a Symbolist poet
    b. a reclining nude*
    c. a fiancée of Munch
    d. a Tahitian princess

36. The techniques of dream construction apply most obviously to which style?

    a. Post-Impressionism
    b. Symbolism
    c. Surrealism*
    d. Aestheticism

37. Which author does <u>not</u> match the work?

    a. Freud -- <u>The Call of the Wild</u>*
    b. Forster -- <u>A Room with a View</u>
    c. Chekhov -- <u>The Cherry Orchard</u>
    d. Wharton -- <u>The House of Mirth</u>

38. Which artist does <u>not</u> match the work?

    a. Cézanne -- *Temptation of Saint Anthony*
    b. Van Gogh -- *The Potato Eaters*
    c. Gauguin -- *The Yellow Christ*
    d. Munch -- *The Scream*
    e. Moreau -- *Idol with Seashell*

39. Which artist <u>does</u> match with the work?

    a. Van Gogh -- *Bedroom at Arles*
    b. Klimt -- *Salomé with the Head of John the Baptist*
    c. Moreau -- *The Dream*
    d. Cézanne -- *Galatea*
    f. Rousseau -- *La Goulue at the Moulin Rouge*

CHAPTER 24:
Turn of the Century: Early Picasso, Fauvism, Expressionism, and Matisse

Key Works

Pablo Picasso, *Old Guitarist*, 1903
Henri Matisse, *Notre-Dame in the Late Afternoon*, 1902
Henri Matisse, *Madame Matisse (The Green Line)*, 1905
Ernst Ludwig Kirchner, *The Street*, 1907
Ernst Ludwig Kirchner, *Five Women in the Street*, 1913
Emil Nolde, *Still Life with Masks*, 1911
Emil Nolde, drawing of an Oceanic canoe prow, 1911, for left hand mask in *Still Life with Masks*
Vassily Kandinsky, *Panel for Edwin R. Campbell No. 4* (formerly *Painting Number 201, Winter*), 1914
Vassily Kandinsky, *Several Circles, Number 323*, 1926
Franz Marc, *Large Blue Horses*, 1911
Käthe Kollwitz, *Whetting the Scythe*, 1905
Henri Matisse, *Harmony in Red*, 1908 – 1909
Henri Matisse, *Dance I*, 1909
Henri Matisse, *Piano Lesson*, 1916
Henri Matisse, *Jeannette V*, 1916
Seated figure, Bambara, Mali
Henri Matisse, *Decorative Figure in an Oriental Setting*, 1925
Henri Matisse, *Icarus*, plate 8 from *Jazz*, Paris, E. Tériade, 1947

Key Terms

crayon
glyptic art

Window on the World
African Art and the European Avant-Garde

Key Works

Male Ancestor statue, eyema-o-byeri, Gabon, northern Fang, Ndoumou substyle
Copper mask, Ife, Nigeria, 12th – 13th century
Baule ancestor, Ivory Coast
Bakota figure, Gabon
Bronze Oba head, Benin, mid-19th century
Head for an altar dedicated to Idia, the queen mother, Benin

Maps, Diagrams, and Projections

Map of Africa

Videos

African Art
47 min, Clearvue

African Art and Sculpture
1971, 21 min, Carousel Film & Video

African Carving: A Dogon Kanaga Mask
1975, 19 min, Phoenix

After Matisse
1979, 30 min, WNET/Thirteen

Art of the Western World, 4-Pack
Volume 4: Into the Twentieth Century
55 min, VM

Art History: A Century of Modern Art (10 programs)
15 min, 1989, AIT

Bauhaus: Its Impact on the World of Design (1919–1923)
19 min, 1991, TRC, Applause

Bonnard
49 min, 1990, HVC

Elements of Sculpture: Modern Sculpture, filmstrip
15 min, Clearvue

Emil Nolde
12 min, 197?, TRC

Expressionism
26 min, 1971, IFB

Franz Marc
21 min, 1987, TRC

Henri Matisse
16 min, 1971, IFB

History Through Art: The Twentieth Century
32 min, Clearvue

Kandinsky
8 min, 1987, TRC

Kathe Kollwitz
16 min, 1987, TRC

Matisse Voyages
57 min, MFA

Portrait of An Artist: Kandinsky
60 min, 1987, Clearvue, HVC, Crystal

Portrait of An Artist: Matisse
57 min, 1990, Clearvue

Picasso and Things: The Still Lifes of Picasso
15 min, Clearvue

Seminars in Modern Art: Part 3: Exploring the Heart and the Mind
15 min, Clearvue

Twentieth-Century Artistic Revolutions
32 min, Clearvue

CD-ROMs

Exploring Modern Art
Windows, Clearvue

History Through Art: The Twentieth Century
Mac/Windows, Clearvue

The Twentieth Century
Mac/Windows, Clearvue

Multiple-Choice Questions

1. 1917 marks the

   a. beginning of World War I
   b. onset of the Russian Revolution*
   c. the first years of the Great Depression
   d. the rise of National Socialism

2. The term "avant-garde" refers to

   a. newness*
   b. advancing troops in World War I
   c. the technological changes that led to urbanization
   d. the turn-of-the-century art dealers

3. Picasso's earliest distinctive style is referred to as

   a. Surrealist
   b. Rose Period
   c. Cubist
   d. Blue Period*
   e. Fauve

4. Which of the following do not match?

   a. Ife -- Nigeria
   b. Baule -- Benin*
   c. Fang -- Gabon
   d. Bakota -- Ivory Coast
   e. Bambara -- Mali

5. Which is not a reason that African sculptures influenced European artists in the early 20th century?

   a. they are geometric
   b. they are abstract
   c. they are naturalistic*
   d. they are magical

6. What was the most striking quality of Fauvism?

   a. line
   b. abstraction
   c. light

d. color*

e. jungle subject matter

7. Fauve artists looked to

    a. Polynesian and African sculpture
    b. the colors of Gauguin and van Gogh
    a. folk textiles and ceramics
    b. all of the above*

8. _____ exhibited with the Fauves but went his own way with his own religious art

    a. Henry Matisse
    b. Pablo Picasso
    c. Georges Rouault*
    d. Ernst Barlach

9. *The Green Line* is a painting of

    a. Mme. Matisse*
    b. a Paris street
    c. Horses
    d. Icarus
    e. a still life

10. As far as joy and spontaneity, _____'s art followed its own muses.

    a. Barlach
    b. Tatlin
    c. Matisse*
    d. Picasso

11. Matisse worked toward _____ in his art.

    a. balance
    b. purity
    c. serenity
    d. all of the above*

12. *Die Brücke* refers to

    a. a German painting of a bridge
    b. a German painting of a street
    c. a German art movement*
    d. a German artist

13. Kirchner was influenced by

    a. African sculpture
    b. medieval woodcuts
    c. the city and its crowd
    d. all of the above*

14. Worringer is the author of

    a. *Abstraction and Empathy**
    b. *The Principles of Art History*
    c. *Die Brücke*
    d. *Der Blaue Reiter*

15. Nolde's style is best described as

    a. Fauve
    b. Cubist
    c. Symbolist
    d. Expressionist*

16. The NKV refers to

    a. the Bridge
    b. the New Artists' Association*
    c. the Blue Rider
    d. the Bolshevik party

17. Which is true of Franz Marc's views of color?

    a. yellow was sunny and cheerful
    b. blue was depressive
    c. red was aggressive*
    d. gray was reserved for trees

18. Which is <u>not</u> true of Kollwitz?

    a. she came from a financially comfortable family
    b. she thought of herself as an Expressionist*
    c. she depicted the problems of the working classes
    d. she sympathized with German peasants
    e. her textures tend to be harsh

19. Matisse's *arabesques* refer to

    a. dancers
    b. musicians
    c. a kind of black curve*
    d. bright colors

20. *Salle Pleyel* refers to

    a. a dance hall
    b. a café
    c. an artist
    d. an author
    e. a concert hall*

21. Matisse's *Decorative Figure in an Oriental Setting* is set in

    a. Morocco*
    b. the Far East
    c. Easter Island
    d. Oceania
    e. Tahiti

22. Matisse's *Jazz* imagery is an example of

    a. Symbolism
    b. Fauvism
    c. *découpage**
    d. Cubism
    e. the Blue Rider

23. The Oba was a

    a. tribal magician
    b. divine king*
    c. Benin shaman
    d. Fang god

24. The "Punitive Expedition" sent to Benin was

    a. Portuguese
    b. French
    c. Dutch
    d. British*
    e. Nigerian

25. Which artist is correctly matched with his or her nationality?

    a. Marc -- French
    b. Matisse -- Moroccan
    c. Kandinsky -- Russian*
    d. Nolde -- Dutch
    e. Picasso -- French

26. As far as one can tell, the first completely non-figurative painter was

    a. Kandinsky*
    b. Marc
    c. Matisse
    d. Picasso
    e. Nolde

27. _____ admired animals and celebrated them in his work in Der Blaue Reiter

    a. Ernest Barlach
    b. Paul Gauguin
    c. Wassily Kandinsky
    d. Franz Marc*

28. 1914–1918 are the dates of

    a. World War II
    b. the American Civil War
    c. the Russian Revolution
    d. World War I*
    e. the Franco-Prussian War

29. Which artist is correctly matched with his work?

    a. Kirchner -- *The Large Blue Horses*
    b. Matisse -- *Jeannette V**
    c. Kandinsky -- *Notre-Dame in the Late Afternoon*
    d. Picasso -- *Still Life with Masks*
    e. Gauguin -- *Drawing of an Oceanic Canoe Prow*

30. The first Fauve exhibit was held in

    a. 1905*
    b. 1906
    c. 1900
    d. 1910

Turn of the Century: Early Picasso, Fauvism, Expressionism, and Matisse

CHAPTER 25:
Cubism, Futurism, and Related Twentieth-Century Styles

Key Works

Pablo Picasso, *Gertrude Stein*, 1906

Pablo Picasso, *Les Demoiselles d'Avignon*, June – July 1907

Mask from the Etoumbi region, People's Republic of the Congo

Mbuya (sickness) mask, Pende, Zaire

Marie Laurencin, *Group of Artists*, 1908

Georges Braque, *Violin and Pitcher*, 1909 – 1910

Pablo Picasso, *Head of a Woman*, 1909

Pablo Picasso, *Man with a Hat*, after December 3, 1912

Pablo Picasso, *Bull's Head*, 1943

Pablo Picasso, *Three Musicians*, 1921

Pablo Picasso, *Girl Before a Mirror*, 1932

Pablo Picasso, *Guernica*, 1937

Pablo Picasso, study for *Guernica*, 1937

Umberto Boccioni, *Unique Forms of Continuity in Space*, 1913

Fernand Léger, *The City*, 1919

Piet Mondrian, *Amaryllis*, 1909

Piet Mondrian, *Broadway Boogie Woogie*, 1942 – 1943

Marcel Duchamp, *Nude Descending a Staircase, No. 2*, 1912

Constantin Brancusi, *Mademoiselle Pogany*, Version I (1913) after a marble of 1912

Stuart Davis, *Lucky Strike*, 1921

Aaron Douglas, *From Slavery through Reconstruction* (from the series *Aspects of Negro Life*), 1934

Kazimir Malevich, *Composition with the Mona Lisa*, 1914

Kazimir Malevich, *Black Square*, 1929

Kazimir Malevich, *Self-Portrait*, 1933

Constantin Brancusi, *The Gate of the Kiss*, 1938

Constantin Brancusi, *The Kiss*, 1912

Constantin Brancusi, *The Endless Column*, 1937

Installation view, "Brancusi + Mondrian" exhibition, December 1982 – January 1983, Sidney Janis Gallery, New York

Frank Lloyd Wright, Robie House, Chicago, 1909

Perspective drawing and plan of the second floor of the Robie House

Frank Lloyd Wright, Fallingwater, Bear Run, Pennsylvania, 1936

Frank Lloyd Wright, Taliesin West, begun 1938, Arizona

Gerrit Rietveld, Schroeder House, Utrecht, The Netherlands, 1923 – 1924

Walter Gropius, plan of the Bauhaus, Dessau, Germany, 1925 – 1926

Vassily Kandinsky, *Composition 8*, 1923

Walter Gropius, the Bauhaus workshop wing, 1925 – 1926

Le Corbusier, Villa Savoye, Poissy-sur-Seine, France, 1928 – 1930

Le Corbusier, Notre-Dame-du-Haut, Ronchamp, France, 1950 – 1954

Ludwig Mies van der Rohe, Lake Shore Drive Apartment Houses, Chicago, 1950 – 1952

Maps, Diagrams, and Projections

Perspective drawing and plan of the second floor of the Robie House

Key Terms

assemblage
cantilever construction
collage
found object (or *objet trouvé*)
functionalism
installation
pre-stressed concrete
reinforced concrete
serigraphy
skeletal (or steel-frame) construction

Videos

African-American Art: Past and Present
3 videos, 30 min each, 1992, Clearvue

Albert Gleizes
16 min, 1971, IFB

Ansel Adams: Photographer
60 min, 1981, AA, PAV

The Avant-Garde in Russia: 1910–1930
60 min, 198?, Films for the Humanities

Breaking Free of the Earth: Kasmir Malevich 1878–1935
50 min, 199?, MFA

Cubism
6 min, 1957, Phoenix

Cubism
21 min, 1970, CFD

Cubist Epoch
53 min, VM

Die Brucke: The Birth of Modern Art in Germany

Chapter 25
Cubism, Futurism, and Related Twentieth-Century Styles

24 min, 196?, TRC

Fernand Leger (1881–1955)
14 min, 1987, TRC

Frank Lloyd Wright
75 min, 1990, Crystal

Frank Lloyd Wright: The Mike Wallace Interviews
53 min, 1957, TVC

Guernica—Genesis of a Painting (B&W)
60 min, 1963, CATA

Le Corbusier
46 min, VM

Malevich
54 min, Crystal

Malevich Suprematism (B&W)
9 min, 1970, MOMA

Mondrian
30 min, 1992, VM

Mondrian: From Naturalism to Abstraction
52 min, 1988, MFA

Picasso: War, Peace, Love
51 min, VM

Piet Mondrian: Mister Boogie Woogie Man
49 min, 1997, MFA

Portrait of An Artist: Picasso
81 min, Clearvue

Shock of Futurism
23 min, 199?, VM

Multiple-Choice Questions

1. *The Autobiography of Alice B. Toklas* is

    a. a book about Picasso
    b. a book about Alice B. Toklas
    c. a book about Gertrude Stein*
    d. a book about Cubism

2. Gertrude Stein was

    a. an art collector
    b. a writer
    c. a salonnière
    d. all of the above*
    e. none of the above

3. 1911 was the year of

    a. the opening of the Museum of Modern Art in New York
    b. the Cubist show in Paris*
    c. the first Cubist sculpture
    d. the beginning of World War I

4. Which is the correct order for Picasso?

    a. Blue Period, Rose Period, Surrealism, Collage, Cubism
    b. Analytic Cubism, Synthetic Cubism, Collage, Rose Period
    c. Analytic Cubism, Collage, Synthetic Cubism, Surrealism*
    d. Rose Period, Collage, Surrealism, Analytic Cubism

5. Picasso's *Bull's Head* is an example of

    a. collage
    b. assemblage*
    c. *découpage*
    d. non-figuration

6. The title "Women of Avignon" refers to

    a. Spanish prostitutes*
    b. Women in the South of France
    c. Parisian prostitutes
    d. African women in Madrid

7. In *Girl Before a Mirror*, Picasso aims at achieving

    a. formal reality
    b. figurative reality
    c. spiritual reality
    d. psychological reality*
    e. historical reality

8. 1936 to 1939 are the dates of

    a. World War II
    b. the Spanish Civil War*
    c. the Italian Civil War
    d. the rise of Communism

9. Which is <u>not</u> alluded to in the iconography of *Guernica*?

    a. the Pietà
    b. the Minotaur
    c. the Crucifixion
    d. the Resurrection*
    e. the sun

10. Nonobjective art is

    a.   abstract, as drawn from nature but changed
    b.   unrelated to the outward, physical world
    a.   highly controversial
    b.   b and c but not a*

11. Which was <u>not</u> a feature of Futurism?

    a. the destruction of the museums
    b. the elimination of archaeology
    c. the exaltation of technology
    d. the promotion of feminism*

12. The author of the Futurist Manifesto was

    a. Marinetti*
    b. Boccioni
    c. Léger
    d. Mondrian
    e. Duchamp

13. 1913 is the date of

    a. the Futurist Manifesto
    b. the Armory Show*
    c. the end of World War I
    d. the Cubist show in Paris

14. Match the artist with his work

    a. Davis -- *Broadway Boogie Woogie*
    b. Duchamp -- *Mlle. Pogany*
    c. Malevich -- *Black Square**
    d. Leonardo -- *Composition with the Mona Lisa*
    e. Brancusi -- Villa Savoye

15. Who said "What is real is not the outer form, but the idea, the essence of things"?

    a. Barlach
    b. Brancusi*
    c. Matisse
    d. Morissot

16. "Orderly heap of broken violins" referred to

    a. Braque -- *Violin and Pitcher*
    b. Davis -- *Lucky Strike*
    c. Picasso -- *Women of Avignon*
    d. Brancusi -- *Endless Column*
    e. Duchamp -- *Nude Descending a Staircase, No.2**

17. "Lines to a Lady Egg" was written about

    a. *The Women of Avignon*
    b. *Mlle. Pogany**
    c. Gertrude Stein
    d. Marie Laurencin
    e. The girl in *Girl Before the Mirror*

18. The Harlem Renaissance refers to

    a. a 15th century Dutch city
    b. Italian 15th-century style
    c. a revival of Classics in New York City
    d. a black American cultural movement*
    e. African American 15th-century painting

19. Match the artist with his style

    a. Brancusi -- Suprematism
    b. Mondrian -- De Stijl*
    c. Wright -- Cubism
    d. Gropius -- Prairie Style

20. *The Non-objective World* was written by

    a. Malevich*
    b. Kandinsky
    c. Mondrian
    d. Duchamp
    e. Le Corbusier

21. "Brancusi + Mondrian" was

    a. a poem on the avant-garde
    b. a book on art
    c. an exhibition*
    d. a manifesto of modernism

22. Match the structure with its location

    a. the Robie House -- Ohio
    b. the Gate of the Kiss -- Romania*
    c. the Schroeder House -- Germany
    d. the Bauhaus -- Holland
    e. Taliesin West -- Colorado

23. The Chrysler Building is in the _____ style.

    a. Art Nouveau
    b. Abstract Expressionist
    c. Bauhaus
    d. Art Deco*

24. Which is <u>not</u> a feature of Fallingwater?

    a. cantilever construction
    b. reinforced concrete
    c. glass walls
    d. skeletal construction*
    e. local rock

25. Which best fulfills the description "a machine for living?"

    a. Villa Savoye*
    b. the Bauhaus
    c. Taliesin West
    d. Lake Shore Drive Apartments

26. Which work and author do <u>not</u> match?

    a. Pearl Buck -- *The Good Earth*
    b. Erich Maria Remarque -- *All Quiet on the Western Front*
    c. Marcel Proust -- *Zuleika Dobson**
    d. Sinclair Lewis -- *Main Street*
    e. Margaret Mead -- *Coming of Age in Samoa*

27. Which of the following shows no influence of African masks?

    a. Picasso, *The Women of Avignon*
    b. Brancusi, *Mlle. Pogany*
    c. Picasso, *Bull's Head*
    d. Picasso, *Gertrude Stein*
    e. Malevich, *Self-portrait**

28. 1939–45 are the dates of

    a. World War II*
    b. the Spanish Civil War
    c. the Franco-Prussian War
    d. the American Civil War
    e. the Vietnam War

29. The first Cubist sculpture was a bronze cast by

    a. Braque
    b. Léger
    c. Boccioni
    d. Picasso*
    e. Brancusi

CHAPTER 26:
Dada, Surrealism, Fantasy, and the United States between the Wars

Key Works

Marcel Duchamp, Replica of *L.H.O.O.Q.*, from "Boîte-en-Valise," Paris, 1919

Marcel Duchamp, *Fountain (Urinal)*, 1917

Marcel Duchamp, *To Be Looked at (From the Other Side of the Glass) with One Eye, Close to, for Almost an Hour*, Buenos Aires, 1918

Jean Arp, *The Dancer*, 1928

Man Ray, *Indestructible Object (or Object to be Destroyed)*, 1964, replica of the original of 1923

Giorgio de Chirico, *Place d'Italie*, 1912

Man Ray, *Le Violon d'Ingres*, 1924

Paul Klee, *Mask of Fear*, 1932

Zuni war god from Arizona or New Mexico

Salvador Dalí, *The Persistence of Memory*, 1931

Joan Miró, *Dog Barking at the Moon*, 1926

Joan Miró, *Spanish Dancer*, 1945

René Magritte, *The False Mirror*, 1928

René Magritte, *Time Transfixed (La Durée poignardée)*, 1938

Max Ernst, *The King Playing with the Queen*, 1944

Mossi whistle, Upper Volta

Max Ernst with his Kachina doll collection, 1942. Photograph by James Thrall Soby

Alberto Giacometti, *Large Standing Woman III*, 1960 and Piet Mondrian, *Composition with Red, Yellow, and Blue*, 1935 – 1942

Henry Moore, *Reclining Figure*, New York, 1957 – 1958

Henry Moore, *Helmet Head No. 1*, 1950

Alexander Calder, *Big Red*, 1959

Grant Wood, *American Gothic*, 1930

Jacob Lawrence, *Harriet Tubman Series, No. 7*, 1939 – 1940

Edward Hopper, *Gas*, 1940

James van der Zee, *Portrait of Couple, Man with Walking Stick*, 1929

James van der Zee, *Garveyite*, c. 1924

Walker Evans, *Shoeshine Sign in a Southern Town*, 1936

Dorothea Lange, *Migratory Cotton Picker, Eloy, Arizona*, 1940

Diego Rivera, *Ancient Mexico*, from the *History of Mexico* fresco murals, 1929 – 1935

Frida Kahlo, *Marxism Will Give Health to the Sick*, 1954

Alfred Stieglitz, *Equivalent*, 1923

Edward Weston, *Two Shells*, 1927

Arthur Dove, *Goin' Fishin'*, 1925

Arthur Dove, *Fog Horns*, 1929

Georgia O'Keeffe, *Black and White*, 1930

Georgia O'Keeffe, *Cow's Skull with Calico Roses*, 1931

Alfred Stieglitz, *Georgia O'Keeffe: A Portrait: Hands and Bones (15)*, 1930

Agnes Pelton, *The Blest*, 1941

Anna Mary Robertson (Grandma) Moses, *Old Checkerboard House*, 1944
Horace Pippin, *Domino Players*, 1943

Key Terms

Automatism
beaverboard
casein
conceptual art
found object
frottage
mobile
Rayograph
stabile

**Window on the World
Hopi Kachinas**

Ansel Adams, *Winnowing Grain*, Taos Pueblo, c. 1929.
Black Ogre, Hopi Kachina.
Butterfly Maiden, Hopi Kachina.

Videos

The Age of Steel: Diego Rivera
28 min, WNET/Thirteen

Armory Show
59 min, 1963, NY State Education Dept

Bernier on Ernst
30 min, 1974, NY State Education Department

Dada
31 min, 1969, IFB

Definitive Dali: A Lifetime Retrospective
75 min, 1988, AA, HVC

Femme/Woman: A Tapestry by Joan Miró
15 min, 1981, NGA

Balthus at the Pompidou

Dada, Surrealism, Fantasy, and the United States between the Wars

28 min, 1984, MOMA

Birth of a Bronze (with Jacques Lipschitz)
18 min, 1959, Coronet/MTI

The Frescoes of Diego Rivera
35 min, 1986, HVC, Crystal

Georgia O'Keeffe
59 min, VM, HVC

Germany-Dada
55 min, 199?, VM, Crystal

Henry Moore
52 min, 1990, MFA, Crystal

Henry Moore and Landscape
26 min, 1989, NDM

Hopi Pottery
65 min, 1990, VM

Hopper's Silence
46 min, 1981, Phoenix

Indian Crafts: Hopi, Navajo and Iroquois
1980, 11 min, Phoenix

Jacob Lawrence: An Intimate Portrait
25 min, Crystal

Joan Miró: Constellations – The Color of Poetry
52 min, 1994, MFA

Klee
25 min, 1992, VM

Marcel Duchamp: A Game of Chess
56 min, 1963, MFA, HVC, Crystal

Max Ernst: Journey into the Subconscious
12 min, 1987, TRC

Mona Lisa to Dada
17 min, Phoenix

Monsieur Rene Magritte
50 min, MFA

Portrait of An Artist: Diego Rivera
35 min, Clearvue

Portrait of An Artist: Duchamp
56 min, Clearvue

Portrait of An Artist: Frida Kahlo
62 min, 1986, Clearvue, HVC

Portrait of An Artist: Georgia O'Keeffe
60 min, 1977, Clearvue

Portrait of An Artist: Joan Miró
60 min, 1987, Clearvue

Portrait of An Artist: René Magritte
60 min, 1991, Clearvue

Surrealism
7 min, 1961 Phoenix

Surrealism in Art and Music
38 min, Clearvue

CD-ROMs

Surrealism
Mac/Windows, Clearvue

The Celebrative Spirit: 1937–1943
Mac, MFA

Multiple-Choice Questions

1. "The Wars" in the title of this chapter refer to

      a. World War II and the Vietnam War
      b. the Spanish Civil War and World War II
      c. World War I and World War II*
      d. The Spanish Civil War and the Vietnam War

Dada, Surrealism, Fantasy, and the United States between the Wars

2. "The lost generation" was a phrase coined by

    a. Ernest Hemingway
    b. F. Scott Fitzgerald
    c. Zelda Fitzgerald
    d. Gertrude Stein*
    e. Frank Lloyd Wright

3. The Cabaret Voltaire was located in

    a. Zurich*
    b. Paris
    c. Avignon
    d. Madrid
    e. Utrecht

4. Who of the following was not a Dadaist?

    a. Arp
    b. Man Ray
    c. Duchamp
    d. Ball
    e. Pelton*

5. *L.H.O.O.Q.* is an example of a

    a. collage
    b. Ready-made
    c. graffiti poster
    d. Ready-made-Aided*
    e. found object

6. The first Ready-made was

    a. a urinal
    b. a shovel*
    c. a seashell
    d. a poster of the *Mona Lisa*

7. Which is least characteristic of Dada?

    a. nonsense
    b. nihilism
    c. punning
    d. Classicism*
    e. iconoclasm

8. Match the author with the correct work

    a. Breton -- *The Guest Expulsed*
    b. Arp -- *Jokes and their Relation to the Unconscious*
    c. Stieglitz -- *Camera Work**
    d. Man Ray -- *Wrong Wrong*
    e. Apollinaire -- *The Interpretation of Dreams*

9. Which is true of the Rayograph?

    a. it is a black and white photograph made with a camera
    b. it is a black and white photograph made without a camera*
    c. it is a black and white collage
    d. it is the name of a painting by Man Ray

10. "Violin d'Ingres" is a French expression

    a. referring to a painting by Ingres
    b. which is the title of a painting by Man Ray
    c. meaning "hobby"*
    d. meaning "modern odalisque"

11. Match the artist with his country of birth

    a. Klee -- Germany
    b. Ernst -- Holland
    c. O'Keeffe -- Ireland
    d. Lawrence -- England
    e. Magritte -- Belgium*

12. Which is <u>not</u> a Surrealist element in Miró's *Dog Barking at the Moon*?

    a. the colors of the ladder
    b. the colors of the dog
    c. the placement of the dog*
    d. the space occupied by the ladder

13. Which of the following is not Surrealist?

    a.   Salvador Dalí
    b.   Giorgio de Chirico
    c.   Réne Magritte
    d.   Georges Braque*

14. "I believe in the future resolution of the states of dream and reality, in appearance so contradictory, in a sort of absolute reality, or surreality." Who said this?

    a. André Breton*
    b. Gustave Caillebotte
    c. Gustave Moreau
    d. Gustave Courbet

15. Surrealists

    a. used titles that were intentionally provocative
    b. felt dreams were another level of reality
    c. embraced Jungian symbolism
    d. all of the above*

16. Dalí's "paranoiac-critical" method

    a. inner truth
    b. inner irrationality as reflected in dreams
    c. showed the cruel reality of the world as it was
    d. a and b but not c*

17. Simultaneous viewpoint is an element of

    a. Cubism and Surrealism*
    b. Surrealism and Futurism
    c. Cubism and Pointillism
    d. Dada and Futurism

18. The so-called veristic Surrealism of Magritte means that

    a. his forms are imaginary
    b. his forms are clear and realistic but their combinations are surreal*
    c. his forms are surreal and fantastic
    d. his arrangements make manifest sense but latent nonsense

19. The Surrealist artist who envisioned himself as a shaman was

    a. Magritte
    b. Klee
    c. Miró
    d. Ernst*
    e. Giacometti

20. A Kachina is a

    a. Hopi toy
    b. Hopi paintings
    c. Hopi spirit*
    d. Hopi mask

21. Pueblos are

    a. communal living quarters*
    b. rock-cut houses
    c. Hopi temples
    d. Hopi tombs

22. Which artist is <u>not</u> matched with his work?

    a. Ernst -- *King Playing with the Queen*
    b. Lange -- *Two Shells**
    c. Giacometti -- *Reclining Figure*
    d. Stieglitz -- *Equivalent*
    e. Magritte -- *The False Mirror*

23. Who of the following was most interested in "found objects?"

    a. O'Keeffe
    b. Van der Zee
    c. de Chirico
    d. Moore*
    e. Giacometti

24. Which most accurately describes a mobile?

    a. it moves when its motor is activated
    b. it hangs on a wall
    c. it hangs from the ceiling
    d. it moves when there is an air current
    e. c and d*

25. *American Gothic* is an example of

    a. Gothic Revival
    b. Romanticism
    c. Social Realism
    d. Regionalism*
    e. photography

26. Which work inspired the CBS logo?

    a. *Le Violin d'Ingres*
    b. *The False Mirror**
    c. *Helmet Head No.1*
    d. *Fog Horns*
    e. *Goin' Fishin'*

27. The "underground railroad" was

    a. a subway line in New Orleans
    b. an escape route for Civil War spies
    c. an escape route for slaves*
    d. a tunnel planned for the English Channel

28. Which work are you most likely to see on a box of cereal?

    a. *Gas*
    b. *Winnowing Grain*
    c. *Old Checkerboard House*
    d. *American Gothic**

29. Who of the following was <u>not</u> involved in the Harlem Renaissance?

    a. Harriet Tubman*
    b. Jacob Lawrence
    c. Marcus Garvey
    d. James van der Zee

30. FSA stands for

    a. Foreign Socialist Association
    b. Farmers' Socialist Administration
    c. Farm Security Administration*
    d. Freed Slaves of America

31. _____ photographed the rural poor during the Great Depression

    a. Alfred Stieglitz
    b. Buckminster Fuller
    c. Matthew Brady
    d. Dorothea Lange*

32. Which is not a feature of Rivera's History of Mexico murals?

    a. Cubism
    b. Non-representational forms*
    c. Leftist politics
    d. references to Mesoamerican history
    e. Surrealism

33. Rivera's wife, also a painter, was

    a. Georgia O'Keeffe
    b. Agnes Pelton
    c. Dorothea Lange
    d. Frida Kahlo*

34. Frida Kahlo painted

    a. her own life
    b. her subjective reality as wife of a great Mexican muralist
    c. symbols of her existential pain
    d. all of the above*

35. The 291 was

    a. the address of the Seventh Regiment Armory
    b. the address of the Museum of Modern Art
    c. an avant-garde art gallery in New York*
    d. Gertrude Stein's apartment number in Paris
    e. An issue of *Camera Work*

36. Which is not an element of Dove's *Goin' Fishin'*?

    a. denim
    b. bamboo
    c. bark
    d. buttons*

37. Which is not a subject of American folk art?

    a. pinball machines*
    b. cigar-store Indians
    c. carved gravestones
    d. shop signs
    e. weather vanes

38. Which is <u>not</u> a feature of Grandma Moses' *Checkerboard House*?

    a. the influence of embroidery
    b. references to industrialization*
    c. Romanticism
    d. local imagery

39. Match the author with his work

    a. Kafka -- *Truth and Logic*
    b. E.E. Cummings -- *The Enormous Room**
    c. T.E. Lawrence -- *Lady Chatterley's Lover*
    d. Homer -- *Ulysses*
    e. Sean O'Casey -- *A Passage to India*

40. Chagall did not make images

    a. full of symbolism
    b. filled with fantasy
    c. of the cruel hardship of Russian peasant life before the Great Revolution*
    d. for stained glass images for the cathedral at Reims

CHAPTER 27:
Abstract Expressionism

Key Works

Hans Hofmann, *The Gate*, 1959 – 1960
Josef Albers, *Study for Homage to the Square*, 1968
Arshile Gorky, *The Artist and his Mother*, c. 1926 – 1936
Arshile Gorky, *Garden in Sochi*, c. 1943
Jackson Pollock, *Going West*, 1934 – 1935
Jackson Pollock, *Guardians of the Secret*, 1943
Hans Namuth, *Jackson Pollock Painting*, 1950
Michael Heron, *Navajo Crafts*, creating a sand painting
Yei god, sand painting, (Navajo) 20th century
Jackson Pollock, *White Light*, 1954
Franz Kline, *Mahoning*, 1956
Willem de Kooning, *Woman and Bicycle*, 1952 – 1953
Helen Frankenthaler, *The Bay*, 1963
Mark Rothko, *Baptismal Scene*, 1945
Mark Rothko, *Number 15*, 1957
Adolph (Ad) Reinhardt, *Abstract Painting (Black)*, 1965
Frank Stella, *Empress of India*, 1965
Frank Stella, *Tahkt-i-Sulayman I*, 1967
Ellsworth Kelly, *Spectrum III*, 1967
Installation view of *Classic Modernism: Six Generations*, r to l: Ellsworth Kelley, *Red, Yellow, Blue*, 1965; Piet Mondrian, *Trafalgar Square*, 1939. Exhibition held November 15 – December 29, 1990, Sidney Janis Gallery, New York.
Richard Diebenkorn, *Ocean Park No. 129*, 1984
Jean Dubuffet, *The Reveler*, 1964
Spirit figure from Wapo Creek, Papua New Guinea
Francis Bacon, *Portrait of Isabel Rawsthorne Standing in a Street in Soho*, 1967
Isamu Noguchi, *Kouros*, 1944 – 1945
David Smith, *Cubi XVIII* and *Cubi XVII*, 1963 – 1964
Louise Nevelson, *Black Wall*, 1959

Key Terms

acrylic
airbrush
drip technique
stain painting

Videos

20th Century American Art: Highlights of the Whitney Permanent Collection
26 min, 1982, Clearvue

20th Century Art at the Metropolitan Museum
60 min, 198?, Clearvue

Abstract Expressionism
40 min, 1990, Crystal

American Art '85
28 min, 1985, HVC

American Art Today: Whitney Biennial Exhibitions
28 min, 1987, HVC, Crystal

Expressionism
7 min, 1961, Phoenix

Francis Bacon
55 min, 1985, HVC

Frankenthaler: Toward a New Climate
30 min, 1977, HVC

Franz Kline Remembered
29 min, Direct Cinema

In Search of Rothko
22 min, Direct Cinema

Jackson Pollock: Ideas in Paint
51 min, 1992, HVC

Portrait of An Artist: Isamu Noguchi
54 min, 1990, Clearvue

Portrait of An Artist: Jackson Pollock
52 min, 1992, Clearvue

Portrait of An Artist: Louise Nevelson
30 min, 1987, Clearvue

Seminars in Modern Art: Part 4: Contemporary Trends
15 min, Clearvue, HVC, Crystal

Multiple-Choice Questions

1. In 1942 Peggy Guggenheim opened

    a. the Museum of Modern art in New York
    b. the Paris Museum of Modern Art
    c. the Art of This Century Gallery*
    d. the Venice Guggenheim

2. Hitler's exhibition of "degenerate art" consisted mainly of

    a. Classical statues
    b. avant-garde art*
    c. photography
    d. lithography
    e. Surrealism

3. Which is true?

    a. Albers taught at Black Mountain College in South Carolina
    b. Hofmann taught at Yale
    c. Hofmann taught at Black Mountain College in South Carolina
    d. Albers taught at Yale*
    e. Albers taught at the Art Students' League and in North Carolina

4. "Homage to the Square" is

    a. a series of paintings by Hofmann
    b. a book by Albers
    c. a manifesto written by Kelly
    d. a series of paintings by Albers*
    e. a painting by Hofmann

5. Who of the following is <u>not</u> an action painter?

    a. Albers*
    b. Gorky
    c. Pollock
    d. de Kooning

6. The term Abstract Expressionism was first used to define the style of

        a. Pollock
        b. Kandinsky*
        c. Albers
        d. de Kooning
        e. Frankenthaler

7. Match the artist with the correct country of birth

        a. de Kooning -- Germany
        b. Stella -- Italy
        c. Gorky -- Armenia*
        d. Rothko -- the United States
        e. Noguchi -- China

8. Which artist most often depicted biomorphic shapes?

        a. de Kooning
        b. Noguchi
        c. Gorky
        d. Smith
        e. b and c*

9. The two leading art critics of Abstract Expressionism were

        a. Bloomberg and Rosenberg
        b. Steinberg and Bloomberg
        c. Greenberg and Wölfflin
        d. Worringer and Wölfflin
        e. Greenberg and Rosenberg*

10. Navaho sand painting inspired which artist?

        a. Rothko
        b. Ernst
        c. Pollock*
        d. Frankenthaler
        e. Noguchi

11. "Jack the Dripper" referred to

    a. Frankenthaler
    b. de Kooning
    c. Gorky
    d. Pollock*
    e. Hofmann

12. Which is not true of acrylic?

    a. it is water-based
    b. it can be used on paper but not canvas*
    c. it comes in bright colors
    d. it dries quickly and does not fade
    e. it can be poured, dripped, or splattered

13. Who of the following is not a Color Field painter?

    a. Mondrian*
    b. Rothko
    c. Kelly
    d. Reinhardt
    e. Stella

14. Which artist is correctly matched with his or her work?

    a. Diebenkorn -- *The Artist and his Mother*
    b. Kelly -- *Ocean Park No.129*
    c. Noguchi -- *Kouros**
    d. Nevelson -- *the Cubi Series*
    e. Gorky -- *Homage to the Square*

15. Which is least true of Dubuffet?

    a. he collected non-Western art
    b. he was a monochromatic painter*
    c. he liked textured surfaces
    d. he was a figurative abstractionist
    e. he was French

16. The artist in this chapter who made furniture, playgrounds, and public sculpture gardens was

     a. Smith
     b. Nevelson
     c. Kline
     d. Noguchi*
     e. Bacon

17. Match the author with the correct work

     a. James Baldwin -- *The Double Helix*
     b. Albert Camus -- *Waiting for Godot*
     c. Graham Greene -- *To the Finaland Station*
     d. Jean-Paul Sartre -- *Being and Nothingness**
     e. Ingmar Bergman -- *Lolita*

18. Who of the following most likely used acrylic?

     a. Frankenthaler*
     b. Rothko
     c. Gorky
     d. Smith
     e. Noguchi

Key Works

Richard Hamilton, *Just what is it that makes today's homes so different, so appealing?*, 1956
Jasper Johns, *Three Flags*, 1958
Larry Rivers, *Portrait of Frank O'Hara*, 1961
Robert Rauschenberg, *Retroactive I*, 1964
Andy Warhol, *Campbell's Soup I (Tomato)*, 1968
Andy Warhol, *Elvis I and II*, 1964
Roy Lichenstein, *Torpedo...Los!*, 1963
Roy Lichtenstein, *Little Big Picture*, 1965
Richard Lindner, *Rock-Rock*, 1966 – 1967
R. B. Kitaj, *Juan de la Cruz*, 1967
Tom Wesselman, *Great American Nude No. 57*, 1964
Wayne Thiebaud, *Thirteen Books*, 1992
Claes Oldenburg, *Giant Soft Drum Set (Ghost Version)*, 1972
Claes Oldenburg, *Clothespin,* Central Square, Philadelphia, 1976
George Segal, *Chance Meeting*, 1989
George Segal, *Sidney Janis Looking at a Painting by Mondrian*, 1967
Marisol, *The Last Supper* (installed at the Sidney Janis Gallery), 1982
Niki de Saint-Phalle, *Black Venus*, 1965 – 1967
Bridget Riley, *Aubade (Dawn),* 1975
Donald Judd, *Untitled*, 1967
Dan Flavin, *Untitled (in Honor of Harold Joachim)*, 1977
Agnes Martin, *Untitled #9*, 1990
Eva Hesse, *Metronomic Irregularity I*, 1966
Eva Hesse, *Laocoön*, 1966
Laocoön and his Two Sons
Joseph Beuys, *The Pack*, 1969
Joseph Beuys, *Coyote, I Like America and America Likes Me*, 1974
Joseph Beuys, detail, *Coyote, I Like America and America Likes Me*, 1974
Joseph Kosuth, *Art As Idea as Idea*, 1966

Key Terms

Encaustic
Serial art
silkscreen

Videos

Andy Warhol
53 min, 1973, Michael Blackwood Productions

Andy Warhol
78 min, 1988, HVC

Andy Warhol: Made in China
29 min, 1992, Phoenix

Art Since Pop
29 min, Clearvue

The Artist's Studio (6 programs)
35 min, 1973, Michael Blackwood Productions

Claes Oldenburg
52 min, 1975, MBP

Four Artists: Robert Ryman, Eva Hesse, Bruce Nauman, Susan Rothenberg
45 min, 1988, Blackwood

George Segal
58 min, 1988, Blackwood

Inside the Studio: Roy Lichtenstein
55 min, TMS

Live From New York, It's Roy Lichtenstein
55 min, 1993, HVC

Marisol
13 min, 1984, MOMA

Portrait of An Artist: Andy Warhol
77 min, 1988, Clearvue

Portrait of An Artist: Jasper Johns
56 min, 1992, Clearvue

Pop and Op Art
25 min, Clearvue

Pop Art,
17 min, Phoenix

Multiple-Choice Questions

1. Which is the best definition of an artistic Happening?

    a. an unplanned event
    b. improvisation*
    c. unrestrained self-expression
    d. a café, performance

2. The first Pop Art poster appeared in

    a. New York City in 1960
    b. Paris in 1959
    c. London in 1956*
    d. Dresden in 1920
    e. Moscow in 1917

3. Which was <u>not</u> a feature of Hamilton's Pop Art checklist?

    a. elitism*
    b. youthfulness
    c. mass-production
    d. transience
    e. wit

4. Which is <u>not</u> an influence discernible in *Just what is it that makes today's homes so appealing*?

    a. Flemish 15th-century painting
    b. Classical poses
    c. appliances
    d. black-and-white cinema
    e. Gothic Revival*

5. Which artist is correctly matched with his or her work?

    a. Johns -- *Portrait of Frank O'Hara*
    b. Lichtenstein -- *Great American Nude No.57*
    c. Wesselmann -- *Three Flags*
    d. Hesse -- *Little Big Picture*
    e. Beuys -- *Coyote, I like America and America Likes Me**

6. "I want to be a machine" is a statement made by

     a. Hesse
     b. Warhol*
     c. Rauschenberg
     d. Flavin

7. Match the source of the imagery with the artist

     a. comic books -- Lindner
     b. pinball machines -- de Saint-Phalle
     c. Hollywood pinups -- Lichtenstein
     d. Leonardo's *Last Supper* -- Marisol*
     e. Prehistoric "Venuses" -- Wesselmann

8. Kitaj's *Juan de la Cruz* combines which two political situations?

     a. the Vietnam War and the Spanish-American War
     b. the Spanish-American War and the First World War
     c. the Vietnam War and the Inquisition*
     d. the Inquisition and the American Civil War

9. Which is <u>least</u> a quality of Oldenburg's sculptures?

     a. small objects are enlarged
     b. hard objects are made of soft material
     c. inanimate objects become anthropomorphic
     d. they are humorless*

10. Sidney Janis was

     a. an art dealer
     b. an art collector
     c. an art historian
     d. a portraitist
     e. a and b*

11. The 20th-century artist who wraps living people is

     a. Oldenburg
     b. Beuys
     c. Hesse
     d. Segal*
     e. Marisol

12. The title and of the first significant Pop Art show in New York was

    a. the "New Realists," 1962*
    b. "Pop -- 1960"
    c. "Pop and Op at the Top," 1965
    d. "Art at the Top," 1956
    e. "Top Art -- 1969"

13. The term "Op" is short for

    a. optimum
    b. optical*
    c. opulent
    d. optional

14. Minimalism was a reaction against which of the following?

    a. figuration
    b. nature
    c. the artist's hand
    d. geometry
    e. a, b, and c*

15. The most painterly of the Minimalists was

    a. Hesse
    b. Flavin
    c. Martin*
    d. Judd

16. The most autobiographical of the Minimalists was

    a. Hesse*
    b. Flavin
    c. Martin
    d. Judd

17. The Minimalist whose primary medium was fluorescent lights was

    a. Hesse
    b. Flavin*
    c. Martin
    d. Judd

18. Who of the following created action sculpture?

    a. Hesse
    b. de Saint-Phalle
    c. Marisol
    d. Beuys*
    e. Segal

19. Which was <u>not</u> an element used in *Coyote, I Like America and America Likes Me*?

    a. a felt blanket
    b. newspapers
    c. a pipe*
    d. a crook

20. *Art as Idea as Idea* is an example of

    a. Minimalism
    b. Pop Art
    c. Op Art
    d. Conceptual Art*
    e. Surrealism

21. Match the work with the correct author

    a. Mary McCarthy -- *The Group**
    b. Betty Friedan -- *Annie Hall*
    c. Saul Bellow -- *Silent Spring*
    d. Woody Allen -- *Feminine Mystique*
    e. Rachel Carson -- *Humboldt's Gift*

22. Which Pop Artist was most likely to have painted repetitious advertising images?

    a. Johns
    b. Warhol*
    c. Lichtenstein
    d. Hamilton

CHAPTER 29:
Innovation and Continuity

Key Works

Robert Mapplethorpe, *Self-Portrait*, 1980

Chuck Close, *Self-Portrait*, 1968

Chuck Close, *Self-Portrait*, 1997

Gilbert Proesch and Goerge Passmore, *Singing Sculptures*, 1969

Laurie Anderson, *Nerve Bible Tour*, 1995

Duane Hanson, *The Cowboy*, 1995

Richard Estes, *Williamsburg Bridge*, 1987

Richard Estes, *The Solomon R. Guggenheim Museum*, 1979

Jenny Holzer, untitled (selections from *Truisms, Inflammatory Essays, The Living Cries, The Survival Series, Under Rock, Laments*, and *Mother and Child Text*), Solomon R. Guggenheim Museum, New York, 1989 – 1990

Marcel Breuer, Whitney Museum of American Art, New York, 1966

R. Buckminster Fuller, American Pavilion, Expo '67, Montreal, 1967

Charles W. Moore and William Hersey, Piazza d'Italia, New Orleans, 1978 – 1979

Michael Graves, Public Services Building, Portland, Oregon, 1980 – 1982

I. M. Pei, Louvre Pyramid, Paris, 1988

Richard Rogers, Lloyd's Building, London, 1986

Frank O. Gehry, Solomon R. Guggenheim Museum Bilbao, Bilbao, Spain, 1993 – 1997

Frank O. Gehry, Frederick R. Weisman Museum, Minneapolis, Minnesota, finished 1990

Frank O. Gehry, plan of the Solomon R. Guggenheim Museum Bilbao, finished 1997

Frank O. Gehry, north side elevation of the Solomon R. Guggenheim Museum, Bilbao

Computer-generated Catia image used for the Solomon R. Guggenheim Museum Bilbao

Interior gallery, Solomon R. Guggenheim Museum Bilbao

Robert Smithson, *Spiral Jetty*, Great Salt Lake, Utah, 1970

Nancy Holt, *Stone Enclosure: Rock Rings*, Western Washington University, 1977 – 1978

Detail of 1340 blue umbrellas in Ibraki, Japan from Christo and Jeanne-Claude, *The Umbrellas*, Japan – U.S.A., 1984 – 1991

Detail of 1760 yellow umbrellas in California, U.S.A. from Christo and Jeanne-Claude, *The Umbrellas*, Japan – U.S.A., 1984 – 1991

Christo and Jeanne-Claude, *Wrapped Reichstag* (two views), Berlin, 1971 – 1995

Christo and Jeanne-Claude, *Over the River: Project for the Arkansas River, State of Colorado*, drawing by Christo, 1998

Valerie Jaudon, *Long Division*, 23rd Street Station, IRT Subway Line, New York, 1988

Jean-Michel Basquiat, *CARBON/OXYGEN*, 1984

Judy Chicago, *The Dinner Party*, 1974 – 1979

Kiki Smith, *Mary Magdalene* (front and rear views), 1994

Rona Pondick, *Tree* (model), 1995

Maya Ying Lin, *The Women's Table*, Yale University, 1993

Spiral diagram of Maya Ying Lin, *The Women's Table*, Yale University, 1993, drawing by Ian Hunt

Susan Rothenberg, *IXI*, 1976 – 1977
Anselm Kiefer, *To the Unknown Painter*, 1983
Maya Ying Lin, *Vietnam Veterans Memorial*, the Mall, Washington, D.C., 1981 – 1983
Bruce Nauman, *Model for Animal Pyramid II*, 1989
Jeff Koons, *New Hoover, Convertibles, Green, Blue; New Hoover Convertibles, Green, Blue; Double-Decker*, 1981 – 1987
Nancy Graves, *Morphose*, 1986
Cindy Sherman, *Untitled*, 1989
Raphael, *The Fornarina*, c. 1518
Nam June Paik, *TV Buddha*, 1974
Nam June Paik, *V-yramid*, 1982
Nam June Paik, *Hamlet Robot*, 1996
Vitaly Komar and Alexander Melamid, *Stalin and the Muses*, 1981 – 1982
Vitaly Komar and Alexander Melamid, *America's Most Wanted*, 1994
Vitaly Komar and Alexander Melamid, *America's Most Unwanted*, 1994
Vitaly Komar and Alexander Melamid, *Denmark's Most Wanted*, 1995

Maps, Diagrams, and Projections

Schematic section of Lloyd's Building
Spiral diagram of *The Women's Table*, drawing by Ian Hunt

Key Terms

geodesic dome

Videos

After Modernism
58 min, 1992, Michael Blackwood Productions

Buckminster Fuller: Grandfather of the Future
25 min, 1984, VM

Christo: Ten Works in Progress
55 min (also 28 min version), 1979, MBP

Christo: Wrapped Coast
28 min, 1977, MBP

Christo: Wrapped Walk Ways
25 min, 1977, MBP

Christo's Islands
58 min, 1983, AA

Christo's Running Fence
58 min, 1978, AA

Christo's Valley Curtain
28 min, 1973, Maysles Films

Frank Gehry
58 min, 1988, Blackwood

Frank Lloyd Wright and The Story of the Guggenheim Museum: 1071 Fifth Avenue
55 min, 1993, VM

Maya Lin: A Strong Clear Vision
96 min, 1995, Facets

Right Out of History: The Making of Judy Chicago's "Dinner Party"
1980, 75 min, Phoenix

Multiple-Choice Questions

1. NEA stands for

     a. National Esthetic Association
     b. National Endowment of Aesthetics
     c. National Endowment for the Arts*
     d. National Efforts for Artists

2. In what city was a museum indicted for exhibiting Mapplethorpes?

     a. Cleveland
     b. Cincinnati*
     c. Chicago
     d. Washington, D.C.
     e. Philadelphia

3. Which is least true of Chuck Close's work?

     a. he relies on photography
     b. his main subject is portraiture
     c. his favorite paint is acrylic*
     d. his most usual viewpoint is the close-up

4. Gilbert and George described themselves as

   a. performance artists
   b. impresarios
   c. video artists
   d. living sculptures*
   e. gilded lilies

5. Which least matches?

   a. Hanson's *Artist with Ladder* -- Polykleitos' *Spearbearer*
   b. Close's 1997 *Self-Portrait* -- Mosaics
   c. Graves' *Morphose* -- Surrealism
   d. Estes' *Solomon R. Guggenheim Museum* -- the Robie House*

6. Which artist is correctly matched with his or her work?

   a. The Christos -- *Over the River**
   b. Gilbert and George -- *Williamsburg Bridge*
   c. Frank Gehry -- the Whitney Museum
   d. Buckminster Fuller -- Lloyd's Building
   e. I.M. Pei -- Geodesic Domes

7. Which structure is incorrectly matched with its location?

   a. The Whitney Museum -- New York City
   b. Piazza d'Italia -- New Orleans
   c. Lloyd's Building -- London
   d. Glass pyramid -- Cairo*
   e. The Frederick R. Wiseman Museum -- Minneapolis

8. Who was a graduate of the Bauhaus?

   a. Fuller
   b. Breuer*
   c. Pei
   d. Rothenberg
   e. Nauman

9. What is a fullerene?

   a. a building by Fuller
   b. a unit of a geodesic dome
   c. a Dymaxion
   d. a molecule*
   e. an atom

10. The large central space around which the new Lloyd's building was wrapped is the

    a. atrium*
    b. courtyard
    c. narthex
    d. nave

11. Who of the following is not an environmental artist?

    a. Smithson
    b. Holt
    c. the Christos
    d. Smith*

12. Match the example of environmental art with its location

    a. *Spiral Jetty* -- Oregon
    b. *Blue Umbrellas* -- California
    c. *Long Division* -- New York City*
    d. *Stone Enclosure. Rock Rings* – Washington, D.C.

13. Which is least true of the Christos

    a. they are Conceptual artists*
    b. they recycle their materials
    c. they accept no financial patronage
    d. they raise money by selling drawings, collages and models

14. Which is not a reference in the iconography of *The Dinner Party*?

    a. Hatshepsut
    b. Virginia Woolf
    c. The Last Supper
    d. Stieglitz*
    e. O'Keeffe

15. Which category best matches the artist?

    a. Smith -- Body Art*
    b. Basquiat -- landscape
    c. Kiefer -- Feminism
    d. Paik -- environmental art

16. Nauman prefers Man Ray to Duchamp because

    a. Man Ray is a greater artist
    b. Man Ray is more unreasonable*
    c. Man Ray is more original
    d. Man Ray is more Classical
    e. Man Ray is a photographer

17. Sherman's self-portrait as the Fornarina differs from the Fornarina in being

    a. more accurate because it is a photograph
    b. more idealized
    c. satirical*
    d. anti-women

18. The artist who developed a philosophy of cybernetics is

    a. Christo
    b. Nauman
    c. Lin
    d. Paik*
    e. Kiefer

19. Which is not a conclusion of the poll conducted by Komar and Melamid?

    a. Americans like non-figurative art*
    b. Americans don't know much about art history
    c. Americans are basically conservative in matters of art
    d. Americans like the color blue

20. Match the author with the correct work

    a. Norman Mailer -- *The Right Stuff*
    b. Tom Wolfe -- *The Unbearable Lightness of Being*
    c. Toni Morrison -- *Beloved**
    d. Alice Walker -- *Glengarry Glen Ross*

21. The artist whose imagery suggests graffiti is

    a. Sherman
    b. Basquiat*
    c. Kiefer
    d. Rothenberg
    e. Jaudon